1/12/22

INFORMATION
Representation
and Retrieval
in the Digital Age

Heting Chu

ASIST Monograph Series

Published for the
American Society for Information Science and Technology by

 Information Today, Inc.
Medford, New Jersey

Second printing, February 2005

Information Representation and Retrieval in the Digital Age

Library of Congress Cataloging-in-Publication Data

Chu, Heting, 1957-
    Information representation and retrieval in the digital age / Heting Chu.
        p. cm. -- (ASIST monograph series)
    Includes bibliographical references.
    ISBN 1-57387-172-9
     1. Information organization. 2. Information retrieval. 3. Information storage and retrieval systems. I. Title. II. Series.
Z666.5.C48 2003
025.04--dc21

                                 2003011848

Publisher: Thomas H. Hogan, Sr.
Editor-in-Chief: John B. Bryans
Managing Editor: Deborah R. Poulson
Graphics Department Director: M. Heide Dengler
Book Designer: Kara Mia Jalkowski
Cover Designer: Laura Hegyi
Copy Editor: Pat Hadley-Miller
Indexer: Heting Chu

Contents

CHAPTER 3

CHAPTER 4

CHAPTER 5
Retrieval Techniques and Query Representation **59**

CHAPTER 10
The User Dimension in Information Representation and Retrieval

CHAPTER 11
Evaluation of Information Representation and Retrieval

Figures and Tables

Preface

Another book on information retrieval (IR)? Yes, because there are new topics and developments that need to be discussed in this field as we enter the digital age. In addition, two chapters of this book are devoted exclusively to information representation, a step that must be taken before information becomes retrievable.

We begin with an overview of information representation and retrieval (IRR) in Chapter 1, which reviews key concepts, key people, key events, and major developmental stages of the field. Chapters 2 and 3 examine basic approaches to information representation and other related topics. Given the significance of language in information representation and retrieval, Chapter 4 discusses natural language and controlled vocabulary, the two types of languages used in the field, along with their relationship and characteristics. Chapters 5, 6, and 7 focus on various aspects of retrieval: retrieval techniques, retrieval approaches, and retrieval models. Major types of information retrieval systems are then considered in Chapter 8 with special coverage of Internet retrieval systems, the rising star in the family of IR systems. Chapter 9 explores the retrieval of multilingual information, multimedia information, and hyper-structured information. The user dimension, a fundamental aspect in information representation and retrieval, is covered in Chapter 10. Chapter 11 surveys the complex and multifaceted evaluation issue in the field, including evaluation measures, evaluation methodology, and major evaluation projects. The last chapter of the book, Chapter 12, analyzes the role and potential of artificial intelligence (AI) in information representation and retrieval.

I have attempted to present a systematic, thorough yet nontechnical view of the field by using plain language, wherever possible, to explain complex topics. The emphasis of the book is placed upon the principles and fundamentals of information representation and retrieval rather than on descriptions of specific procedures, systems, or corresponding practices in the field. Once the reader understands these IRR principles and fundamentals, he or she should be able to apply them in different situations and environments. Attention is also paid specifically to topics and developments regarding information representation and retrieval in the digital age.

While *Information Representation and Retrieval* has an orientation toward the user, IRR system designers should find it helpful for understanding the field from the perspective of users. My intent is a book that will be useful to anyone who is interested in learning about the field, particularly those who are new to it. I strongly recommend that beginners read the book in the order in which it is organized, as later chapters are built upon the earlier ones.

Looking back, I might not have written this book at this point in my career if my colleague, Richard Smiraglia, had not initiated the contact for me with the publisher. My gratitude also goes to my students, who have shared my interest and enthusiasm in the field. I appreciate as well the sabbatical leave granted by Long Island University, without which I would not have had the luxury of time for undertaking this project. In addition, I would like to thank Michael Koenig, dean of Palmer School with which I am affiliated, and John Bryans, editor-in-chief of the book publishing division of Information Today, Inc., for making the publication of my manuscript a reality.

This book to a large extent was an integral part of my family life during the time of writing as my husband and daughter were also deeply involved with my work. For example, the book became a regular topic at our dinner table, and my family often had to spend weekend and evening hours without me at home. My daughter, Fangfei, is perhaps exposed more to *information retrieval* than any other kids her age. She continually urged me to work on my book even though, in her heart, she would have preferred I spend the time with her. The love, understanding, and support from my family have continuously been a source of energy and inspiration.

Heting Chu
Long Island, New York
hchu@liu.edu

CHAPTER 1

Information Representation and Retrieval: An Overview

Information representation and retrieval (IRR), also known synonymously as abstracting and indexing, information searching, and information processing and management, dates back to the second half of the 19th century when schemes for organizing and accessing knowledge (e.g., Dewey Decimal Classification [DDC], 1876) were created (Wynar, 1980). However, research on information representation and retrieval did not become a key field in information science until the breakout of World War II. Since then, great minds from various disciplines have been attracted to this emerging field, while information technologies with different degrees of sophistication and maturity are applied to facilitate research and development in information representation and retrieval.

The history and development of information representation and retrieval are illustrated here with a focus on the main features of each period and outstanding pioneers of the field. The key concepts involved in this book are then explained, followed by a discussion of major components in IRR. This chapter is concluded with an exploration of the essential problem of the field, namely, how to obtain the right information for the right user at the right time.

1.1 History and Development of Information Representation and Retrieval

The history of information representation and retrieval is not long. A retrospective look at the field identifies increased demand, rapid growth, demystified phases, and the network era as the four major stages IRR has experienced in its development.

1.1.1 Major Stages

1.1.1.1 Increased Demand (1940s–early 1950s)

WWII denoted the official formation of the field of information representation and retrieval. Because of the war, a massive quantity of technical reports and documents was produced to record the research and development activities surrounding weaponry production. Never before did people confront such an enormous task of information representation and retrieval, without considering other aspects of information processing and management such as selection, dissemination, and preservation. As Bush (1945) wrote:

> There is a growing mountain of research. But there is increased evidence that we are being bogged down today as specialization extends. The investigator is staggered by the findings and conclusions of thousands of other workers—conclusions which he cannot find time to grasp, much less to remember, as they appear. (p. 101)

Indeed, the need for representing and organizing the vast amount of information became quite obvious and pressing. In the fields of chemistry and biology, for example:

> The biomedical press, for example, has been estimated to publish 2 million papers each year. (McCandless, Skweir & Gordon, 1964, p. 147) These papers can be read at the rate of two per hour—assuming that the reader is attentive, can read approximately 70 languages, and has the documents at hand. If journal reading is limited to 1 hour per day and 365 days per year, then it will take more than 27.4 centuries to read the output of 1 year of the world's biomedical press. (Borko & Bernier, 1975, p. 6)

Although the exact amount of technical information produced during the 1940s and 1950s may not be accurately determined, its magnitude can be estimated according to the previously described biomedical field. People could no longer rely exclusively on their own skills, memories, or individual file cabinets for organizing and retrieving information efficiently whenever there was a need. Rather, collective efforts in the area of information representation and retrieval were called for, resulting in systems specifically designed for that purpose even though they were manual ones such as the coordinated indexes introduced in 1951 (Gull, 1956).

1.1.1.2 Rapid Growth (1950s–1980s)

The three decades in this period represent the golden years in the development of information representation and retrieval. Computers were formally introduced to the field between 1957 and 1959 when Hans Peter Luhn used the machine to handle not only the keyword matching and sorting tasks, but also the intellectual work related to the content analysis of written texts (Salton, 1987).

The emergence of online systems such as DIALOG in the 1960s and 1970s signified the shift from manual to computerized information retrieval (IR). Hahn (1996) described the pioneer online systems developed during that period of time. In addition, she pointed out that these systems:

> ... had some remarkable advanced features such as online thesauri, ranked output, automatic inclusion of synonyms in the search formulation, Boolean logic, right and left-hand truncation, cited-reference searching, and natural language free-text searching. Some systems had automatic data collection programs to monitor use and satisfaction. (p. 34)

Along with the growth and maturity of the online systems, automated and automatic techniques for information representation and retrieval had been created and experimented with, supported by the advancements in computing technology. People from different fields, especially those from computer science, devoted their efforts to research and development in this area. However, additional problems were waiting to be researched, just as Salton (1987) summarized in one of his writings:

> Even though great progress has been made in the past 30 years in text processing and information retrieval, especially in the areas of text editing and document production, index term assignment, and dynamic collection search and query formulation, few substantive advances are apparent in the true text understanding areas. (p. 379)

1.1.1.3 Demystified Phase (1980s–1990s)

Although the online systems previously described were built for users with various kinds of information need, they were not designed in such a way that the users could search them directly without any training or assistance from information professionals. In other words, only intermediaries such as librarians and other information professionals were able to perform the search task on behalf of the users. Moreover, it was very costly to use such systems in locating information because a remarkable array of fees (e.g., telecommunication, connection, and database fees) would be charged for every single search. The term *end-users* then referred to those who had some information need but would not conduct the actual online search themselves. The meaning of the term end-user changed gradually when personal computers were employed in information retrieval and when CD-ROM and Online Public Access Catalog (OPAC) systems were implemented in the mid-1980s.

Online IR systems in the past were accessed via assorted means such as printer terminals and Cathode Ray Tube (CRT) terminals. Needless to say, the interaction between the searcher and the system was not inviting or friendly. When personal computers were introduced into IR, end-users would find that the retrieval process seemed much less intimidating as some form of friendly "conversation" or interaction could be carried out between the user and the system.

The implementation of CD-ROM and OPAC systems made it possible for end-users to search for themselves by demystifying IR systems that existed previously in online form only and were geographically located in a remote place. Users no longer needed to be concerned with the online costs when they searched CD-ROM or OPAC systems. Since then, IR systems have increasingly become systems built for and used by end-users.

1.1.1.4 The Networked Era (1990s–present)

IR, up to this point, was a centralized activity, which implies that databases of IR systems were physically managed in one central location. If people intended to use several IR systems, they had to establish connections with respective IR systems individually. In comparison, distributed searching allows people to access database information using the network infrastructure. IR systems are no longer restricted to one single geographical area. The advent of the Internet truly makes networked IR a reality by providing the infrastructure needed for this implementation.

In addition to the feature of distributed searching, the Internet has redefined the field of information representation and retrieval. Never before in the history of information representation have statistical keyword and similar methods been applied so extensively to such a huge amount of hyperstructure and multimedia information. Never before in the history of IR have so many users conducted online searches without the help of intermediaries. As a result, the quality of information representation in this environment seems so mixed that the term *organized chaos* has been coined specifically for describing the status quo. On the other hand, full-text retrieval becomes the norm rather than the exception on the Internet. Retrieval techniques that were previously tested only in lab experiments are readily available in Internet retrieval systems like AltaVista and Google. Overall, research results obtained from controlled environments are now widely applied to information representation and retrieval on the Internet.

The networked era is symbolized by the Internet, which provides a novel platform as well as a showcase for information representation and retrieval in the digital age.

1.1.2 Pioneers of the Field

The field of IRR has been attracting so many talented and devoted people in the past 50 years that it is impracticable to list all of them in the space given. Nevertheless, the following people deserve individual discussion in this book because their contributions to the field are too great to let go without special coverage.

1.1.2.1 Mortimer Taube (1910–1965)

Mortimer Taube earned his doctorate in philosophy at the University of California at Berkeley. He worked as a librarian for circulation, cataloging, and acquisitions before he took a position at the Library of Congress to become the assistant chief of general reference and bibliography in 1945 (Shera, 1978). In 1952, Taube founded Documentation Inc., where he and his colleagues began to explore new methods for information indexing and retrieval under contract to the United States Armed Services Technical Information Agency (Smith, 1993).

The new approach to indexing and searching eventually became the well known "coordinate indexing." Taube, with Alberto F. Thompson, first presented a report entitled "The coordinate indexing of scientific fields" before the division of chemical literature of the American Chemical Society as part of its Symposium on Mechanical Aids to Chemical Documentation. The report was never officially published in a journal or book although Gull (1987) included it later in one of his publications as an appendix.

The need for new indexing and retrieval methods at the time was twofold. First, a huge amount of technical reports and other scientific literature, generated by research conducted for WWII, indicated the inadequacy of the existing indexing and retrieval systems, which were primarily manual. Second, the two established methods of representing information, the alphabetical and the hierarchical (e.g., subject headings and classification schemes), were unable to accommodate the new disciplines, new technologies, and new terminology evolved from WWII–related research and development (Smith, 1993). It was in this particular circumstance that in 1952 Taube and Thompson proposed coordinate indexing (Gull, 1987).

Breaking away from traditional methods for indexing and searching, coordinate indexing is based on the implementation of uniterms and application of Boolean logic in IR. Uniterms are individual terms selected by indexers to represent different facets of a document. Uniterms can, in a sense, be regarded as today's keywords because both are derived from original documents and no effort is made for vocabulary control (e.g., checking synonyms and homographs). Typically, several uniterms are used to represent a single document, as with keyword indexing.

Boolean logic, a subdivision in philosophy, was put forward by George Boole in 1849 based on detailed analyses of the processes of human reasoning and fundamental laws that govern operations of the mind (Smith, 1993). To Boole, the processes of reasoning were either the addition of different concepts, or classes of objects, to form more complex concepts, or the separation of complex concepts into individual simpler concepts (Boole, 1854). The former is summarized as the AND operator while the latter includes the OR and NOT operators. These principles were brought to the field of information representation and retrieval in the form of coordinate indexing by Taube almost a century later.

Taube's cumulative efforts in coordinate indexing laid the foundation for Boolean searching in the computerized environment. If disciplines can be broken down into single ideas represented by uniterms, computers can be used to organize and search for information put in that format. This eventually led to the development of various retrieval systems that performed all types of Boolean searching, a topic that shall be explored further in other parts of this book. Meanwhile, indexes that were developed using the coordination method became known as coordinate indexes. The process of searching these indexes by combining ideas to find needed information was called "concept coordination" (Smith, 1993).

The phrase *coordinate indexing* is, however, a misnomer (Gull, 1987). More accurately, it should be called "coordinate indexing and searching" or, in today's terminology, "coordinate representation and retrieval," because it does not appear to be just an indexing method. Rather, it has been used for searching as well. In addition, the emphasis of the method was put on analysis over synthesis, which led some critics (e.g., Gull, 1987; Pao, 1989) to question whether coordinate indexing combined words or concepts/ideas. The problem of false coordination also caused concern among people because there was no mechanism in the method to prevent false drops. For example, if the desired search topic is *computer desk*, the retrieval results may possibly contain documents related to *computer desk* as well as *desk computer* and other phrases that happen to have the words *computer* and *desk* in them (e.g., *desk-top computer*). As uniterms are assigned without reference to controlled vocabularies, all the cons associated with indexing and retrieval using natural language (see Chapter 4) are present in coordinate indexing. Furthermore, coordinate indexing seems just a restriction imposed on the old alphabetical and hierarchical methods rather than a novel third method for indexing and retrieval if it is limited to single words only (Gull, 1987).

Nevertheless, Taube's contribution to the field is remarkable in that he created coordinate indexing and introduced Boolean logic to indexing and retrieval. As summarized by Gull (1956), the Uniterm System exhibited the following characteristics in comparison with classification and subject catalogues:

- Low in cost

- Smaller in size

- Faster for analysis

- Provides more access points per unit catalogued

- Faster for searching

- Slower for rate of growth

- Slower for rate of obsolescence

- Provides greater specificity

- Provides universality

- Provides logical structure

- Provides neutrality

- Provides simplicity

- Suitable for cumulative publication

There is certainly little doubt that the real impetus to modern methods of information retrieval was given by Mortimer Taube, founder of Documentation Inc. (Lancaster, 1968). As we move from the electronic age to the digital one, the influence and impact Taube had on indexing and retrieval remains apparent.

1.1.2.2 Hans Peter Luhn (1896–1964)

If Taube is regarded as the pioneer who laid the foundation for computers to be applied in information retrieval by incorporating Boolean logic in his uniterm system, Hans Peter Luhn would be the individual who actually created computer-based applications for the field.

Born in Germany, Luhn was an engineer by education who became a famed IBM inventor with more than 80 patents. Luhn's initiation to information science in general and information retrieval in particular came in 1947–1948 when James Perry and Malcolm Dyson approached him and asked if an IBM machine could be designed to search chemical structures coded according to the Dyson notation system (Harvey, 1978). Luhn quickly became interested and joined with them to develop and test a pioneer electronic information searching system that, in 1948, Luhn called an electronic searching selector. This machine later came to be known as the Luhn Scanner (Schultz, 1968). By 1953, he was spending an increasing amount of time in information retrieval and published his first paper in the area entitled "A new method of recording and searching information" (Luhn, 1953). He also became the manager of information retrieval research at IBM. Luhn explored and worked out many of the important computer-based IR applications that now seem common-place in the field.

One such application is the Keyword-in-Context (KWIC) system that encompasses three elements fundamental to information representation and retrieval. The first element is that keywords, rather than terms obtained from conventional classifications and subject headings, are used to represent and retrieve the plural facets of a document. Keywords, in a sense, can be considered as a descendant of Taube's uniterms, although few people have attempted to make this association. This keyword approach has since been widely implemented in applications such as automatic indexing, automatic abstracting, and keyword searching. The second element of the KWIC method derives from the concordances our ancestors created in as early as the 13th century (Wellisch, 1995). While all the sentences in a document make up a concordance, titles and similar artifacts (e.g., topic sentences) form the so-called "context" for KWIC products. For instance, titles are processed to generate Keyword-in-Title (KWIT) indexes, one extension of the KWIC application. The third element of the KWIC approach is the permuta-tion of keywords contained in titles and other equivalents. The permutation typically assumes two display formats: KWIC with a particular keyword aligned within the context, and Keyword-out-of-Context (KWOC) with a par-ticular keyword displayed and left aligned outside the context. KWOC, like KWIT, is another variation of the KWIC application. Luhn, who coined the KWIC terminology in 1958, successfully produced a KWIC index for *Chemical Titles*, bringing his idea to practical results (Fischer, 1966). The KWIC approach unarguably stands for a significant milestone in information rep-resentation and retrieval.

Automatic indexing and abstracting represent major contributions made by Luhn to the IR fields. Using statistical methods, Luhn developed and pro-moted algorithms for producing indexes and abstracts automatically. For automatic indexing, the procedure is mainly based on the selection of signif-icant words (i.e., keywords) that carry meanings from documents. Words that appear frequently (i.e., high frequency words such as articles, conjunctions, and prepositions) or seldom in the document (i.e., low frequency words or words people rarely use in communication) and "noninforming words" (i.e., general nouns such as *report* and *summary* as well as terms constantly used in a particular collection, e.g., *information retrieval* in a document database for information retrieval) can be eliminated by adopting a stop-word list or statistical word-frequency procedure (Luhn, 1958). This approach for producing KWIC indexes, KWIC variations (e.g., KWOC and KWIT), and other keyword indexes became the first and to this day the only fully automatic indexing method. For automatic abstracting, two measures are suggested for identifying significant words and subsequently significant sentences that can be the most representative of a given document. The keyword approach, as described earlier for automatic indexing, furnishes one of the two measures for constructing automatic abstracts. The other measurement relies on the relative position within a sentence of significant words. According to Luhn (1958), proximity of four or five nonsignificant words between significant words appears useful for selecting significant sentences from a document. A combination of the keyword frequency and keyword proximity within a sentence seems a viable methodology for generating auto-abstracts.

Luhn's third notable contribution to the field is the development of Selective Dissemination of Information (SDI) systems. SDI is an application for effective dissemination of new scientific information to target users based on their profiles. Luhn (1959) outlined its components and various steps for operating an SDI system, of which the creation and maintenance of user profiles is the most important and critical task. The profile of user interests includes a list of words along with their current weights, each indicating the balance between additions and subtractions resulting from the profile maintenance procedure. The profile is then checked against document representations (e.g., abstracts and index terms) at a specified temporal interval (e.g., weekly or monthly). As conceived by Luhn, intelligent systems could be built for business, science, and other types of literature with the implementation of the SDI concept (Stevens, 1968).

Obviously, Luhn put quite a few ideas into practice for information representation and retrieval with the aid of computers even though not all of them originated from him (Stevens, 1968; Wellisch, 1995). As all the aforementioned applications are computer-based, the efficiency of those IR-related operations has been drastically improved. However, these applications cannot attain the quality generally associated with indexes, abstracts, and retrieval tasks that are done manually.

Luhn's contributions to the field, especially to computerized information representation and retrieval, earned him an important place in the history of information science of which information retrieval is a key component. Based on an analysis by Carlos Cuadra (1964), Luhn's name led all the rest on three out of four of the listings of major contributions as perceived by four experts in information science. He also ranked fourth among the top 25 authors in publication density, a score calculated by Cuadra using bibliographic data. In addition, he was positioned in the top 10 in the four bibliographies of the most frequently cited authors in the field. All the findings confirm that Luhn stands out as a prominent researcher in information science, particularly in information retrieval, regardless of the evaluation methods (e.g., expert advice, textbook analysis, and citation analysis) used (Cuadra, 1964). It is Luhn who brought computers into our field, pioneered many IRR applications, and catalyzed empirical research in information representation and retrieval.

1.1.2.3 Calvin N. Mooers (1919–1994)

Compared with Taube and Luhn, Calvin N. Mooers' contributions to IRR are recognized later in time. Mooers' areas of study were mathematics and physics, but he did devote a considerable amount of his time to information and computer science after attending Massachusetts Institute of Technology (MIT) in 1946 to capitalize on his computing experience (Corbitt, 1992).

Mooers, in fact, coined in 1950 the term *information retrieval*, which has since been seamlessly integrated into the vocabulary of information science. According to Mooers, information retrieval means finding information whose location or very existence is a priori unknown (Garfield, 1997). Mooers (1960) was also credited with proposing Mooers' Law for information retrieval systems:

> An information retrieval system will tend not to be used whenever it is more painful and troublesome for a customer to have information than for him not to have it. (p. ii)

The same law has been paraphrased, and one version reads, "an information system will only be used when it is more trouble not to use it than it is to use it" (Koenig, 1987). Garfield (1997) further suggested a corollary to Mooers' Law: "The more relevant information a retrieval system provides, the more it will be used." In sum, Mooers' Law indicates quintessentially that systems that reflect users' needs and practices are more apt to be consulted readily (Henderson, 1996).

In addition to coining the term *information retrieval* and authoring Mooers' Law, Mooers also developed the Zatocoding system for storing a large number of document descriptors on a single specially notched card by superimposing random, eight-digit descriptor codes. The use of the Zatocoding system would result in only a small but tolerable number of "false drops" in a bibliographic search (Garfield, 1997). Mooers was also responsible for creating two applications oriented toward computer science: the Text Reckoning and Compiling (TRAC) and VXM computer languages. TRAC was designed specifically for handling unstructured text in an interactive mode as opposed to the batch mode. VXM was used for multicomputer network systems (Corbitt, 1992; Henderson, 1996).

In recognition of his outstanding contributions to the field of information science, Mooers was honored with the American Society for Information Science (ASIS) Award of Merit in 1978. The award citation states that he "has affected all who are in the field of information and his early ideas are now incorporated into today's reality" (Henderson, 1996). Indeed, Mooers was one of the great pioneers in the growing field of information representation and retrieval.

1.1.2.4 Gerard Salton (1927–1995)

Everyone in the IR community agrees that Gerard Salton was one of the preeminent figures in the field. He was the man "most responsible for the establishment, survival, and recognition of IR..." by spending 30 years of the latter part of his life, "carefully nurturing it and sustaining it when the professional climate was inhospitable, and defending it until it could support itself" (Crouch, et al., 1996). If the entire field of IR were regarded as a domed architecture, Salton would be the "dome" while his colleagues and protégés would serve as pillars or other supporting parts of the structure.

Salton's main research tool was the System for the Manipulation and Retrieval of Texts (SMART), which is also humorously known as "Salton's Magical Automatic Retriever of Text." His ideas in this work fundamentally changed full-text processing methods on computers and provided the field of information retrieval with solid underpinnings (Anonymity, 1995). "His research contributions span the gamut of information retrieval: the vector space model, term weighting, relevance feedback, clustering, extended Boolean retrieval, term discrimination value, dictionary construction, term dependency, text understanding and structuring, passage retrieval—and, of course, automatic text processing using SMART" (Crouch, et al., 1996). Each of the contributions can easily be a topic for extensive discussion, some of which appear in other parts of this book. Nevertheless, it is not exaggerating to say that Salton brought computer science and introduced contemporary techniques to information retrieval.

Information retrieval systems that operated commercially in the 1960s were basically using Boolean logic and other pre-SMART retrieval technology. Today, dozens of well-known commercial systems use the ideas and technology developed in SMART. For example, Individual (a news clippings service) licensed the SMART technology directly. Others such as the Wide Areas Information Server (WAIS) and DOWQUEST, a tool for the Dow Jones newswire, are directly derived technology. Many new systems have leveraged off the years of research, including WIN, a legal retrieval system run by the West Publishing Company, and INQUERY, another eminent research tool

(Anonymity, 1995). IR techniques, previously only tested in SMART, are now commonly implemented even in the newest species of IR systems: Internet retrieval systems.

All these systems show the influence and application of Salton's IR concepts and research in the electronic and digital environments. In addition, Salton was a prolific writer. He published five texts on information retrieval and more than 150 research articles in the field throughout his career (Anonymity, 1995). He also dedicated his outstanding services to the field. In return, Salton received numerous awards.

1.2 Elaboration on Key Concepts

The title of this book contains four distinct concepts: information, information representation, information retrieval, and digital age. Each of the four concepts, without exception, has synonyms and can be interpreted and comprehended differently in different contexts. The following discussion is intended to explain and clarify the meaning and connotation of the concepts used in this book.

1.2.1 Information

Information, as a concept, has been considered and contrasted extensively with such terms as *data*, *knowledge*, and *wisdom* (e.g., Meadow, 1992). Hence, there seems little need for this book to repeat or continue the discussions or debates. On the other hand, the words *information*, *text*, and *document* are often used interchangeably in the field (e.g., *text retrieval* and *document representation*). According to Larsen (1999):

> In our field, documents are characterized by having a "price," they can be counted in "numbers," and are in that capacity the basic components of library statistics. Most of them "take up space," they can be "damaged in use," and they may "deteriorate" over time. (p. 1020)

In addition to Larsen's definition, documents may also contain multimedia. If *text* refers to textual information only, *document* could include multimedia information (i.e., any combination of audio, video, image, and textual information). It appears that *information* encompasses both *text* and *document*, having the broadest connotation among the trio.

In recent years, research has been done on passage retrieval as opposed to document retrieval (Sparck Jones, 2000). Passage retrieval, also phrased as *information retrieval*, denotes finding the very information or document passage (e.g., a paragraph or an arbitrary length of document segments) the end-user needs. In contrast, document retrieval implies getting a full document for the end-user, even though only one short passage is needed. If the word *information* is treated as a synonym of *passage* as in *passage retrieval*, one exception must be made to the previous discussion regarding the implication of *information*.

1.2.2 Information Representation

No matter which format a piece of information may take, it needs to be represented before it can be retrieved. Information representation includes the extraction of some elements (e.g., keywords or phrases) from a document or the assignment of terms (e.g., descriptors or subject headings) to a document so that its essence can be characterized and presented. Typically, information representation can be done via any combination of the following means: abstracting, indexing, categorization, summarization, and extraction. *Information processing* and *information management*, though having different meanings, are often regarded as synonyms of *information representation*. While *information processing* refers to how information is handled for retrieval purposes, *information management* deals with the full range of activities associated with information: from information selection to information preservation.

In this book, the term *information representation* will be used to cover the various aspects and methods of creating surrogates or representations (e.g., indexes and abstracts) for information retrieval purposes.

1.2.3 Information Retrieval

Information retrieval has been treated, by and large, as a subject field covering both the representation and retrieval sides of information (Sparck Jones & Willett, 1997). The retrieval dimension is further referred to as *information access, information seeking*, and *information searching*. These terms can be considered as synonyms for *retrieval*. However, each of them does have its different orientation with regard to implications. The term *information access* emphasizes the aspect of getting or obtaining information. In contrast, the focus of *information seeking* is placed on the user who is actively involved in the process. As for *information searching*, the center of attention appears to be on how to look for information.

In addition to the aforementioned terms, *data mining* and *resource discovery* can often be found in the information professional's vocabulary in recent years when the theme of discussion is information retrieval. Both terms are normally used in the business and networked environment. At this time, it remains to be seen whether *data mining* and *resource discovery* will be incorporated into the permanent vocabulary of people from the field of information retrieval.

Another layer of meaning in *information retrieval* is *information storage*, which mainly deals with the recording and storage of information. However, such usage gradually becomes a past practice because *information storage* is no longer a major concern, thanks to the advances made in information storage and access technology. Therefore, information retrieval in this book encompasses information seeking, information searching, and information access, but excludes information representation and information storage.

1.2.4 Digital Age

The word *digital*, as opposed to *analog*, is a relatively new concept. Both *digital* and *analog* are terms related to electronic technology, but, according to the account provided at Whatis.com (2000), a Web site devoted to defining terminology in information technology:

> Digital describes electronic technology that generates, stores, and processes data in terms of two states: positive and non-positive. Positive is expressed or represented by the number 1 and non-positive by the number 0. Thus, data transmitted or stored with digital technology is expressed as a string of 0's and 1's. ... Prior to digital technology, electronic transmission was limited to analog technology, which conveys data as electronic signals of varying frequency or amplitude that are added to carrier waves of a given frequency. Broadcast and phone transmission has conventionally used analog technology.

With the advent of the computer, the Internet, and other information technologies, we have apparently been entering into a digital age. Activities, including research and development, related to information representation and retrieval are increasingly done in the digital environment. This book is thus titled accordingly, signifying the state-of-the-art for the field.

1.3 Major Components

Information representation and retrieval, in its totality, can be divided into several major constituents, which include database, search mechanism, language, and interface. People (including the user, information professional, and system developer), information, and systems are the three intertwining entities that function jointly in the process of information representation and retrieval although they are not discussed specifically in this section.

1.3.1 The Database

Databases in information representation and retrieval comprise information represented and organized in a certain manner. In the traditional sense, a database (e.g., online database and CD-ROM database) is typically made of records that can be further decomposed into fields, the smallest and most natural units for sorting, searching, and retrieving information. In a database of journal publications, for instance, author and title are two examples of fields. Traditional databases consist of two parts: sequential files and inverted files. The sequential file is the database source, containing information organized in the field-record-database structure. It is called *sequential file* because the records in it are ordered according to the sequence they take when being entered into the database. The inverted file, also known as indexes, provides access to the sequential file according to given search queries. It is called *inverted file* because the order in which information is presented (i.e., access point first and locator second) is the reverse of that in sequential files (i.e., locator first and access point second).

In a nontraditional sense, a database (e.g., as in Internet retrieval systems) may still have sequential and inverted files. But, for example, the composition of the sequential file for an Internet retrieval system is different from its counterpart of traditional IR systems (e.g., online systems) in that the composition of the sequential file does not take the field-record-database structure. Rather, the sequential file is made of field-less information presented in prose-like format. In addition, information contained within is not a surrogate (e.g., abstract) but a part or the full content of an original Internet document (e.g., Web page). In traditional IR systems, however, information in sequential files is usually some type of representation in the form of bibliographical descriptions, abstracts, summaries, extracts, and the like.

The content and coverage of the database determine what can be retrieved later from the IR system.

1.3.2 The Search Mechanism

Information represented and organized systematically in a database can only be searched and retrieved when a corresponding search mechanism is provided. A search mechanism can acquire any degree of sophistication in search capabilities, which are defined ultimately by the search algorithms and procedures the IR system incorporates. All search procedures can be categorized as either basic or advanced. Basic search procedures are commonly found in the majority of operational information retrieval systems, while advanced search procedures have been tested and experimented with mainly in laboratories or prototype systems. However, in recent years, advanced search algorithms have increasingly been integrated into Internet retrieval systems.

Procedures such as keyword searching, Boolean searching, truncation, and proximity searching belong to the basic search algorithm cluster. As noted earlier, these procedures often form the search mechanism embedded in many information retrieval systems. End-users with little training or search experience should be able to perform simple searching tasks in retrieval environments of this kind. Advanced search procedures, such as weighted searching, are employed mostly in newer retrieval systems and are generally designed for people with professional training and search experience.

The capacity of a search mechanism determines what retrieval techniques will be available to users and how information stored in databases can be retrieved.

1.3.3 The Language

Information relies on language, spoken or written, when being processed, transferred, or communicated. In this context, language is one of the crucial components in information representation and retrieval. Language in information representation and retrieval can be identified as either natural language or controlled vocabulary. What people naturally use for representing information or forming a query is called *natural language.* If an artificial language, whose vocabulary, syntax, semantics, and pragmatics are limited, is applied for information representation and retrieval, that language is termed *controlled vocabulary* (Wellisch, 1995). There are three common types of controlled vocabulary: classifications, subject heading lists, and thesauri, each with its own special usage in information representation and retrieval.

Natural language, generally speaking, allows the highest degree of specificity and flexibility in representing and retrieving information. People do not need any training and practice in using natural language, as it is what they use for oral and written communication every day. In contrast, it is costly to create and maintain a controlled vocabulary and people have to learn how to use it by practice and training. Nevertheless, controlled vocabulary is able to reduce the intrinsic difficulties (e.g., complexity, subtleness, and ambiguity) in using natural language for representing and retrieving information (Lansdale & Ormerod, 1994). The debate about natural language vs. controlled vocabulary has been going on since the end of the 19th century in this field (Rowley, 1994). However, language remains an essential part in information representation and retrieval regardless of debate outcomes.

Language, to a certain degree, determines the flexibility and artificiality in information representation and retrieval. Chapter 4 of this book is devoted to the discussion of language in information representation and retrieval.

1.3.4 The Interface

Interface, according to Shaw (1991), is what the user sees, hears, and touches while interacting with a computer system. In information representation and retrieval, interface refers to the interaction occurring between the user and related activities. Also, with this component of information representation and retrieval, the user dimension appears obvious yet intermingled with the other three components just described, namely: database, search mechanism, and language.

Interface is regularly considered when judging whether or not an information representation and retrieval system is user-friendly. As defined by Mooers' Law, user-friendly systems will attract more people than user-hostile ones in terms of usage. The quality of an interface is decided by interaction mode (e.g., menu selection), display features (e.g., screen layout and font type), and other related factors. Adaptive and affective technologies are beginning to be applied in interface design and implementation as more attention is paid to the human dimension in IRR. Interface determines the ultimate success of a system for information representation and retrieval, especially if the system operates in the digital environment.

In sum, database, search mechanism, language, and interface constitute the major components in information representation and retrieval while they interact with the human dimension at one stage or another during the IRR process.

1.4 The Essential Problem in Information Representation and Retrieval

The essential problem in information representation and retrieval remains how to obtain the right information for the right user at the right time despite the existence of other variables (e.g., user characteristics or database coverage) in the IRR environment. Before exploring the essential problem any further, we should first consider the process of information representation and retrieval.

1.4.1 The Process of Information Representation and Retrieval

In §1.3, we discussed the major components in information representation and retrieval: database, search mechanism, language, and interface. In information representation and retrieval process, the user initiates the search and receives any results retrieved, while the information professional is responsible for designing, implementing, and maintaining the IRR systems. Figure 1.1 illustrates the IRR process.

Any information retrieved from the database must first be represented by the information professional according to the language chosen for IRR. Discrepancies are likely to occur during the course of information representation, and can be a serious problem if a controlled vocabulary is used for the following reasons. First, when information recorded in such form as journal articles or technical reports is represented as abstracts, indexing terms, and the like, a genuine rendering of the original information does not seem achievable. One could argue that we represent, for example, a big circle with a smaller one. Even so, the size dimension has been distorted. Second, any controlled vocabulary is merely a subset of the natural language with which the original documents are created. It is therefore often hard to find, for

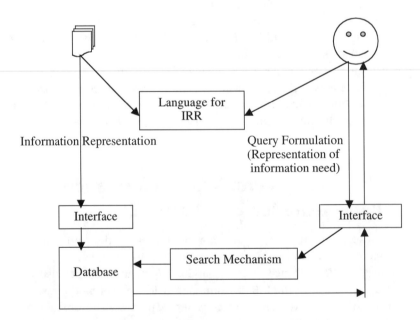

Figure 1.1   Process of Information Representation and Retrieval

example, an exact match between a term in a document and a descriptor from a thesaurus. The indexer then has to choose from related terms, narrower terms, or broader terms listed in the thesaurus for representation purpose. Third, inconsistency in information representation (including concept analysis) appears inevitable especially if more than one person or system handles the task. Cleverdon (1984) reported that even two experienced indexers, using the same controlled vocabulary, could only assign 30 percent of terms in common to the same document. Similarly, Humphrey (1992) found that inter-indexer consistency in MEDLINE by selecting terms from Medical Subject Headings (MeSH) was under 49 percent.

On the other hand, users are required to transform their information needs, based on the chosen IRR language, into queries that can then be executed in the database with the searching mechanism provided. Researchers have long been aware of the complexity involved in this task. For instance, Blair and Maron (1985) pointed out: "It is impossibly difficult for users to predict the exact words, word combinations, and phrases that are used by all (or most) relevant documents."

In addition, any usage of controlled vocabularies and search features (e.g., Boolean operators) will add to the difficulty. Natural language searching, i.e., searching with complete phrases or sentences as used in everyday communication without forming any structured queries (e.g., why is the sky blue), is becoming available on the Internet, but there is still a long way to go before researchers in natural language processing—a subdivision of artificial intelligence (AI)—make substantial breakthroughs in their endeavors.

In other words, whether a search will be successful or not depends solely on if a match is found between the represented information in the system and a query submitted by the user. To be more specific, a search is successful if a match is made between a query and the information represented in the database chosen for the task. Otherwise, a search cannot turn up any useful results. Matching is, therefore, the fundamental mechanism in information representation and retrieval. As shown in Figure 1.1, there are several points in the IRR process that can cause discrepancies in the matching. The ultimate goal for quality information representation and retrieval is to minimize or even eliminate the discrepancies that can occur during the process by using different methods and techniques. These are discussed at length in later chapters.

1.4.2 The Limits of Information Representation and Retrieval

While a great amount of research has been done on information representation and retrieval, there are certain limits that appear insurmountable. Swanson (1988) stated that by borrowing the term *postulates of impotence* (PI) from E. Taylor Whittaker, what cannot be done in the form of nine PIs when he pondered the prospect for automatic indexing and retrieval. Most of the statements, though made more than a decade ago and with reference to the automatic domain, still seem quite relevant as they are cited selectively below:

> PI 1:   An information need cannot be fully expressed as a search request ... the question cannot be precisely formed until the answer is found.

> PI 3:   ... Relevance is not fixed, it is judged within a shifting framework.

> PI 4: It is never possible to verify whether all documents relevant to any request have been found ...

> PI 9: In sum, the first eight postulates imply that consistently effective fully automatic indexing and retrieval is not possible. The conceptual problems of IR—the problems of meaning—are no less profound than thinking or any other forms of intelligent behavior. (p. 96)

The conceptual problems of IR, as Swanson puts it, are critical to the understanding and development of the field. With a close examination of the IRR process, it is apparent that what information representation and retrieval implies is essentially term matching rather than concept searching in the digital environment. When the search term is, for example, *public transportation*, documents indexed under *buses* or *subway* are not likely to be retrieved unless cross-references are made in the controlled vocabulary. Will information representation and retrieval one day move beyond term matching and closer to concept searching? The answer is being sought and explored vigorously via trial and error (Swanson, 1977).

References

Anonymity. (1995). Gerard Salton: In memoriam. *IRLIST Digest, 12(34)*. http://www.cs.virginia.edu/~clv2m/salton.txt/. (April 28, 2000)

Blair, D.C., and Maron, M.E. (1985). An evaluation of retrieval effectiveness for a full-text document-retrieval system. *Communications of the American Computing Machinery, 28(3)*, 289–299.

Boole, George. (1854). *An investigation into laws of thought, on which are founded the mathematical theories of logic and probabilities*. London: Walton and Maberley.

Borko, Harold, and Bernier, Charles L. (1975). *Abstracting concepts and methods*. New York: Academic Press.

Bush, Vannevar. (1945). As we may think. *Atlantic Monthly, 176(1)*, 101–108.

Cleverdon, C.W. (1984). Optimizing convenient online access to bibliographic databases. *Information Services and Use, 4*, 37–47.

Corbitt, Kevin D. (1992). Calvin N. Mooers Papers, 1930–1978 (CBI 81). Minneapolis: Center for the History of Computing, Charles Babbage Institute, University of Minnesota. http://www.cbi.umn.edu/inv/mooers. htm. (April 20, 2000)

Crouch, Carolyn, et al. (1996). In memoriam: Gerard Salton, March 8, 1927–August 28, 1995. *Journal of the American Society for Information Science, 47(2)*, 108–115.

Cuadra, Carlos A. (1964). Identifying key contributions to information science. *American Documentation, 15(4)*, 289–295.

Fischer, M. (1966). The KWIC index concept: A retrospective view. *American Documentation, 17(2)*, 57–70.

Garfield, Eugene. (1997). A tribute to Calvin N. Mooers, A pioneer of information retrieval. *The Scientist, 11(6)*, 9.

Gull, Cloyd Dake. (1956). Seven years of work on the organization of materials in the special library. *American Documentation, 7(1–5)*, 320–329.

Gull, Cloyd Dake. (1987). Historical note: Information science and technology: From coordinate indexing to the global brain. *Journal of the American Society for Information Science, 38(5)*, 338–366.

Hahn, Trudi Bellardo. (1996). Pioneers of the online age. *Information Processing and Management, 32(1)*, 33–48.

Harvey, John F. (1978). Luhn, Hans Peter (1986–1964). In Bohdan S. Wynar. (Ed.), *Dictionary of American library biography* (pp. 324–326). Littleton, CO: Libraries Unlimited.

Henderson, Madeline M. (1996). In Memoriam: Calvin N. Mooers, October 24, 1919–December 1, 1994. *Journal of the American Society for Information Science, 47(9),* 659–661.

Humphrey, S. (1992). Indexing biomedical documents: From thesaural to knowledge-based retrieval systems. *Artificial Intelligence in Medicine, 4,* 343–371.

Koenig, Michael E.D. (1987). The convergence of Moore's/Mooers' Laws. *Information Processing & Management, 23(6),* 583–592.

Lancaster, F.W. (1968). *Information retrieval systems: Characteristics, testing and evaluation.* New York: Wiley.

Lansdale, Mark W., and Ormerod, Thomas C. (1994). *Understanding interfaces: A handbook of human-computer dialogue.* London: Academic Press.

Larsen, Poul Steen. (1999). Books and bytes: Preserving documents for prosperity. *Journal of the American Society for Information Science, 50(11),* 1020–1027.

Luhn, H.P. (1953). A new method of recording and searching information. *American Documentation, 4(1),* 14–16.

Luhn, H.P. (1958). The automatic creation of literature abstracts. *IBM Journal of Research and Development, 2(2),* 159–165.

Luhn, H.P. (1959). Selective dissemination of new scientific information with the aid of electronic processing equipment. In Claire K. Schultz. (Ed.), (1968), *H.P. Luhn: Pioneer of information science. Selected works* (pp. 246–254). New York: Spartan Books.

McCandless, R.F.J., Skweir, E.A., and Gordon, M. (1964). Secondary journals in chemical and biological fields. *Journal of Chemical Documentation, 4(2),* 147–153.

Meadow, Charles T. (1992). *Text information retrieval systems.* San Diego: Academic Press.

Mooers, Calvin N. (1960). Mooers' Law: Or, why some retrieval systems are used and others are not. *American Documentation, 11(3),* ii.

Pao, Miranda Lee. (1989). *Concepts of information retrieval.* Englewood, CO: Libraries Unlimited.

Rowley, Jennifer. (1994). The controlled versus natural indexing languages debate revisited: A perspective on information retrieval practice and research. *Journal of Information Science, 20(2),* 108–119.

Salton, Gerard. (1987). Historical notes: The past thirty years in information retrieval. *Journal of the American Society for Information Science, 38(5),* 375–380.

Schultz, Claire K. (Ed.). (1968). *H.P. Luhn: Pioneer of information science. Selected works.* New York: Spartan Books.

Shaw, Debora. (1991). The human-computer interface for information retrieval. *Annual Review of Information Science and Technology, 26,* 155–195.

Shera, Jesse H. (1978). Taube, Mortimer (1910–1965). In Bohdan S. Wynar. (Ed.), *Dictionary of American library biography* (pp. 512–513). Littleton, CO: Libraries Unlimited.

Smith, Elizabeth S. (1993). On the shoulders of giants: From Boole to Shannon to Taube: The origins and development of computerized information from the mid-19th century to the present. *Information Technology and Libraries, 12(2),* 217–226.

Sparck Jones, Karen. (2000). Further reflections on TREC. *Information Processing & Management, 36,* 37–85.

Sparck Jones, Karen, and Willett, Peter. (Eds.). (1997). *Readings in information retrieval.* San Francisco: Morgan Kaufmann.

Stevens, Mary Elizabeth. (1968). H.P. Luhn, Information scientist. In: Schultz, Claire K. (Ed.). *H.P. Luhn: Pioneer of information science. Selected works* (pp. 24–30). New York: Spartan Books.

Swanson, Don R. (1977). Information retrieval as a trial-and-error process. *Library Quarterly, 47(2),* 128–148.

Swanson, Don R. (1988). Historical note: Information retrieval and the future of an illusion. *Journal of the American Society for Information Science, 49(2),* 92–98.

Wellisch, Hans H. (1995). *Indexing from A to Z*. 2nd ed. New York: H.W. Wilson.

Whatis.com. (2000). Digital. TechTarget.com. http://whatis.com/. (June 28, 2000)

Wynar, Bohdan S. (1980). *Introduction to cataloguing and classification*. 6th ed. Littleton, CO: Libraries Unlimited.

CHAPTER 2

Information Representation I: Basic Approaches

Information, recorded formally in different types of documents (e.g., proceeding papers and technical reports), needs to be represented before it can be retrieved. In no case can information retrieval be performed with the original documents themselves. Rather, the retrieval activity takes place with document surrogates in the form of indexes, abstracts, summaries, and the like. Representation in this book refers to the essence or the subject content of the document via a certain approach although the end product can take a variety of forms. Ideally, the representation process should be conducted simply and efficiently; however, as Lesk (1997) noted:

> If we had a single knowledge representation scheme that let us put each idea in one place, and if the users knew this scheme and could place each of their queries in it, subject retrieval would be straightforward. ... In practice, it seems unlikely that any single knowledge representation scheme will serve all purposes. (p. 99–100)

Furthermore, how the representation scheme could be applied consistently and precisely still poses challenges to information professionals even if the choice of schemes is not a concern and some methods (e.g., abstracting) do not require a scheme to get implemented. Information representation, in a nutshell, means challenge, complexity, and subtlety.

2.1 Indexing

Indexing has been a widely adopted method for information representation. It uses terms (i.e., words or phrases), either derived or assigned, to represent important facets of the original document. The number of index terms used to represent a document ranges from several terms in bibliographical databases to hundreds in full-text systems.

Conceptual analysis and translation of the document to be indexed constitute the intellectual portion of the indexing practice. To be more specific, conceptual analysis in indexing involves the identification of key concepts covered in the document whereas the translation phase actually converts a chosen concept to index terms based on a preselected indexing language.

Indexing language will specifically be discussed together with retrieval language in Chapter 4.

2.1.1 Types of Indexing

Indexing type is normally dependent on how the terms are obtained. If the terms are extracted from the original text of a document, it is called derivative indexing. Correspondingly, if the terms are assigned to a document, it is labeled as assignment indexing. Derivative indexing can also be treated as a synonym for keyword indexing because index terms are selected directly from keywords in the text and no controlled vocabulary is consulted. By comparison, a controlled vocabulary must be used in assignment indexing for choosing appropriate terms.

Indexing terms assigned from a controlled vocabulary are customarily called descriptors even though the controlled vocabulary used might not be a thesaurus. If a concept to be indexed is new or happens to be a proper name (e.g., *Great Wall*) and no equivalent can be found in the controlled vocabulary, an identifier can be created in assignment indexing. In other words, identifiers are terms assigned by the indexer but not taken from a controlled vocabulary. As mentioned earlier, terms selected in the derivative indexing process are called keywords.

Indexing without a controlled vocabulary is sometimes referred to as free indexing (Fugmann, 1993). Free indexing is generally applied in derivative indexing. Similarly, assignment indexing is typically performed by using a controlled vocabulary. Whether a controlled vocabulary should be used in indexing has been an issue over the years, and the debate continues. Overall, as more information becomes available digitally, controlled vocabulary will be applied less in indexing because of quality and quantity factors.

2.1.2 Automated and Automatic Indexing

All the activities involved in indexing can be categorized into two types: intellectual and mechanical. The intellectual part of indexing is already described in §2.1. As far as the mechanical elements in indexing are concerned, they mainly include activities such as alphabetizing and formatting index entries. While the intellectual portion of indexing remains to be accomplished by human beings most of the time, given the current state of research in artificial intelligence, indexing operations of mechanical nature can be completed satisfactorily by computers. If computers are used to handle both the mechanical and intellectual parts of indexing, we have automatic indexing. If computers are used only for the mechanical operations of indexing and human indexers are responsible for the intellectual portion of indexing, we have automated indexing.

Automatic indexing, also known as machine indexing, appears to be a very attractive solution to the inconsistency problem and high cost associated with manual indexing. However, the intrinsic weakness of automatic indexing is that the computer can only deal with the intellectual part of indexing as well as the human indexer, and in most of the cases, much worse than the information professional. The reason is obvious because the computer in truth cannot think and does not have the analytical power of a human being. In comparison, automated indexing can relieve human indexers from the tedious and repetitive indexing tasks so that they are able to concentrate more on the intellectual undertakings of indexing.

On the other hand, the value of automatic indexing should not be understated especially when the amount of information to be indexed is gigantic. Automatic indexing usually relies on a variety of algorithms among which the keyword frequency approach seems the most popular and has been implemented extensively. Other automatic indexing approaches are generally based on keyword proximity, location, probability, and linguistics. Controlled vocabularies are incorporated in some automatic indexing practices as well. But the successfulness of such a method is again negatively affected by the mechanical nature of computerized indexing.

2.1.3 Indexing in the Hyperstructure Environment

More and more information becomes available in the hyperstructure environment, which is symbolized by the World Wide Web. For Web-based information, index terms are most naturally presented as hyperlinks that embody both the index term and the locator mechanism. In other words, hyperlink names serve as index terms whereas the hyperlink mechanism seamlessly leads the user to where the index terms are pointing. In comparison with other indexing environments, this setting is unique in the following aspects.

First, index terms in the hyperstructure environment are imbedded within the document itself rather than separate entities outside the context. Second, index terms and locators are merged into one unit instead of being listed individually. Third, the subject hierarchy or the concept of subentries in traditional indexing is not exactly reflected in the hyperstructure environment. Fourth, only content-based links in the hyperstructure can be regarded as index terms while organizational links such as "Next page" and "Top of document" should not (Chu, 1997). Fifth, authors assume the role of indexing when they prepare hyperstructure documents, and indexing is done simultaneously, if not before, as the document is created. As a result, terms (e.g., *click here*) that are unlikely to be chosen by an indexer would often appear as link names in the hyperstructure environment. Sixth, less discrepancy will occur between the original document and the index terms in this process of information representation as the author decides which terms should become links while the document is being written, unlike in traditional indexing where the author writes a document, and then an indexer tries to analyze it for representation purpose.

Given the unique features of indexing in the hyperstructure environment, hyperdocuments should be indexed with methods appropriate to them. For example, choose link names carefully when writing hyperdocuments (Chu, 1997).

2.2 Categorization

Categorization denotes the successive and hierarchical representation of information by categories. Two types of categorization exist depending on whether a systematically developed scheme is used.

2.2.1 Types of Categorization

Traditionally, categorization is done according to an established classification scheme such as Dewey Decimal Classification (DDC) and Library of Congress Classification (LCC). Such categorization practices are thus universally called classification, which is generally applicable to publications collected by libraries and information services. Notations for classification include numbers, alphabets, or alpha-numerals.

With the advent of the Internet, a lot of information has been posted to that new platform. Information on the Internet overall shares the following attributes: ephemeral, mixed quality, and huge quantity. The classification method therefore seems too costly, inappropriate, or unjustified for representing information on the Net. Rather, taxonomy based on loosely structured categories appears the right framework for organizing information of that nature. Yahoo! is undoubtedly a pioneer in this practice, which has become one model for representing information on the Internet, especially on the Web. Categories in taxonomies for representing Web-based information are listed directly as hyperlinks. No notations (e.g., numbers, alphabets, and alpha-numerals) are used to reflect the hierarchical or other relationships in the framework of taxonomy.

2.2.2 Principles of Categorization

When categorization is chosen as the information representation method, one category, occasionally two for items covering interdisciplinary topics, will be assigned to a given document. In other words, a given document should be assigned to a specific category listed in an existing system for categorization. This practice requires that categories selected for the categorization system must conform to the following:

- Exhaustive

- Mutually exclusive

That is to say, all categories possibly needed for representing information should be included in the categorization system. On the other hand, these categories should be mutually exclusive among themselves. If the first point is not satisfied, some information cannot be represented by categories available in the scheme. If the second point is not observed, more than one category can be chosen to represent the same document. Other principles such as flexibility and ease of use, though important, are not as fundamental as the two previously discussed.

2.2.3 The Convergence of the Two Categorization Approaches

What differentiates one categorization approach from another lies mainly in the nature of the framework adopted for the purpose of information representation. Classification, having endured tests of various kinds, has established itself as a plausible method for representing information. Taxonomy, in contrast, has been regarded as a quick and rough approach to information representation. As more substantive and quality information becomes available on the Internet, classification is beginning to be utilized to categorize network-based information (e.g., McKiernan, 2001). In the meantime, frameworks developed for taxonomy purpose are improved and enhanced by incorporating time-tested features originated from classification schemes such as hierarchical representation.

In addition, text categorization using automatic means (e.g., Boley et al., 1998; Yang, 1999) has increasingly been explored with an orientation toward taxonomy rather than classification, as a growing amount of information is available digitally. While automatic classification once attracted a lot of attention from researchers, the brainpower needed for rigorous classification seems unattainable in purely machine-based algorithms.

2.3 Summarization

Summarization, unlike indexing and categorization, tries to represent a document with a paragraph or two—a précis or a condensed copy of the original. The degree of condensation and method used define different summarization approaches.

2.3.1 Types of Summarization

2.3.1.1 Abstracts

An abstract is a concise and accurate representation of the contents of a document. Abstracting, the act of writing an abstract, has basically been carried out by human beings although automatic efforts (e.g., Luhn, 1958) had been attempted in the past. Abstracts ideally should be written in a style similar to the original. But that criterion is hard to meet because of the inevitable loss of authenticity during the abstracting process.

Abstracts can be further divided into three kinds: informative abstracts, indicative abstracts, and critical abstracts. Informative abstracts contain substantial information from the original document, so they may serve as a substitute. People can decide based on an informative abstract whether or not they need to read the full document. Indicative abstracts, by comparison, simply describe the "aboutness" of the original document, excluding specific details such as methodology and findings, and therefore cannot be treated as a replacement for the original. People have to consult the original document to get a thorough understanding of it. Critical abstracts are so named because they not only represent the document's contents under consideration but also try to evaluate it. This form of abstract is not recommended because abstracts by definition should be free of any interpretation and judgment. Generally speaking, no critical abstracts should be written unless one is required to do so.

As mentioned earlier, researchers have explored ways of producing automatic abstracts. However, the end products at present look essentially more similar to auto-summaries or auto-extracts than auto-abstracts because they consist of purely key sentences extracted from the original document.

2.3.1.2 Summaries

A summary is a restatement of the main points of the original document, placed either in the beginning or at the end of a document. Although very close to an abstract, a summary usually assumes that the reader will have the opportunity to peruse the full document. Hence, certain elements essential to a complete understanding of the document, such as sections on background, purpose, and methodology, tend to be absent from a summary (Rowley, 1992).

Algorithms for automatically summarizing texts, especially those in digital format, have been developed in recent years (e.g., Sparck Jones &

Endres-Niggemeyer, 1995). Some researchers may label their end products of representation as abstracts. However, it is well known that only artificial intelligence (AI) research will be able to make automatic abstracting a reality, and such AI algorithms have not been successfully worked out.

2.3.1.3 Extracts

An extract comprises one or more portions of a document selected to represent the whole. Extracts are unlikely to offer a good representation of the original document. Nevertheless, they may be valuable to the reader who is interested in the outcome of a particular study. In no case can extracts be regarded as substitutes for original documents.

Extracts, though their representativeness is inferior to both summaries and abstracts, can be constructed entirely by using automatic methods. The majority of Internet retrieval systems such as AltaVista and HotBot employ auto-extracts for information representation purpose. An infamous feature of auto-extracts produced by Internet retrieval systems is that the extract often ends with an ellipsis because that is the cut-off point set up by the system. The quality of auto-extracts, therefore, is a serious concern when they are used to represent documents.

2.3.2 The Issue of Representativeness

All three different forms of summarization, i.e., abstracts, summaries, and extracts, are legitimate means for information representation. As described previously, however, they differ from each other in terms of representativeness. To rank the trio by that criterion, abstracts would be scored the highest. Extracts appear to have the least representativeness in this group, and summaries would be ranked somewhere between abstracts and extracts. This comparison exercise, although brief, can shed some light on how each summarization method can be best applied for different tasks of information representation.

2.4 Other Methods of Information Representation

If indexing, categorization, and summarization are considered the conventional methods of information representation, the techniques discussed here are unique and atypical.

2.4.1 Citations

Citations are references that authors make when they compose their writings. In general, a citation implies a relationship between a part or the whole of the cited document and a part or the whole of the citing document (Malin, 1968). Ever since Eugene Garfield, founder of the Institute for Scientific Information (ISI), which publishes citation indexes, introduced this novel approach to the field of information representation and retrieval, a great deal of discussion has been devoted to deciphering the implication of the citation relationship or determining why a citation is made. Garfield tried in 1965 to summarize reasons for the citation practice in 15 points, which include, for example, paying homage to pioneers and giving credit for related work (Garfield, 1965).

Although the real motivation for citing others' works might be different from person to person, citations can be regarded as what the citing authors select to represent in their own publications. The representations in this context take up the form of citations rather than the usual surrogates such as abstracts and index terms. Citations are in fact bibliographical information about documents, which can be further decomposed into smaller units such as titles and authors. In other words, citations provide a rich source for representing information. Moreover, there is no need to create and maintain a framework (e.g., thesaurus or classification scheme) for representation purposes while it is a must in classification and controlled vocabulary indexing.

Citing authors index their own work with the readily available resources, namely, references or citations. The elimination of intermediaries in citation indexing, however, has both positive and negative impacts on the representation. The positive impact is that the author, as the indexer, knows his/her own work the best, and no efforts are needed to interpret the original document. The negative impact results from the fact that the true reason for citation is really unknown. Therefore, we can always question if the right citations have been used to represent a document. Another related concern about citation indexing as a method for information representation is the limited coverage of ISI citation databases. Yet, people customarily use them because manually creating one often seems impractical and too time-consuming.

Since citation indexing involves little human intelligence in the process, the whole procedure can be easily automated. Indeed, the entire process of citation indexing can be completed without any human intervention, which appears unachievable in the cases of other methods for information representation.

2.4.2 Strings

While citations can serve as surrogates for original documents, string indexing (Craven, 1986) would be another approach for information representation. Strings can be a phrase, a group of phrases, or a statement, all specifically prepared for representing a document. *Use of World Wide Web for distributed learning in higher education* is an example of such strings.

There are many different types of string indexes, but they share two main characteristics: 1) manually create a string to summarize the theme of a document, and 2) mechanically generate index entries based on the given string for representation purpose. String indexing, therefore, is a distinctive case of automated indexing, briefly depicted in §2.1.2.

PREserved Context Index System (PRECIS) and NEsted Phrase Indexing System (NEPHIS) are two of the best-known systems developed for string indexing. In both systems, a string is first prepared by a human indexer. A PRECIS string is a mini-abstract loaded with relevant indexing terms while a NEPHIS string is a summary statement for indexing a document. These strings will then be coded to indicate which terms could become access points and determine the composition of index entries. The actual displaying algorithms adopted by each string indexing system may vary greatly. But all the mechanical tasks in string indexing can be effectively handled by automatic means.

The integration of the human selection of index strings with computer-assisted manipulation of index displays makes string indexing an appealing method for information representation. On one hand, it retains the quality associated with human indexing by having human beings prepare index strings. On the other, string indexing can preclude the dissatisfaction associated with the tedium, inefficiency, and inconsistencies of manual approaches. The digital age is, after all, rapidly emerging. Computers are expected to play an increasingly important role in information representation as well as information retrieval.

2.5 A Review of Basic Approaches to Information Representation

As shown in previous sections, there are various methods for information representation. Table 2.1 recapitulates the major representation approaches discussed so far, from the perspectives of representation type, entities represented, representation framework (if a controlled vocabulary is used), and production method. Each of these approaches has strengths and weaknesses.

Table 2.1 Basic Approaches to Information Representation

Approach / Feature	Indexing		Categorization		Summarization			Other	
	Derivative	Assignment	Classification	Taxonomy	Abstract	Summary	Extract	Citation	String
Representation Type	Derivative	Assignment	Classification	Taxonomy	Abstract	Summary	Extract	Citation	String
Entity Represented	Part		Whole		Whole		Part	Whole	
Representation Framework	No	Yes	Yes	No	No			No	Maybe
Production Method	Automatic	Manual & Automatic	Manual	Manual & Automatic	Manual	Manual & Automatic		Automatic	Automated

When a particular method is selected for representing information, as Meadow (1992) states, it should:

> (1) discriminate between different entities, (2) identify similar entities, (3) allow accurate description of entities, and (4) minimize ambiguity in interpretation. (p. 41-43)

As anticipated, not a single method can completely fulfill the requirements Meadow specified. One method's weakness may be another's strength. For instance, indexing alone can only reveal certain facets of a document while abstracting is meant to represent a document in its entirety. Therefore, methodological pluralism (i.e., using more than one method) has been the choice when one needs to select from the diverse approaches to information representation. In practice, an assortment of representation methods (e.g., classification with abstracting or summarization with indexing) has been implemented.

References

Boley, Daniel, et al. (1998). A client-side Web agent for document categorization. *Internet Research: Electronic Networking Applications and Policy, 8(5)*. http://www.emerald-library.com/brev/17208eb1.htm. (February 6, 1999)

Chu, Heting. (1997). Hyperlinks: How well do they represent the intellectual content of digital collections? *Proceedings of the 60th Annual Meeting of the American Society of Information Science, 34*, 361–369.

Craven, Timothy C. (1986). *String indexing*. New York: Academic Press.

Fugmann, Robert. (1993). *Subject analysis and indexing: Theoretical foundation and practical advice*. Frankfurt/Main: Indeks Verlag.

Garfield, Eugene. (1965). Can citation indexing be automated? In Mary E. Stevens, et al. (Eds.). *Statistical methods for mechanized documentation* (pp. 189–192). Washington, DC: National Bureau of Standards.

Lesk, Michael. (1997). *Practical digital libraries: Books, bytes and bucks.* San Francisco: Morgan Kaufmann.

Luhn, H.P. (1958). The automatic creation of literature abstracts. *IBM Journal of Research and Development, 2(2),* 159–165.

Malin, Morton V. (1968). The Science Citation Index: A new concept in indexing. *Library Trends, 16,* 374–397.

McKiernan, Gerry. (2001). Beyond bookmarks: Schemes for organizing the Web. http://www.public.iastate.edu/~CYBERSTACKSCTW.htm. [Continuous updating]

Meadow, Charles T. (1992). *Text information retrieval systems.* San Diego: Academic Press.

Rowley, Jennifer E. (1992). *Organizing knowledge: An introduction to information retrieval.* Brookfield, VT: Gower.

Sparck Jones, Karen, and Endres-Niggemeyer, Brigitte. (Eds.). (1995). Summarizing text [Special issue]. *Information Processing & Management, 31(5).*

Yang, Yiming. (1999). An evaluation of statistical approaches to text categorization. *Information Retrieval, 1(1/2),* 69–90.

CHAPTER 3

Information Representation II: Other Related Topics

In Chapter 2, basic approaches to information representation were discussed with an emphasis on traditional practices and their variations or extensions. In this chapter, other topics related to information representation are explored, including metadata, full-text, and multimedia representation.

3.1 Metadata

Metadata is a term coined in recent years for referring to those descriptions that are specifically created to represent digital information accessible on the Net. That is to say, metadata was initially applied only to electronic resources and networked information. The connotation of the term has been expanded to include all practices for information representation because *metadata* has become a very fashionable term and the Internet is increasingly becoming a platform for accessing a wide variety of information.

3.1.1 What Is Metadata?

Metadata nowadays can be defined in two different ways: one is narrower in scope, implying descriptions provided for networked information and digital resources by following a standard or framework (e.g., Dublin Core) that is specifically created for this purpose. The other is broader in coverage, including cataloging and indexing data created for any kind of documents by using traditional methods for describing and organizing information. In this sense, for example, cataloging data produced with Dewey Decimal Classification (DDC) and Anglo-American Cataloging Rules/Machine Readable Cataloging (AACR/MARC) is also regarded as metadata.

Metadata can be derived or assigned by authors, repository managers, and third party creators (Dempsey & Heery, 1998). Some metadata information can also be embedded in the hyperstructure environment in the form of HTML tags or hyperlinks. While metadata provides frameworks for representing information, especially for networked resources, in addition to the existing ones (e.g., classifications and cataloging rules), Wool (1988) believes that metadata provision is essentially an extension of the traditional cataloging process. As briefly mentioned in Chapter 2, the traditional cataloging process is not feasible for organizing digital resources on the Net because of the unique features discussed in the following sections.

3.1.2 Characteristics of Digital Information on the Net

Digital information, as compared with printed resources, has its own characteristics. One must rely on certain hardware and software in order to view the content of digital information. In addition, digital information must be recorded in some kind of format that changes constantly as the hardware and software are upgraded. Sometimes, different versions of the same software program are compatible while other times and more often they are not. The compatibility issue becomes worse if one works with digital information generated using different software packages.

Furthermore, digital information on the Net is commonly recorded in the form of hyperstructure, which contrasts sharply with the flat structure of printed information. The advent of the Internet makes it easy for people to communicate and share resources. But the absence of a quality control mechanism on the Net results in the flooding of information whose quality has a large variance. Therefore, different methods should be adopted for describing and organizing digital information on the Net because existing standards (e.g., DDC and AACR/MARC) are designed primarily for representing printed information and before digital information was produced in huge quantities. Metadata emerges just to cope with the problem of representing digital information that is uniquely formatted, constantly changing, uneven in quality, and gigantic in quantity.

3.1.3 Examples of Metadata Standards

Although the concept of metadata is relatively new in the realm of information representation, a number of metadata standards have been developed and more are being conceived. Dublin Core and Resource Description Framework are some examples of metadata standards.

3.1.3.1 Dublin Core (DC)

Dublin Core (DC) is a simple content description model for electronic resources (Weibel, 1997). DC is a joint effort among experts from the library world, the networking and digital library research communities, and a variety of content specialists in a series of focused, invitational workshops called the Dublin Core Workshop series. Dublin Core consists of 15 elements: title, creator, subject, description, publisher, contributor, date, type, format, identifier, source, language, relation, coverage, and rights. As Weibel (1997) explained:

> ... the Dublin Core is not intended to replace richer description
> models such as AACR2/MARC cataloging, but rather to provide a
> core set of description elements that can be used by catalogers or
> non-catalogers for simple resource description. (p. 9)

In practice, Dublin Core is mainly used to provide simple descriptions for networked resources like Web sites. It seems to be the best-known standard among all the metadata models. Moreover, Dublin Core is the prototype application that drove the development of the Resource Description Framework (RDF) in the World Wide Web Consortium (W3C). Developers of the Dublin Core are closely involved in the W3C's RDF effort.

3.1.3.2 Resource Description Framework (RDF)

Resource Description Framework (RDF) was developed under the auspices of the W3C, becoming a W3C recommendation in February 1999. According to Shafer (1998):

> RDF is an infrastructure for encoding, modeling and exchanging
> metadata. At the heart of RDF is a simple three-part model:
> metadata is about a resource, the resource has one or more prop-
> erties, and each property has a value. (p. 21)

RDF uses eXtensible Markup Language (XML) as the transfer syntax. RDF is evolving to support the many different metadata needs of vendors and information providers (Weibel, 1997). RDF does not stipulate semantics, but rather provides the ability for each resource description community to define a semantic structure that reflects community requirement. In other words, unlike Dublin Core, RDF does not specify the particular elements the framework should have. Rather, it lets users choose and define the specifications within its framework based on their needs. RFD is therefore a foundation for processing metadata. According to Lassila (1997), RDF can be used in a variety of application areas: for example, in resource discovery to provide better search engine capabilities; and in cataloging for describing the content and content relationships available at a particular Web site, Web page, or digital library.

Other metadata standards (e.g., Digital Object Identifier [DOI]) have also been or are being developed for describing digital information on the Net. The need for such metadata standards is growing, and so are the concerns and questions.

3.1.4 Some Questions and Concerns about Metadata

As indicated earlier, metadata is created basically for describing and organizing digital resources. But in consideration of the nature of digital information or Internet resources, what is having metadata worth? In the printed world, every publication in a library collection is cataloged. The same practice apparently does not seem applicable for digital information on the Net because of the aforementioned reasons. A similar question also surfaces: Who would create the metadata given the huge quantity and mixed quality of networked resources?

The life expectancy of digital information to a large extent depends on the availability of the technology (e.g., hardware and software) used for information creation and access. As information technology develops rapidly, how can we ensure that digital resources, once described, can be located and retrieved throughout their lifetime?

In the printed world, the content of a publication remains the same until a new edition is released. But in the digital environment, the content of a document can be changed constantly. Then how do we deal with the dynamic contents of many of these resources when we try to provide metadata for them?

As discussed earlier, there are metadata standards for representing digital information on the Net. Meanwhile, we also have standards such as DDC and AACR/MARC that we have been using over the years for describing printed resources. Now, how should metadata be incorporated with other existing frameworks? Dempsey and Heery (1998) point out that the library community is only beginning to address how to bring "book world" metadata and "network" metadata into the same context of use. One attempt of this kind is OCLC's efforts in enhancing DDC with tools like WordSmith, which extracts new and emerging concepts and terminology from unrestricted text and then links them to the DDC (Vizine-Goetz, 1997).

The questions and concerns enumerated here have by no means exhausted all the challenges we face in representing digital data on the Net with the metadata approach. There is no general plan to specifically deal with these questions and concerns. Selective description, scheduled updating, and planned archiving are some of the current practices used in providing metadata for digital resources. Metadata, no matter how the current and future practices may change, is ultimately intended to facilitate the representation of digital information so that it can be more effectively retrieved later.

3.2 Full Text

When computer space was precious and computing time was costly, only surrogates of full text (e.g., bibliographical and indexing) information could be stored digitally for retrieval purposes. Today, even a regular desktop computer can be powerful in terms of storage space and computing capacity. In the digital age, full text storage and retrieval is no longer a rare commodity.

3.2.1 Representation of Full-Text Information

Representation of full-text information stored digitally is apparently a result of information technology advancement (Meadow, 1992). However, representation of full text is neither "Every word a descriptor" (Fugmann, 1993) nor "No indexing necessary." Either "invisible" or embedded representation other than the full text itself is needed to make the information retrievable. Representation of full text shares most of the properties of derivative indexing by adopting a stop-word list plus stemming and other similar techniques. This approach is nothing else but what Luhn called *keyword indexing*, which typically can be done automatically. Popular Internet retrieval systems such as AltaVista use the same method of keyword indexing to represent the full text they collect in their databases.

3.2.2 Difficulties in Representing Full Text

While representation of full text appears desirable to users, the outcome is often mixed and overwhelming because of the low precision problem. A pertinent example would be the results turned out by most Internet retrieval systems. More often than not, a keyword search on the Web will retrieve at least several thousand sites, among which only a few are probably relevant to the input query. Fugmann (1993) wrote:

> Full text storage imposes particularly high demands on storage space and on search time. The latter does not only comprise machine time consumption, but also, more important, the human's time and patience for weeding out the excessive amount of retrieval noise. (p. 99)

Full-text storage, as explained earlier, is no longer an issue in information representation and retrieval, thanks to the advancement of computing technology. However, the quality of representation for full-text information remains far from satisfactory, which reflects unmistakably in results produced by the majority of Internet retrieval systems. Future breakthroughs in solving this fundamental problem largely depend on research in natural language processing (NLP). Some of the important tasks NLP researchers must undertake include: 1) determine the syntactic structure of a sentence, also known as parsing (e.g., Time flies like an arrow), and 2) determine the meaning of a word in context or multiple meanings of a word (e.g., duty) (Knight, 1999). Further discussion of natural language processing will be provided in Chapter 12, Artificial Intelligence in Information Representation and Retrieval.

Typically, nontextual information such as diagrams, tables, etc. is inaccessible for retrieval in full-text information systems (Fugmann, 1993) if the representation is done automatically. But how about other types of multimedia information such as sound and moving images that are available in the digital format? How is multimedia information represented in a retrieval system? This is the topic examined in the next section.

3.3 Representation of Multimedia Information

More and more multimedia information is produced in the digital age, and the advent of the World Wide Web makes access to such information much easier than before. The booming of multimedia information, however, also presents unprecedented challenge to the field of information representation and retrieval.

3.3.1 Types of Multimedia Information

Multimedia is any combination of sound, image, and textual information in which images include both still and moving images. The words *sound* and *audio* can be treated as synonyms; however, there is a tendency to replace the term *audio* with *sound*. Sometimes, the phrase *spoken document* is also used for referring to textual information recorded orally (e.g., speeches and talks). As for image information, still images comprise pictures, photos, posters, and the like. Moving images can be with or without sound. Images without sound are animation or silent movies. Moving images with sound become video or movies. Text could appear in sound information as annotations, and in images as captions and subtitles. Figure 3.1 illustrates the different types of multimedia information.

3.3.2 Two Major Representation Approaches

In the past, multimedia was usually represented by descriptions based on, for instance, creator's name, image size, captions/subtitles, and keywords. This approach was thus called description-based, and has long been

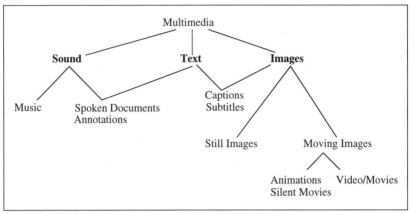

Figure 3.1   Taxonomy of Multimedia Information

employed by librarians and other information professionals to represent multimedia. However, the description-based representation of multimedia must always be done by people, yet the quality of end products fluctuates because, among other things, multimedia in some cases can hardly be explicitly and objectively described. For example, how can one describe explicitly an image that looks like a sunset or a piece of music that sounds soothing and peaceful? In addition, how can people have consistent and accurate representation of multimedia information by assuming this subjective approach?

The so-called content-based approach, i.e., representing multimedia by their own properties such as image color and sound pitch, is developed to overcome the limitations of the description-based approach. Dictated by the key technologies (e.g., speech recognition, pattern recognition, and image understanding) used in analyzing multimedia for representation purposes, the content-based approach is normally adopted by researchers in computer science. This approach also symbolizes a paradigm shifting in multimedia representation. If the description-based representation of multimedia is accomplished by describing the "ofness" (e.g., creator's name and publication year) and "aboutness" (e.g., keyword and subject) of the object, the content-based representation is attained by analyzing multimedia properties or attributes such as image color and sound pitch.

Multimedia attributes are multifaceted. Common attributes of still images include color, shape, and texture, which can further be decomposed by directionality, randomness, roughness, contrast, and the like. For sound information, properties like pitch and speed are often considered for representation purpose. These primitive or low-level features can usually be abstracted automatically or semi-automatically, thus eliminating the need for the costly, yet not always rewarding, process of human involvement in the representation process. Attributes for video information can be scaled down to those for still images and sound after the segmentation procedure.

Between these two distinctive approaches for multimedia representation, which one is used more often than the other in research and practice? Chu (2001) conducted a citation analysis of the literature published in the field of image indexing and retrieval, and found that the content-based approach had been dominating in the area especially in recent years. The complexity associated with the adoption of the description-based approach and the advancement of the key technologies employed in the content-based approach explain in part the emergence and flourish of the content-based method for multimedia representation. Chu's findings do not imply, however, that the content-based approach should be the only method chosen for representing multimedia. To the contrary, the description-based approach, if used properly and consistently, is able to achieve quality representation that would be hard for the content-based approach to attain. An integration of the two different approaches by combining the jewels of both seems to be an ideal road to take in representing multimedia.

3.3.3 Challenges in Representing Multimedia

Aside from the aforementioned problems associated with both representation approaches, moving image segmentation and speech parsing appear to be major stumbling blocks in representing multimedia. Moving image segmentation is a step necessary for decomposing moving images into, for instance, element units (e.g., camera operations and salient stills) and keyframes (i.e., frames that are representative of each shot) that would then serve as the basis for content analysis and representation (Zhang, et al., 1995). Other methods may use different algorithms and techniques for moving image segmentation. But the essence of the process remains the same; i.e., dividing moving images into smaller and meaningful entities so they could be adequately and accurately represented.

Speech segmentation refers to the process of segmenting full-length speeches into paragraphs, sentences, phrases, and words so that their subject contents can be examined and represented. The criteria for either moving image or speech segmentation are hard to formulate because of the very nature of moving images and sound information. That is, moving images are continuous in time and space. Yet, boundaries between consecutive camera shots cannot always be relied on for segmentation. Similarly, speech information does not contain punctuations and blank spaces as in written (e.g., English) information for natural segmentation. In addition, many constraints that pertain to speech information make the segmentation task more difficult. Some examples of speech constraints are nonspeech events (e.g., loud breath and tongue clicks), disfluencies (e.g., partially spoken words, pauses, and hesitations), and functional events or components (e.g., and, in addition) (Sparck Jones, et al., 1996). Because of these difficulties, more research is needed before we have quality and automatic methods for segmenting speech and moving images. Human involvement still seems necessary at present in representing multimedia even using the content-based approach.

Generally speaking, less research has been done in multimedia representation compared with that for text information. Of all the different kinds of multimedia, sound information appears the least studied in terms of representation. Meanwhile, the digital age has been witnessing the increasing amount of multimedia information. How to represent multimedia information therefore poses a serious challenge if we would like to make multimedia information accessible when needed.

3.4 Further Elaboration on Information Representation

Information representation is essential in information retrieval because of the following two points: first, information must be represented before it can be retrieved; second, representation quality directly affects retrieval performance. We generally base our representation on the ofness and aboutness of information with the exception of the content-based approach for representing multimedia. Ofness includes attributes such as author, language, and publication year while aboutness deals with the subject content of the information contained within. In comparison, information representation based on ofness is straightforward and less challenging, whereas representations concerning the aboutness judgment are much harder to accomplish.

We understand that retrieval performance suffers when information representation is not properly done. The importance of having quality information representation cannot be overemphasized. We should therefore aim for quality information representation so that we can find what we are looking for in the world of digital information.

References

Chu, Heting. (2001). Research in image indexing and retrieval as reflected in the literature. *Journal of the American Society for Information Science and Technology, 52(12)*, 1011–1018.

Dempsey, Lorcan, and Heery, Rachel. (1998). Metadata: A current view of practice and issues. *Journal of Documentation, 54(2)*, 145–172.

Fugmann, Robert. (1993). *Subject analysis and indexing: Theoretical foundation and practical advice*. Frankfurt/Main: Indeks Verlag.

Knight, Kevin. (1999). Mining online text. *Communications of the ACM, 42(11)*, 58–61.

Lassila, Ora. (1997). Introduction to RDF metadata: W3C note 1997-11-13. http://www.w3.org/TR/NOTE-rdf-simple-intro-971113.html. (June 22, 1998)

Meadow, Charles T. (1992). *Text information retrieval systems*. San Diego: Academic Press.

Shafer, Keith. (November/December 1998). Mantis project provides a toolkit for cataloging. *OCLC Newsletter*, 21–23.

Sparck Jones, Karen, et al. (1996). Experiments in spoken document retrieval. *Information Processing and Management, 32*, 399–419.

Vizine-Goetz, Diane. (1997). From book classification to knowledge organization: Improving Internet resource description and discovery. *Bulletin of the American Society for Information Science, 24(1)*, 24–26.

Weibel, Stuart. (1997). The Dublin Core: A simple content description model for electronic resources. *Bulletin of the American Society for Information Science, 24(1)*, 9–11.

Wool, Gregory. (1998). A meditation on metadata. *The Serials Librarian, 33(1/2)*, 167–178.

Zhang, H.J., et al. (1995). Video parsing, retrieval and browsing: An integrated and content-based solution. *Proceedings of ACM Multimedia* (pp. 15–24). New York: ACM Press.

CHAPTER 4

Language in Information Representation and Retrieval

As briefly discussed in §1.3.3, language is a fundamental component in both information representation and information retrieval (e.g., query formulation). Language in IRR assumes the form of either natural language or controlled vocabulary. Whenever there is a choice, a question arises as to which type of language one should use for representing and retrieving information.

4.1 Natural Language

Natural language is the language people speak and write. In natural language, no effort is made in IRR to limit or define vocabulary, syntax, semantics, and inter-relationships among terms. What people use for representing information or forming a query without consulting a controlled vocabulary is called natural language.

Natural language is commonly used in three ways for information representation and retrieval. One is to use terms taken from titles (e.g., KWIC), topic sentences, and other important components of a document for representation of information. The other is to use terms derived from any part of the document for information representation (e.g., derivative indexing). The third way is to use words or phrases extracted directly from people's questions for query representation, a topic discussed in Chapter 5.

Natural language basically consists of two kinds of words: significant words and function words. Significant words refer to those terms that carry substantial meanings or subject concepts whereas function words include articles, prepositions, and conjunctions such as *an, a, the, and, for, of, to, this, that, her,* and *their*. When natural language is applied in automatic IRR, a stop-word list (or stop-list for short) is usually compiled and stored in the system to prevent those stop words from becoming indexing or query terms. The stop-list contains all possible function words plus those significant terms that are too general or common to be suitable representations. Such terms are sometimes called trade words. For example, the word *engineering* would be meaningless either as an indexing term or a query term in an engineering database. Terms of ephemeral nature, known as buzzwords, are included in the stop-list as well because they would not last long as candidates for indexing or query terms. Most buzzwords appear as technology-related, for example, *Gopher* and *Denial of Service*. All the terms in the stop-list would not be used either for representation or retrieval purposes. However, each IRR system should have its own stop-list, created specifically for the system by considering its target audience and other factors.

As a counterpart of the stop-list, a go-list can also be created for natural language IRR (Rowley, 1992). All significant words, minus trade words and buzzwords, are eligible to the membership of a go-list. Like the stop-list, the go-list is also machine-readable and can be checked against at the time of representation and retrieval. In general, the go-list in natural language seems to be implemented less often than the stop-list for two reasons. First, the stop-list is shorter and easier to manage, and this mechanism would generally check the usage of natural language in IRR. Second, go-lists are mostly used for controlled vocabulary IRR in the form of thesauri, subject heading lists, and classification schemes.

In recent years, word lists as a semi-controlled vocabulary have increasingly been used in automatic IRR. Since word lists at most include synonyms and antonyms for terms contained in the documents and have little other vocabulary control, they appear to be another form of the go-list. Some Internet retrieval systems create and maintain a word list or go-list for their own use.

4.2 Controlled Vocabulary

Controlled vocabulary is an artificial language while its vocabulary, syntax, semantics, and pragmatics are limited and defined (Wellisch, 1995). The same word in different controlled vocabularies might have a different meaning given the orientation of the vocabulary. Controlled vocabulary must be constructed and maintained with specific subject area(s) in mind. Terms to be included in controlled vocabulary are selected by following the principle of either literary warrant or user warrant. Literary warrant means that terms to be included in the controlled vocabulary must be chosen from existing literature. Similarly, user warrant implies that terms to be selected for the inclusion in a controlled vocabulary must have been used in the past. Thesauri, subject heading lists, and classification schemes are the three major types of controlled vocabularies.

4.2.1 Thesauri

A thesaurus is a controlled vocabulary of terms in natural languages that are designed for postcoordination (National Information Standards Organization, 1993). Rowley (1992) further defines a thesaurus as:

... a compilation of words and phrases showing synonyms, hierarchical and other relationships and dependencies, the function of which is to provide a standardized vocabulary for information storage and retrieval systems. (p. 252)

Postcoordination is manipulative and has a shorter history than precoordinated languages such as classification schemes. Postcoordinated languages like thesauri allow users to coordinate terms at the time of representation and retrieval. The main drawback of postcoordination is false coordination. One example is that the two words *computer* and *desk* can be coordinated as either *computer desk* or *desk computer*, depending on what the original intention is. If *desk computer* is intended, coordinated results like *computer desk* will be considered as false coordination.

Standard notations are used in thesauri to specify the hierarchical, associative, homographic, and other relationships among the terms included. USE and UF (Used for) identify which terms in the thesaurus are preferred descriptors while SN (Scope Note) defines the meaning of a descriptor. NT (Narrower Term) and BT (Broader Term) display the hierarchical relationships among descriptors. The associative relationships among descriptors are expressed by the notation of RT (Related Terms). Thesauri are usually displayed alphabetically and hierarchically. Rotated or permuted display, systematic or classification display, and graphic display are sometimes seen in certain thesauri as well (Aitchison, Gilchrist & Bawden, 1997).

Thesauri are the most commonly used controlled vocabulary in nonmonograph information representation and retrieval for their specificity, flexibility, and ability to handle complex concepts. The thesaurus of Educational Resources Information Center (ERIC) Descriptors is an example in point.

4.2.2 Subject Heading Lists

A subject heading list is a controlled vocabulary of terms in natural language that are designed for both precoordination and postcoordination. Precoordination, predominant before the 1940s, combines terms before they are used for representation and retrieval. If one intends to, for example, represent or retrieve documents about *Internet retrieval systems*, the three-word phrase would appear exactly in a precoordinated language. Precoordinated controlled vocabularies are thus nonmanipulative. Since subject heading lists allow both pre- and postcoordination, their flexibility seems better than classification schemes but not as good as thesauri.

Terms in subject heading lists are called subject headings and are arranged alphabetically. Notations for subject headings include "See" for pointing to preferred terms from nonpreferred ones while "X," meaning "See from," presents the reciprocal expression of the "See" statement. For example, *handicapped* See *physically challenged*, and *physically challenged* X *handicapped*. Another set of notations for subject heading lists is "See also" and "XX," which stands for "See also from." "See also" indicates both the hierarchical and associative relationships among the chosen subject headings. That practice, however, undermines the specificity of subject heading lists. Similar to the X notation, XX shows the reciprocal expression of the "See also" statement.

Generally, subject heading lists are used for both information representation and retrieval although they appear to be applied less frequently as thesauri for representing and retrieving nonmonograph information. Sears' List of Subject Headings is one example of subject heading lists. Another well-known example is the Library of Congress Subject Headings, whose notations for the 11th edition, however, look more like that for thesauri.

4.2.3 Classification Schemes

A classification scheme is a controlled vocabulary of terms in alphanumeral that are designed mainly for precoordination. Units in classification schemes are called classes, which are further labeled numerically or alphabetically or alphanumerically. As the first type of controlled vocabulary being developed, classification schemes have witnessed and weathered the changes over the 20th century. On the other hand, they have been updated and revised again and again as time passes.

Unlike thesauri and subject heading lists, classification schemes are built on an artificial framework of knowledge. For instance, Dewey Decimal Classification (DDC) chooses to present the world of knowledge on the basis of 10 classes. Exactly 10 classes are formed at each level within the scheme, which indicates its rigidity. The hierarchical relationship among classes is displayed using indentations or different lengths of classification notations. That is, the longer a classification notation, the deeper the class locates in the hierarchical structure. Associative relationships among the terms are displayed via the "See" and "See Also" mechanism, which is only used occasionally.

Traditionally, classification schemes are most often selected for representing and retrieving monograph information. DDC and Library of Congress Classifications (LCC) are two examples of classification schemes.

4.2.4 A Comparison of Thesauri, Subject Heading Lists, and Classification Schemes

Table 4.1 summarizes the features for each of the three types of controlled vocabularies (CV). In addition to what has been discussed, analysis method

Table 4.1 Comparisons of Controlled Vocabularies

CV Feature	Thesauri	Subject Heading Lists	Classification Schemes
Term Component	Descriptors	Subject Headings	Classification Labels
Reference Notation	U, UF, SN BT, NT, RT	See, See also X, XX	See, See also
Analysis Method	Synthesis ⟷ Enumeration		
Coordination Method	Postcoordination ⟷ Precoordination		
Specificity	More ⟷ Less		
Flexibility	More ⟷ Less		
Target Document Type	Nonbooks	Books, nonbooks	Books

is another feature associated with controlled vocabularies. Enumeration, as an analysis method, means simply providing a list of terms without the ability to combine them to express something more complex. In contrast, synthesis allows some combination of terms to form more complex ones, either at the representation or the searching stages (Lancaster, 1986). Analysis method is in close relationship with the coordination method. That is, the precoordinate vocabulary is enumerative whereas the postcoordinate language is synthetic. Analysis and coordination methods also determine the specificity and flexibility of the controlled vocabulary. A synthetic and postcoordinate vocabulary appears more specific and accommodating than an enumerative and precoordinate language.

According to Table 4.1, thesauri seem to have more specificity and flexibility than classification schemes while subject heading lists fall in between on this spectrum of measurements, which explains why thesauri have been the most widely used controlled vocabulary among the trio in information representation and retrieval.

4.3 Natural Language vs. Controlled Vocabulary

Having discussed in the previous two sections the features and characteristics of both natural language and controlled vocabulary, it is time to contrast how they differ from each other and what they have in common as IRR languages.

4.3.1 Different Eras of IRR Languages

Controlled vocabulary is a latecomer compared with natural language in the history of information representation and retrieval. Four different eras can be identified so far in consideration of the IRR language.

The first era refers to the time before any controlled vocabulary was introduced. Natural language was the only language applied in information representation and retrieval, which was forming as a field. People began to realize the limitations (e.g., homographs and synonyms) of natural language when it was applied for representing and retrieving information.

The second era is signified by the introduction of controlled vocabulary to information representation and retrieval. In the beginning, precoordination systems such as classification schemes were heavily used. Other types of controlled vocabularies, i.e., subject heading lists and thesauri, were implemented later in the field. Both kinds of IRR languages coexisted in this era with a slant toward controlled vocabulary. Also, the debate on natural language vs. controlled vocabulary started then and has been continuing thereafter.

The third era is symbolized by the resurgence of natural language due to the keyword retrieval technique and the development of full-text systems. Controlled vocabulary is still applied for information representation and retrieval but most often to bibliographic IRR systems. Will controlled vocabulary remain a viable IRR language? More debates have been provoked in this era regarding the issue of natural language vs. controlled vocabulary.

The fourth era started when natural language interface was implemented in information representation and retrieval while the vocabulary control mechanism was employed behind the scenes. Since the vocabulary control mechanism is invisible to the end-user, Milstead (1995) called it invisible controlled vocabulary in a natural language retrieval environment. One example is to hide the controlled vocabulary behind the shell of natural language. Advances in natural language processing have also contributed significantly to this development. Some IR systems, for example Westlaw's WIN, have begun providing retrieval services in natural language.

Although the boundaries among the different eras do not appear very obvious and clear-cut, information representation and retrieval today apparently passed the first two eras and spans over the third and fourth eras in terms of the IRR language.

4.3.2 Why Natural Language or Why Controlled Vocabulary?

As language in IRR has been evolving through the four eras described, there must be reasons behind the coexistence of natural language and controlled vocabulary. The reasons are nothing else but the complementary pros and cons of the two kinds of IRR languages.

4.3.2.1 The Synonym Issue

The issue of synonyms is one of the most cited reasons against using natural language in IRR. In natural language, there are synonyms that use different terms referring to the same entity. For example, *microcomputers, personal computers, PCs, desktops, notebooks, Pentiums,* and the like are all synonyms. But which term in this partial list of synonyms should be chosen and used for representation and retrieval purposes? This is an issue in the debate about IRR languages. When controlled vocabulary is the selected IRR language, synonyms are not a source of concern because one and only one term is chosen from the controlled vocabulary as the preferred term. The rest of the synonyms are treated as nonpreferred terms and cross-referenced to the preferred term.

4.3.2.2 The Homograph Issue

Homographs, also known as polysemy, seem to be another argument often presented in the debate on natural language vs. controlled vocabulary. Homographs are terms spelled the same but carrying different meanings in different contexts. Terms such as *record, subject, drug, spring, bank,* and *duty* are just a few examples of homographs. In natural language representation and retrieval, homographs can produce problems such as ambiguity, due to the lack of context. However, Lancaster and Warner (1993) point out that the retrieval problem of ambiguity caused by homographs is often more theoretical than actual. Words that may be ambiguous on their own are no longer ambiguous when used in association with other words. It is true that homographs would not become ambiguous in meaning if used in conjunction with other words, but the conjunct usage may or may not happen in natural language representation and retrieval. By comparison, the context for interpreting homographs is always provided via assorted means in controlled vocabulary. One common method is to use parentheses to specify the context for homographs, for example, *duty* (responsibility) and *duty* (tax).

4.3.2.3 The Syntax Issue

Language has syntax. But how can syntax be expressed when natural language is selected for representing and retrieving information? Suppose a document is represented by the three terms *USA, automobiles,* and *Japan* in natural language; this document can be about, for example, Japan exporting automobiles to the USA, or the opposite, the USA exporting automobiles to Japan. It is unclear which country is the exporter when given only these three terms without any syntax information. This problem can be solved easily in controlled vocabulary with devices such as roles, which are symbols or numbers that indicate the syntax relationship between or among terms. In this example, we may define the number 1 as the role of exporter and then put it next to the term *Japan*, i.e., *Japan* (1). Similarly, we can designate the number 2 as the role of importer and then assign it to the term *USA* (2). The mechanism provided in controlled vocabulary allows people to tackle the syntax issue while natural language cannot.

4.3.2.4 The Accuracy Issue

It is always desirable to have an IRR language that could accurately represent information and search queries. That objective appears attainable if natural language is chosen as the IRR language. The rationale for the statement seems twofold. First, no additional manipulation (e.g., explanation) is needed in using natural language for IRR. Second, interpretation is unnecessary in natural language representation and retrieval because what the author/user uses will be the language for IRR. In comparison, controlled vocabulary is artificial, not reflecting the richness of natural language used for composing documents and expressing search queries. Controlled vocabulary also lacks specificity as a result of the language manipulation process. Interpretation of controlled vocabulary seems indispensable as the connotation and denotation of every term are defined with a particular target audience in mind. Such interpretation could inevitably introduce inaccuracy in IRR using controlled vocabulary.

4.3.2.5 The Updating Issue

Natural language needs no updating while controlled vocabulary does. New terms can be used for IRR purposes as soon as they appear in natural language while any change in controlled vocabulary cannot take effect until it goes through the rigid and lengthy updating process. Consequently, terms in controlled vocabulary are not always up-to-date. Requests that contain new terminology could hardly be satisfied if controlled vocabulary is chosen as the IRR language.

4.3.2.6 The Cost Issue

It takes time to create, maintain, and learn how to use a controlled vocabulary in information representation and retrieval. The time needed for these activities will eventually get translated as cost for information representation and retrieval. In comparison, natural language is just the language people commonly use. Neither training nor maintenance is required for doing IRR in natural language.

4.3.2.7 The Compatibility Issue

There are times when an IRR system needs to change its language during the course of its development or when a user would like to perform multiple database searching. The compatibility issue thus emerges for controlled vocabulary IRR as each controlled vocabulary has its own unique features and characteristics. It seems impossible, for example, to use Dewey Decimal Classification to perform IRR tasks in an OPAC that actually chooses Library of Congress Classification as its controlled vocabulary. If the systems are built on natural language, the switching or migration from one system to another would typically be seamless because natural language should always be compatible with itself.

In summary, the strengths for controlled vocabulary in synonyms, homographs, and syntax are weak points for natural language. Likewise, the weaknesses for controlled vocabulary in accuracy, updating, cost, and compatibility are strong points for natural language. Just as Rowley (1994) reiterated in one of her writings:

> There is a general recognition that controlled vocabulary and natural language should be used in conjunction with one another, and there is some agreement as to the relative merits of each of these systems. (p. 116)

In other words, both natural language and controlled vocabulary have found their own places in information representation and retrieval. But will this continue to be the case?

4.4 Language for IRR in the Digital Age

In the printed world, controlled vocabulary and natural language are used in parallel for information representation and retrieval. In the online world, close human involvement in IRR is still required and controlled vocabulary has taken a dominant position as an IRR language. In the digital age, natural language becomes the norm for information representation and retrieval while controlled vocabulary is only used occasionally or on a much smaller scale because of the unique features of digital information.

A large percentage of digital information is available on the Net where a quality control mechanism is absent, the life expectancy of the information is short, and the magnitude of information increases exponentially. Any application of the costly controlled vocabulary in the digital IRR environment therefore requires justification and rationalization. The popular Internet retrieval systems that undertake the bulk of IRR tasks on the Net make no use of controlled vocabulary. The use of word lists by a few Internet retrieval systems appears to be the closest example of vocabulary control in digital IRR.

However, natural language should not be the only IRR language in the digital environment because the lack of vocabulary control could be one of the major reasons for the poor results from Internet retrieval systems. In general, the task of controlling vocabulary could shift from the shoulders of information professionals to that of end-users when natural language is chosen as the IRR language. When controlled vocabulary is formally adopted, it is the information professional's responsibility to assume the task of vocabulary control. Otherwise, the end-user must assume the role of vocabulary control informally, for instance, by thinking about synonymous terms needed in a search query. The increased interaction between the end-user and the IRR system in the digital environment should not become an excuse for placing the responsibility of vocabulary control on the end-user's shoulders because even information professionals can only do a mediocre job in that respect.

So what will be the future of controlled vocabulary as an IRR language in the digital age? The answer does not seem certain at all. In retrospect, there are four different ways in which controlled vocabulary can be used in information representation and retrieval (Lancaster & Warner, 1993).

1. Controlled vocabulary for both representation and retrieval.

2. Natural language for both representation and retrieval but with the help of such controlled vocabulary devices as roles and precoordination.

3. Controlled vocabulary for representation only. The control for retrieval is done by means such as imbedded or invisible controlled vocabulary in the system.

4. Controlled vocabulary for retrieval only. This approach is implemented by the use of a search-only thesaurus, which is also known as postcontrolled vocabulary.

In consideration of the IRR features in the digital environment, the second approach appears more feasible than others. Both the third and fourth approaches store controlled vocabulary online for look-up or searching, which also seems to be a viable option for employing controlled vocabulary.

Vocabulary switching, i.e., a mechanism for automatically changing from one IRR language to another across different subject domains, is being researched and explored as a promising scheme for resolving the debate on natural language vs. controlled vocabulary. Once implemented, people can choose to use an IRR language at will without being confined to a predesignated selection, and will not be limited to the vocabulary in a specific subject domain. Rather, users can break the bondage of their near specialties and effectively utilize the whole of scientific information in the research (Schatz, 1997). Vocabulary switching is different from the "invisible controlled vocabulary" in two aspects. First, vocabulary switching relies heavily on research in natural language processing. Second, vocabulary switching deals with IRR languages from multiple (much more than two) domains while invisible controlled vocabulary basically handles translation between natural language and one controlled vocabulary stored online. For example, Chen, Schatz, and their colleagues generated concept spaces for 10,000,000 journal abstracts across 1,000 subject areas covering all engineering and science (Schatz, 1997). Concept spaces have been found effective for interactive term suggestion and vocabulary switching (Chen, et al., 1997).

In short, automatic representation and retrieval with scalable semantics appear to be the future as far as the language issue in the digital age is concerned.

References

Aitchison, Jean, Gilchrist, Alan, and Bawden, David. (1997). *Thesaurus construction and use: A practical manual.* 3rd ed. London: Aslib.

Chen, Hsinchun, et al. (1997). A concept space approach to addressing the vocabulary problem in scientific information retrieval: An experiment on the Worm Community System. *Journal of the American Society for Information Science, 48(1),* 17–31.

Lancaster, F.W. (1986). *Vocabulary control for information retrieval.* 2nd ed. Arlington, VA: Information Resources Press.

Lancaster, F.W., and Warner, Amy J. (1993). *Information retrieval today.* Arlington, VA: Information Resources Press.

Milstead, Jessica L. (1995). Invisible thesauri: The year 2000. *Online & CD ROM Review, 19(2),* 93–94.

National Information Standards Organization. (1993). *Guidelines for the construction, format, and management of monolingual thesauri.* Bethesda, MD: NISO Press. (ANSI/NISO Z39.19-1993).

Rowley, Jennifer E. (1992). *Organizing knowledge: An introduction to information retrieval.* Brookfield, VT: Gower.

Rowley, Jennifer E. (1994). The controlled versus natural indexing languages debate revisited: A perspective on information retrieval practice and research. *Journal of Information Science, 20(2)*, 108–119.

Schatz, Bruce R. (January 17, 1997). Information retrieval in digital libraries: Bringing research to the net. *Science, 275,* 327–334.

Wellisch, Hans H. (1995). *Indexing from A to Z.* 2nd ed. New York: H.W. Wilson.

CHAPTER 5

Retrieval Techniques and Query Representation

Now that the issue of language in IRR has been discussed in Chapter 4, it is time to move onto the next topic—retrieval techniques that should be considered in performing searches. Query representation, or query formulation, will be explained thereafter.

5.1 Retrieval Techniques

Retrieval techniques are designed to help users locate the information they need effectively and efficiently. A variety of techniques are available to users as information technology develops and as research on retrieval techniques advances. Of all the retrieval techniques, one group is called basic approaches, while the others are called advanced methods.

5.1.1 Basic Retrieval Techniques

Retrieval techniques such as Boolean searching, case sensitivity, truncation, proximity searching, and field search are basic approaches because they are generally supported by most IR systems. In the following sections, the functionality and features of basic approaches will be examined one by one.

5.1.1.1 Boolean Searching

As described briefly in §1.1.2.1, Boolean searching was named after the Englishman George Boole who conducted mathematical analysis of logic. Boole used three operators, namely, AND, OR, NOT, to summarize the logical operations of the human mind: the addition (AND) of different concepts to form more complex ones, the separation (NOT) of complex concepts into individual simpler ones (Smith, 1993), and the inclusion (OR) of more concepts to expand their connotation. All these logical operations are also known as Boolean logic. When Boolean logic is applied to information retrieval, the three operators, called Boolean operators, assume the following functionality:

- The AND operator for narrowing down a search
- The OR operator for broadening a search
- The NOT operator for excluding unwanted results

The AND operator combines two or more terms in a search statement, and requires all the terms be present in the documents found. For example, a search statement *filtering* AND *controversy* should get results about filtering as a controversy only. Any results about filtering in general or other controversies such as gun control would not meet the search requirement. The AND operator is especially helpful in searching for information covering complex concepts.

The OR operator expands a search by including more terms in the search statement. Terms being OR'ed together are in most cases synonyms or related terms. Documents that have any one of the terms are regarded as hits or anticipated results. For example, a search statement *filtering* OR *controversy* would turn out results about all kinds of filtering and controversies in addition to documents on filtering as a controversy. Obviously, the OR operator aims to expand search scope and increase retrieval outcome.

The NOT operator is more restrictive if compared with OR. NOT limits the search scope by excluding term(s) listed after the NOT operator. For instance, a search query *filtering* NOT *controversy* would retrieve information about all kinds of filtering (e.g., *water filtering* and *air filtering*) as long as it is not a controversy. The NOT operator can be used purposely to exclude unwanted results at the time a search query is formed.

When only one type of Boolean operator is used in a single search statement, it is called simple Boolean searching. When a single search statement includes more than one type of Boolean operator, it is called compound Boolean searching; the natural order for processing the three Boolean operators in most IR systems is:

- First: the NOT operator

- Second: the AND operator

- Third: the OR operator

In the example of compound Boolean search statement *filtering* OR *censorship* AND *controversy* NOT *libraries*, the NOT operator will be first processed to exclude any documents about controversies involving libraries (i.e., *controversy* NOT *libraries*). Then the AND operator will combine the two terms *censorship* and *controversy* with the *library* concept NOT'ed out already. Finally, the term *filtering* will be OR'ed with the document set generated in the previous searches. If the search results do not meet one's expectation, the end-user can use parentheses to change the natural order of processing or specify the intended order of processing. In the previous search statement, for instance, we can have ((*filtering* OR *censorship*) AND *controversy*) NOT *libraries* by applying parentheses. As a result, the order of processing for this statement would be OR, AND, NOT by following the rule that the most inner parentheses are processed first, the outer ones next, and so on. The retrieved documents will be on *filtering* or *censorship* as a *controversy* but not related to *libraries*. As shown, multiple pairs of parentheses can be used to specify a particular order of processing in a compound Boolean search statement. For this reason, compound Boolean searching is sometimes called nested Boolean.

As a retrieval technique, Boolean searching is by far used the most often among all the existing retrieval facilities. However, it takes time and practice to master Boolean search techniques, especially the compound Boolean search technique.

5.1.1.2 Case Sensitive Searching

For languages such as English, French, and Spanish where upper and lower cases make a difference, case sensitive searching allows the end-user to pinpoint exactly how a term is represented in a query and the system. For example, the word *Web* and *web* refer to two different entities. The upper case *Web* means the Internet application of World Wide Web while the lower case *web* is simply the web woven by spiders. Once the distinction between the two cases is made, the user can decide if case sensitive searching is needed. If one intends to look for information about the World Wide Web, the upper case *Web* should be chosen as query term. Otherwise, the lower case *web* can be used instead.

The application of case sensitive searching is on a much smaller scale when compared with Boolean search. However, it accomplishes specific types of retrieval tasks that no other retrieval techniques are able to.

5.1.1.3 Truncation

Truncation, known variously as wildcard, stemming, stripping, term masking, and conflation algorithm, is a technique for retrieving different forms of a term but all with one part in common. IR systems usually designate a particular symbol (e.g., question mark ? or asterisk *) for truncation purpose. For example, use of the truncated term of *network** as a query results in retrieving documents on *networks* and *networking*.

Truncating the term suffix, as just described, is called right truncation, which accounts for the majority of truncation practices. Truncation can also be done by taking away the prefix or infix (i.e., some characters in the middle of a term). Taking away the prefix is called left truncation whereas taking away the infix of the term is called middle or internal truncation. Left truncation is rarely seen, and few IR systems now support it. Middle truncation can be used to handle terms obeying different spelling conventions. For instance, truncated query term *col*r* will retrieve both *color* and *colour*.

Similarly, searching on *organi*ation* will get information on both *organiza-tion* and *organisation*.

It is important to truncate the right portion of a term if one intends to apply this retrieval technique. At one extreme, too much truncation (e.g., truncate *catalog* to *cat**) can lead to a lot of unwanted information. At the other end, truncating too little (e.g., truncate *catalogue* to *catalogu*) will not achieve the goal for truncation. To provide some control over truncation, many IR systems also allow the user to specify the exact number of charac-ters to be truncated.

5.1.1.4 Proximity Searching

While the AND operator can indicate which terms should be included in search results, it cannot specify how far apart these search terms are positioned in a document. For example, the Boolean search statement *filtering* AND *controversy*; these two terms could appear next to each other, several hundreds of words apart, or anywhere in between in the target document. Proximity searching, also known as adjacency search-ing, allows the user to specify precisely the proximity or distance between two search terms and their relative positions by using the WITH and NEAR operators. Notations for proximity searching may vary from system to system.

The WITH operator implies that the two linked terms should appear in the system next to each other and in the same order as stated in the search query. For instance, a search statement *information* WITH *technology* indi-cates that documents retrieved by the query must contain *information technology* as a phrase rather than anything else (e.g., *information and technology, technology information*). In addition, the extension of the WITH operator—nWITH can further request that the terms linked by the operator be within n (n=1, 2, ... n) words of each other and in the order specified. For example, a search statement *information* 2WITH *technology* would yield documents about *information and technology, information and network technology*, and the like.

The NEAR operator functions similar to the WITH operator, i.e., the two terms it links should be adjacent. But unlike the WITH operator, the terms linked by the NEAR operator can appear in any order as long as they are next to each other. For example, the search statement *information* NEAR *technol-ogy* would produce results on either *information technology* or *technology information*. The nNEAR operator requires that terms linked by the operator be within n (n=1, 2, ... n) words of each other but in any order. Thus, docu-ments containing the following sample phrases are all legitimate results of the search statement *information* 2NEAR *technology*:

- *information and technology*

- *information and network technology*

- *technology and information*

- *technology and business information*

Phrase searching, as opposed to word searching, is just one particular application of proximity searching if the original information gathered for IR systems is only represented by words (i.e., word indexed). To be more specific, the WITH operator can accomplish exact phrase searching while the rest of the proximity operators support searches using different juxtapositions of the terms specified in the search statement. The juxtapositions can also be extended beyond the range of n words but to a same field or paragraph in some IR systems. For example, DIALOG, an online IR system, allows the user to specify that search terms must appear within a same field (e.g., title field or abstract field) or paragraph.

5.1.1.5 Field Searching

Traditionally, document information is represented by attributes such as author, title, publication date, and document type. These attributes are called fields once they are represented in IR systems. When information or documents are represented by field, they can be retrieved later the same way. Field searching, by definition, restricts searches to one field or multiple fields instead of the entire document.

Field searching performs two functions. One function is to zero in on the information one is looking for if the field attribute (e.g., author's name) is known. For example, if we wish to learn about Hans Peter Luhn's work related to information retrieval, we may search by the term *information retrieval*. But we would immediately realize that such a search would inevitably bring out much more information than expected because all the works, including those by Luhn, will be retrieved as search results. If we conduct a search by the author's name, i.e., search by the author field, we should be able to get all the publications by Luhn on information retrieval as well as other topics. We can then use the AND operator to combine the previous search results with the term *information retrieval* to exclude Luhn's work in areas other than IR.

In addition to what we just depicted, field searching can also narrow down a search effectively. Assuming that a search on information retrieval is conducted in a system created for information science, the outcome could contain several thousand records. Few users would be willing to go over search results of that magnitude. At this point, field attributes such as publication year, language type, or document type can help narrow the search effectively.

Subject or concept searching (i.e., searching by the aboutness of information) followed by field searching (i.e., searching on the ofness of information) is a common approach to refine retrieval results.

Most information available on the Internet is not represented by field attributes in Internet retrieval systems because of the reasons we discussed in previous chapters. Therefore, field searching is generally not applicable to information retrieval on the Internet. Nevertheless, other basic retrieval techniques discussed in this section are either fully or partially supported by Internet retrieval systems, a theme explored further in Chapter 8, Information Retrieval Systems.

5.1.2 Advanced Retrieval Techniques

The basic retrieval techniques described earlier are implemented in most, if not all, IR systems. By contrast, advanced retrieval techniques are provided selectively in a small portion of existing IR systems after they have been tested and experimented in research laboratories.

5.1.2.1 Fuzzy Searching

Fuzzy searching sounds related to truncation but with a major difference. While truncation is intended to retrieve different forms of a term when they share some parts in common, fuzzy searching is designed to find terms that are spelled incorrectly at data entry or query input. For example, the term *computer* could be misspelled as *compter, compiter, comptuer,* or *compyter.* Optical Character Recognition (OCR) or compressed texts could also result in erroneous contents. Fuzzy searching is thus designed particularly for detection and correction of spelling errors or errors that result from OCR and text compression (Grossman & Frieder, 1998).

N-gram is one special technique for the implementation of fuzzy searching. Simply put, n-grams are a fixed length consecutive series of n (n=2, 3, ... n) characters in a term (Kowalski, 1997) or a term decomposed into word fragments of size n. Take the term *fuzzy searching* as an example, we can have:

- Bi-grams (n=2): fu uz zz zy se ea ar rc ch hi in ng

- Tri-grams (n=3): fuz uzz zzy sea ear arc rch chi hin ing

Other types of n-grams (e.g., quart-grams or penta-grams) are also available. These n-grams, not necessarily representing the semantic meaning of the term, become the basic units for identifying possible errors. Matching algorithms are then used to determine whether or not a match exists between the representation and a query (Grossman & Frieder, 1998). If all the n-grams for a term match the query but one or two do not, an error is detected and the correct outcome can be presented.

In other words, fuzzy searching can tolerate errors made at the time of data entry or query input. Documents containing errors due to misspelling, OCR, or similar causes would not have been retrieved if there were no fuzzy searching technique.

5.1.2.2 Weighted Searching

There are times when the user wishes to put different emphases on each term in a query. For example, in the search query *filtering* AND *controversy*, the user is more interested in the *controversy* aspect rather than *filtering* per se. Weighted searching is devised specifically for that purpose.

For weighted searching, weights are assigned to terms when a search query is composed to indicate proportionally their significance or the emphasis the user placed upon them. Weights can be given in the form of either symbols (e.g., symbol * in the ERIC system denoting major descriptors) or numerals (both decimals and integers). The weighting scale (e.g., a weighting scale of 1 to 5 with 5 being the highest point) is also variously defined by individual IR systems. Of course, a prerequisite for conducting weighted searching is that weighting has been applied at the representation, or more specifically, the indexing stage. For instance, in executing the weighted search query *filtering3* AND *controversy6*, the user would expect to get documents in which these two terms are represented using the same weighting scale; i.e., a weight of 3 and 6 is assigned respectively to the terms *filtering* and *controversy*.

Threshold, a concept closely related to weighted searching, can be used to specify when search results satisfy the weighted query. Assuming the threshold for the above weighted searching is set to 9, then any results with a threshold less than 9 (e.g., a document on the same topic but with a weight of 3 for *filtering* and 5 for *controversy*) would not be regarded as hits in this case.

Obviously, determining a weight to be assigned to terms is crucial in weighted searching. There are different weighting algorithms in usage. Term location, term proximity, term frequency, inverse document frequency, and individual judgment are the major criteria for weight assignment. Of those criteria, however, mainly individual judgment or the deterministic method (Davis, 1997) can be practically implemented for weighted searching because the user, at the time of assigning weights to query terms, has no knowledge about the documents to be retrieved. Yet, all the other criteria for weight assignment are dependent on the attributes of terms derived from the original documents. Therefore, weighting techniques based on term location and other criteria seem applicable only to weighted indexing.

Weighted searching based on individual judgment sounds very subjective. Nevertheless, its implementation actually relies further on a combination of such factors as information need, the nature of IR systems, and kinds of results expected. In other words, the user decides the weights for query terms by taking into consideration those specific factors. The weight assignment at the time of query formation is therefore not merely an arbitrary exercise.

As indicated earlier, there are more weight assignment criteria to choose from for weighted indexing than for weighted searching. Among those criteria, term location refers to where the term appears in a document. As a rule of thumb, a term that appears in such places as the title, section headings, and topic sentences would receive a higher weight than those present in other parts of a document. Term proximity means the distance between indexing terms in a document. Generally speaking, the shorter the distance, or the closer the proximity between the terms under consideration, the higher the indexing weight the terms will be given. Term frequency (tf), on the other hand, is defined as the number of times a term appears in a document. As discussed previously, terms with high frequency alone are not necessarily good indexing term candidates because they could be function words or words of insignificant meaning in retrieval. Rather, the best indexing terms, or terms that should be given high weights, are those that occur frequently in individual documents but rarely in the rest of the database (Salton, 1989). So the number of documents to which a particular term is assigned should also be considered in determining weights. This measure is known as inverse document frequency (idf) because the weights assigned are in reverse proportion to the document frequency. Namely, the fewer documents a term is assigned to, the higher weight it receives.

Since term frequency is often used in conjunction with inverse document frequency to determine the weight to be assigned to terms, this practice is called the tf.idf weighting technique. Document length (dl) is also considered sometimes in combination with the tf.idf weighting technique, adding another parameter in determining term weights. If tf and idf are held constant, the longer the document that contains the term, the higher weight the term will receive. The tf.idf.dl weighting technique is widely adopted in the Text REtrieval Conference (TREC) projects (Sparck Jones, 2000). Detailed discussion of the TREC series is provided in Chapter 11.

Other weighting techniques, e.g., probability approaches, are used in practice as well. Moreover, these weighting techniques are often implemented in various combinations with other methods. For example, term location could be applied jointly with term proximity in a weighting algorithm. Weighted searching opens up another avenue for effective retrieval of information.

Figure 5.1 Process of Query Expansion

5.1.2.3 Query Expansion

Even if careful thought has been given to query formation, a topic explored in §5.3, the user cannot guarantee that the search query needs no revision or expansion once it is formed. Query expansion is a retrieval technique that allows the end-user to improve retrieval performance by revising search queries based on results already retrieved. Searches using query expansion are iterative and interactive, as shown in Figure 5.1.

Results obtained from searches after each query submission are examined to find out if any information from the results can be derived and incorporated into a newer version of the query. Theoretically, the process of query expansion can be repeated until satisfactory results are obtained. Interaction between the IR system and user during the query expansion process can help improve retrieval performance.

Query expansion can be implemented manually and automatically. For manual query expansion, the user decides how the search results can be utilized to modify the query. For automatic query expansion (also known as relevance feedback), the top-ranked documents in the search results are assumed relevant, and thus included in query revision. The end-user is not directly involved in the process of modifying the query (Salton, 1970; Grossman & Frieder, 1998). By this point, we can see that query expansion is not a very precise expression for describing this process as the query will not necessarily be expanded but will always get modified. Therefore, query modification appears to be a more appropriate terminology for naming this process.

The ranking of outputs done by many IR systems is a vital mechanism for relevance feedback or automatic query expansion. Similar to the weighting techniques discussed previously, ranking algorithms are based most often on criteria such as term location, term proximity, and term frequency. Typically, each individual IR system implements its own ranking algorithms by choosing certain criteria. Such ranking algorithms are usually not published and in the public domain. A new ranking criterion called the backlink approach was introduced in 1998 by Google, an Internet retrieval system, to rank Web search results (Vidmar, 1999). The backlink approach judges the quality of a Web page by, among other things, counting how many other Web sites provide hyperlinks to it. More discussion on the backlink approach is in Chapter 8, Information Retrieval Systems.

Query by example is one implementation of query expansion where the term *example* refers to the results already retrieved; in other words, results that have been retrieved will be treated as examples for further queries. In sound and image information retrieval, the example could come directly from the user, e.g., a hand-drawn sketch of a flower, rather than information extracted from the search results. When searching on the Internet, the user can do relevance feedback by simply clicking on hyperlinks such as "More like this."

Query modification is often needed in information retrieval as it can help improve retrieval performance by revising the search query based on results already obtained. As a retrieval technique, query expansion, and especially relevance feedback, have wide application and great potential in information retrieval in the digital age.

5.1.2.4 Multiple Database Searching

Multiple database searching means searching in more than one IR system simultaneously. The term database here is customarily considered a synonym for system. The need for searching multiple databases seems threefold. First, searching in a single IR system may not get what the user is looking for because every IR system has its own coverage, orientation, and features. In this case, other IR systems should be tried for the search. Second, multiple database searching can serve as a selection tool if the user is not sure which system(s) would be the best choice for a given query. Third, the results obtained from multiple database searching can also suggest or indicate suitable systems for the user to conduct further searches.

In searching multiple databases, one must pay specific attention to the differences in query syntax, language, and search capabilities each system provides. A feature quite common and basic in one system may not be supported in others. Furthermore, the same feature supported in both systems may not be expressed the same. For example, the Boolean operator AND is used in one system, while another system uses the plus sign +. The languages used in multiple systems are likely dissimilar as well. Possibilities include natural language vs. controlled vocabulary, different controlled vocabularies, and natural language used in different disciplines.

Another challenge that multiple database searching faces is how to handle data of different formats (e.g., ASCII, MAchine Readable Cataloging [MARC]) stored in multiple databases. Z39.50, a standard for Information Retrieval Service Definition and Protocol Specification for Library Applications, is set up to, among other things, handle data of all formats for retrieval tasks. Therefore, IR systems that are Z39.50 compliant can be searched simultaneously regardless of their format differences and geographical proximity (Michael & Hinnebusch, 1995). Approved by the American National Standard Institution (ANSI)/National Information Standard Organization (NISO), Z39.50 is widely applied in Web-based OPACs (WebPACs) and some other types of IR systems. With Z39.50, the end-user can also retrieve information using a uniform interface no matter what interface an IR system originally had.

Aside from the aforementioned problems and challenges associated with multiple database searching, how to merge results retrieved from multiple databases poses another concern. For example, ranked outputs become increasingly the norm in presenting search results. Yet ranking algorithms vary from one IR system to another. It is unrealistic to expect that a ranking of 0.90 for one document retrieved from one system is the same as a result of the same ranking but from a different system. Data fusion, the combination of results from differing systems using certain methods, appears a possible solution to this problem. Belkin and his colleagues, for instance, suggested a group of techniques for merging results of multiple search strategies on multiple databases to produce the best possible response to a query (Belkin, et al., 1995). The Database Merging track of TREC, discussed in Chapter 11, is devoted to tackling the problem of merging data from heterogeneous sources to present a uniform output (Voorhees & Harman, 2000).

Multiple database searching is usually supported by IR services or vendors (e.g., DIALOG) that manage multiple databases rather than a single IR system. The so-called metasearch engines on the Internet perform a similar function for retrieving information from various sources on the Net. This topic is discussed further in Chapter 8, Information Retrieval Systems.

5.2 Selection of Retrieval Techniques

As shown in the previous section, there are different retrieval techniques for the end-user to choose from for a given search task. Many factors need to be considered when selecting retrieval techniques. In this section, however, the discussion on the selection of retrieval techniques is focused on their functions and retrieval performance.

5.2.1 Functions of Retrieval Techniques

Each retrieval technique functions in certain ways so that the user can rely on it to achieve the right search objective. For instance, the use of truncation technique retrieves various forms of a term if they share a common portion in their spellings. In comparison, fuzzy searching accommodates spelling and OCR errors if some matches can still be found between the two different versions of a term. Therefore, the first question a user should ask when choosing a retrieval technique is what the retrieval technique (e.g., weighted searching) can accomplish. It is only after this question is answered that the user knows if the retrieval technique under consideration is suitable for a given query.

5.2.2 Retrieval Performance

Retrieval performance is traditionally and most often measured by precision and recall although these two measures are continuously the foci of controversial discussions. For presentation clarity purpose, the following discussion concentrates only on precision and recall as retrieval performance measures, while the controversies around them are examined in Chapter 11, Evaluation of Information Representation and Retrieval.

Precision, by definition, is the ratio between the number of relevant documents retrieved and the total number of documents retrieved from a system. It measures the discriminating ability of an IR system, i.e., the ability of separating the irrelevant from the relevant. If 100 documents are retrieved from a search of which 35 are judged relevant, the precision ratio for this search is 35 percent. On the other hand, recall is defined as the ratio between the number of relevant documents retrieved and the total number of relevant documents in a system. It measures the retrievability of an IR system. Suppose that there are 100 relevant documents on a given topic in a system, of which 45 are retrieved; the recall ratio for this search would be 45 percent. For both precision and recall, the higher the percentage number is, the better the retrieval performance. But it is impossible to get search results high in both precision and recall because of the inverse relationship between the two measurements.

As far as retrieval performance is concerned, all the retrieval techniques depicted in §5.1 can be categorized as either precision improving (e.g., Boolean operator AND, weighted searching) or recall improving (e.g., Boolean operator OR, fuzzy searching). Therefore, the selection decision of retrieval techniques should also be made in consideration of the retrieval performance the user anticipates. If search results of high precision are expected, corresponding retrieval techniques need to be chosen, and vice versa.

5.2.2.1 Retrieval Techniques for Improving Precision

Boolean operator AND improves precision by combining two or more terms in a search query for specifying the precise implication of a search request. For example, if there are three terms *filtering*, *controversy*, *Web* in a search request, precise results can be expected by AND'ing all three together. If only two of the terms are included in a search query, the results will increase in number but decrease in precision because the restriction on the third term is relaxed.

The Boolean operator NOT enhances the precision of a search by eliminating unwanted terms from a query. Suppose the user wants to search for documents on filtering controversy with regard to Web materials but not about TV programs, the NOT operator can be used to achieve that purpose.

Case sensitive search increases the precision of a search by differentiating the upper and lower cases of term spellings. The terms *Web* and *web* illustrate the case in point. If the user is only interested in finding materials on *Web* as an Internet application, case sensitive searching should retrieve exactly what the user intends to get. If an IR system does not support case sensitive searching, the user would have no way of making a distinction between the two different cases of the term. Consequently, documents on both *Web* and *web* will be retrieved as legitimate results and the precision of the search will be negatively affected.

The WITH operator of proximity searching is also a method for improving precision because it specifies the order in which the search terms the WITH operator links appear in the original document or its representation. If a search statement reads as *information* WITH *technology*, these two terms specified must appear exactly in the same order in the retrieval system. Any other compositions of the terms (e.g., *technology information, information and technology*) would not produce precise results but search noise. The nWITH operator functions similarly as the WITH operator in terms of precision improvement except that it allows variations within the range of n words between the two terms the operator links.

Field searching ensures the precision of a search by limiting it to a particular field. Each field is established to represent one attribute of a document. If a query is about one document attribute (e.g., author), the search will be more precise when it is restricted in that field than having a comprehensive search in all the fields. It is possible that other fields contain the author's name for various reasons, but these fields are not intended to reflect the author attribute of documents.

Weighted searching, another precision-improving technique, assigns weights to query terms. By doing so, the user can specify the emphasis of a query and thus get results that match more precisely with expectations. Take the search statement of *filtering* AND *controversy* again as an example, the user can put different emphases on the two terms by assigning different weights to them. If a higher weight is assigned to the term *controversy*, then the emphasis of this query is on *filtering* as a *controversy*. In other words, the user can be more precise about a particular query when using weighted searching.

In summary, the AND and OR operators of Boolean searching, case sensitivity searching, the WITH operator of proximity searching, field searching, and weighted searching can all be used in their various capacities to improve the precision of retrieval tasks. Retrieval techniques for improving recall will be explained and recapitulated in the next section.

5.2.2.2 Retrieval Techniques for Improving Recall

The Boolean operator OR, as described before, only requires either of the two terms it links appearing in the document to match a query. As a result, search results increase in number and so does the recall, presumably. If either term in the search statement *filtering* OR *controversy*, for example, appears in the system, the query will get a hit. The restrictions on the OR search seem to be much less compared with the other two Boolean operators. The less the restriction a search has, the higher the recall it gets.

Truncation expands search results by allowing a specific part of a term to take various forms as long as they share one common component (e.g., word stem). In that case, all the variations of a word stem are counted in the search. For example, a search query of *e-journal** will retrieve documents containing the term of either *e-journal* or *e-journals*. Obviously, the recall for this search is consequently higher than that for the search in which the query term is not truncated. When a search term is not truncated (e.g., *e-journal*), the search results will only contain those documents having the term spelled exactly as in the query.

The NEAR operator of proximity searching provides opportunity for retrieving more relevant results by permitting the terms the operator links to appear in either order in the system database. So a search on *information* NEAR *technology* will retrieve documents about either *information technology* or *technology information*, and thus increase the possibility of improving recall. The nNEAR operator works in a similar manner as the NEAR operator but is even more accommodating by allowing variations within the range of n words between the two terms the nNEAR operator connects.

Fuzzy searching has the potential to improve recall by detecting and correcting errors that result from spelling, OCR, and other sources. If a document is about *cellular phone* but the term is misspelled as *celluler phone*, a search using the fuzzy technique will still be able to retrieve the document. Recall for this search is thus increased.

Query expansion aims to retrieve more relevant results by modifying a query based on the previous batch of search results. As known, this modification process can be repeated until enough relevant results are obtained. Recall, a measurement for the proportion of relevant documents retrieved out of all those that exist in a system, is clearly the parameter to be improved in query expansion. For example, the first round of a search only retrieved five documents relevant to the query of *vector space model*. After viewing the results just obtained, Salton's name (e.g., *Salton, G.)* is chosen to be incorporated in forming a new query for the second round of search. If six more relevant documents are retrieved as a result, this would be a remarkable increase in recall.

Multiple database searching offers another opportunity for improving recall because more databases are used in the search. When a query is searched in multiple databases, the chance for obtaining more relevant results becomes bigger than from a single IR system. Moreover, each single IR system can only include certain amounts and selected types of information. But a group of IR systems can undoubtedly cover a wider variety of information in larger quantity.

As shown, the OR operator of Boolean searching, truncation, the NEAR operator of proximity searching, fuzzy searching, query expansion, and multiple database searching can all expand searches in one way or another. Although more results would not necessarily result in higher recall for information retrieval, they can increase the possibility of getting a more relevant outcome for a given query. In addition, having known how each retrieval technique affects the recall and precision measurement of a search task, users can then make educated decisions in choosing the right retrieval techniques for their searches.

5.3 Query Representation

An information need must be expressed verbally or in writing before a search can be performed to satisfy it. The expressed information need is called a search request or retrieval question, usually in natural language. The search request can then be transformed into a query using the IR system's facilities such as query syntax, retrieval techniques, and controlled vocabulary if one is adopted. That transformation process is labeled as query representation—the most critical factor in retrieval (Sparck Jones, 2000).

5.3.1 General Steps

Query representation is an intellectual exercise that typically consists of the following steps:

1. Conduct a concept analysis of the search request by decomposing it into concept groups or facets

2. Think about synonyms, broader terms, and narrower terms of the concepts identified

3. Translate these terms into controlled vocabulary if one is used

4. Use Boolean logic to OR all the synonyms (terms) in every concept group, AND relevant facets, and then NOT out unwanted facet(s)

5. Apply other retrieval techniques where needed

Although these steps are not carved into stone, they comprise the essence in query representation. There could be some variations in practice. The following is a step-by-step discussion of the query representation process in consideration of its crucial role in information retrieval.

5.3.1.1 Concept Analysis

The first step in query representation is to parse a search request into concept groups or facets. The search request, for example, is to locate documents discussing Web filtering as a controversy rather than an information technology. We find, after analysis, that there are three discrete concepts in the search request as shown in Table 5.1.

Table 5.1   Concept Analysis of a Search Request

Concept 1	Concept 2	Concept 3
Web filtering	Controversy	Information technology

In this case, the terms included in the request happened to be the same as the concepts involved. However, there are situations where the two do not exactly match. For instance, a search request may contain the terms *buses* and *subways*, but the underlying concept is about *public transportation*. Therefore, *public transportation* rather than *buses* and *subways* should be used for representation purpose here. In addition, only nouns or noun phrases should be used to represent the concepts. Verbs, if there are any in the request, will be represented by Boolean operators. Other parts of speech should not be selected for representing concepts identified in a search request at all.

5.3.1.2 Term Variations

Terms, in most cases, have synonyms, broader terms, narrower terms, and other variations. The objective of this step in query representation is to think

Table 5.2   Concept Groups for Query Representation

Concept 1	Concept 2	Concept 3
Web filtering	Controversy	Information technology
Filtering Censorship Filtering on the Web Filtering on the WWW Censorship on the Web Censorship on the WWW	Debate Dispute	Network technology Computer technology

about as many variations as necessary for the concepts previously identified so that the concepts will be represented comprehensively. Table 5.2 shows possible variations for the three concepts identified in the previous step.

As shown in Table 5.2, not all the possible term variations are exhausted because of certain reasons such as popularity and brevity. Under Concept 1, for instance, we did not list *World Wide Web* as a variation for *Web*. The decision on whether a particular term should be listed depends on several subjective criteria such as anticipated recall and familiarity with the topic. While not all the term variations suggested will be included in the final query for a search, listing a number of possibilities can help select candidate query terms. This practice of listing term variations can also provide entry terms for choosing the rights terms from controlled vocabulary if one is used.

5.3.1.3 Term Conversion

If a controlled vocabulary is used as the IR language, the terms expressed in natural language in the previous step should be converted accordingly into the chosen vocabulary. Otherwise, the user can skip this step in query representation and move to the next one. The conversion requires familiarity with the controlled vocabulary in use, and can take any of the following approaches:

- Exact equivalent—The term listed has an exact equivalent in the controlled vocabulary, which appears to be the easiest choice among all the conversion approaches.

- Synonyms or related terms—The term under consideration only has synonyms or related terms in the controlled vocabulary. Efforts should then be made to choose the one that is the closest in meaning to the term being converted.

- Broader terms—The term listed only has broader terms in the controlled vocabulary. Specificity of the original term will be negatively affected as a result of this conversion.

- Narrower terms—The term under consideration only has narrower terms in the controlled vocabulary. Breadth of the original term will be reduced as a consequence of this conversion.

- Unlisted terms—The term to be converted is either a proper name (i.e., corporate name, personal name, or place name) or a new term, having no counterpart in the controlled vocabulary. A new term, called identifier, has to be created for conversion purpose if the user happens to be an information professional. It is very likely in this case that the newly created term is the same as the one being converted.

Except for the exact equivalent approach, all other conversion approaches require the interpretation of terms. The accuracy of the interpretation determines the accuracy of the conversion practice.

5.3.1.4 Application of Boolean Operators

Suppose all the terms grouped under each concept in Table 5.2 are in the right form they should be, the task for this step of query representation is to apply Boolean operators to link the terms and concepts identified previously according to the relationships among them. Although there might be some deviations in implementation, there are two general rules for applying the Boolean operators:

1. Link the terms in a same concept group (e.g., all the terms in a column in Table 5.2) with the OR operator.

2. Link every concept in a search request (i.e., in the row of Table 5.2) with the AND or NOT operator, depending on the need.

Figure 5.2 illustrates this process symbolically with the concept groups enumerated in Table 5.2 for the search request example we used in this section.

Apparently, a couple of points need to be clarified about Figure 5.2. First, how many terms from each concept group should be included in the query?

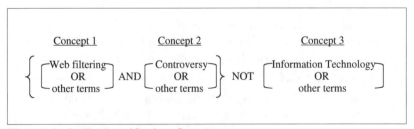

Figure 5.2   Application of Boolean Operators

In other words, how many terms should be OR'ed together to represent each concept identified? The answer relies mainly on the number of results the user expects to get. The more terms are OR'ed together, the more results one will receive. Likewise, the fewer terms are OR'ed together, the fewer results one will obtain. One common practice in making such a decision is to prioritize all the terms listed, and then choose the first few terms in the list to be OR'ed together according to one's need. In Figure 5.2, we do not specify how many terms to use to represent the corresponding concept. Rather, we only indicate that other terms are available for the OR operator.

The second point that needs to be explained in Figure 5.2 is the use of parentheses. In discussing Boolean searching in §5.1.1.1, we introduced the order of processing for compound Boolean searches. The example illustrated in Figure 5.2 is a compound Boolean search, which requires the use of parentheses to change the natural order of processing. If not, the end results will be anything but what the user intends for the search. Assume we take away all the parentheses in Figure 5.2 and keep all the terms we suggested in Table 5.2 as well as in the same order, the first term listed under Concept 3 (i.e., *information technology*) would be excluded from the result set created for the last term shown under Concept 2 (i.e., *dispute*). Other unexpected results would also be generated eventually. Therefore, parentheses have to be used if the natural order of processing is to be changed.

The importance of the Boolean technique in information retrieval is self-explanatory, as Boolean logic has to be applied in query representation unless a search query contains only one single term. However, the application process of Boolean searching actually is more complex than it appears. More discussion on the complexity and difficulties of Boolean searching is in Chapter 7, Information Retrieval Models.

5.3.1.5 Use of Other Retrieval Techniques

There are many other techniques the user can apply to represent a query more precisely and explicitly. Again, taking the request about Web filtering as an example (see Table 5.2), the end-user can consider:

- Whether case sensitive searching is available to differentiate *Web* from *web*

- Whether the term *debate* should be truncated

- Whether proximity operators such as WITH or NEAR should be used to represent *information technology*

- Whether the search should be limited to certain fields, e.g., title field and/or descriptor field

- Whether the chosen IR system supports fuzzy searching

- Whether weights should be assigned to any of the terms selected

- Whether relevance feedback is supported by the system or whether query expansion should be manually applied

- Whether multiple databases should be tried and searched

As indicated before, not many IR systems provide all the search facilities we have discussed so far. Therefore, this list of retrieval techniques serves more as a checklist than as a must-do inventory. By this time, the query should be fully represented and is ready to be submitted for searching.

Query representation, as information representation, is a very complex process. Although we summarized these five steps to illustrate the major points of query representation, the actual practice may not consist of the same number of steps and follow the same order. For example, experienced users tend to combine some of the steps while novice users would be reluctant to take any shortcuts.

To sum up, Step 1 of query representation deals with the parsing of search requests into concepts. Step 2 and Step 3 are concerned with the translation of concepts into query terms. Step 4 and Step 5 focus on the application of various retrieval techniques.

Since each user, search request, and IR system are different, query representation should reflect this phenomenon by taking into consideration the uniqueness of the process.

5.3.2 Difficulties with Query Representation

Query representation, as discussed, is not a mechanical but an intellectual process, which requires thinking and judgment. In addition, there exist several difficulties in this intellectual exercise.

Concept analysis constitutes the first difficulty in query representation. The user should have the right knowledge, experience, and skills to identify and express the concepts contained in a search request. Subjectivity can easily slip into the process. Inaccurate analysis is not an uncommon phenomenon.

The second difficulty in query representation is the language. Natural language is rich, flexible, subtle, and vague while controlled vocabulary is rigid, artificial, and hard to maintain. Yet, a search request must be represented as precisely as possible using either language. This conversion can introduce discrepancy into the representation process, and eventually affect retrieval performance. The use of controlled vocabulary increases the difficulty for query representation as it takes time and effort for the user to become familiar with it. On the other hand, the use of natural language in representing queries has its own drawbacks as discussed in Chapter 4.

Applying the right retrieval techniques presents another difficulty in query representation. Each IR system defines its own specifications and implementations of retrieval techniques (e.g., the + sign in some Internet retrieval systems means the Boolean operator AND while in others as the weighting symbol). Mastering the usage of these techniques also takes time and needs practice.

The aforementioned difficulties are all likely to cause an inaccurate representation of search requests, which in the end lead to mismatches between the query representation and information representation. To overcome these difficulties, we could on one hand educate and train the user, and on the other look forward to breakthroughs in research on automatic query representation.

5.3.3 The Automatic Approach

Automatic representation of queries is very desirable if it can actually be accomplished. Unlike automatic indexing, which includes both mechanical as well as intellectual activities, automatic query representation only has the intellectual component. Therefore, it is not hard to see the difficulties involved in having the intellectual task of query representation done by computers because computers still cannot think like human beings.

The automatic approach of query representation, the same as automatic indexing and other automatic methods for text processing, relies largely on attributes such as keyword frequency, proximity, and location. Algorithms based on probability, linguistics, and artificial intelligence are also adopted sometimes.

IR researchers have tried automatic query representation in the past. The automatic approach has also received close attention in the TREC projects. It was reported, for example, that automatically constructed queries from the topics did as well as or even better than manually constructed ones in TREC-1. There was no clear gain from manual query preparation (Sparck Jones, 1995). In TREC-4, a few automatic results were comparable with the manual ones for short queries. The trend in TREC-5 and TREC-6, however, is for manual query construction, normally done with long topics, to clearly outperform automatic query formation for the same long sources (Sparck Jones, 2000). More discussion of the TREC series is presented in Chapter 11.

Although the TREC results are not conclusive, they demonstrate the limitation of the automatic approach with the current status of research in this area. Further work is needed to improve the automatic method of query representation.

References

Belkin, N.J., et al. (1995). Combining the evidence of multiple query representations for information retrieval. *Information Processing and Management, 31,* 431–448.

Davis, Charles H. (1997). From document retrieval to Web browsing: Some universal concerns. *Journal of Information, Communication, and Library Science, 3(3),* 3–10.

Grossman, David A., and Frieder, Ophir. (1998). *Information retrieval: Algorithms and heuristics.* Boston: Kluwer Academic Publishers.

Kowalski, Gerald. (1997). *Information retrieval systems: Theory and implementation.* Boston: Kluwer Academic Publishers.

Michael, James J., and Hinnebusch, Mark. (1995). *From A to Z39.50: A networking primer.* Westport, CT: Mecklermedia.

Salton, Gerard. (1970). Automatic text analysis. *Science, 168,* 335–343.

Salton, Gerard. (1989). *Automatic text processing: The transformation, analysis, and retrieval of information by computer.* Reading, MA: Addison-Wesley.

Smith, Elizabeth S. (1993). On the shoulders of giants: From Boole to Shannon to Taube: The origins and development of computerized information from the mid-19th century to the present. *Information Technology and Libraries, 12(2),* 217–226.

Sparck Jones, Karen. (1995). Reflections on TREC. *Information Processing & Management, 31(3),* 191–314.

Sparck Jones, Karen. (2000). Further reflections on TREC. *Information Processing & Management, 36(1),* 37–85.

Vidmar, Dale J. (1999). Darwin on the Web: The evolution of search tools. *Computers in Libraries, 19,* 22–28.

Voorhees, Ellen M., and Harman, Donna. (2000). Overview of the sixth Text REtrieval Conference (TREC-6). *Information Processing & Management, 36(1),* 3–35.

CHAPTER 6

Retrieval Approaches

Information retrieval can be accomplished by taking the searching approach, the browsing approach, or the two approaches combined. The selection of an appropriate retrieval approach depends on, among other factors, what kind of information need a particular user has. In this chapter, we explore the three different retrieval approaches along with their features and applications.

Koll (2000) made the following analogy when discussing information retrieval. He describes that finding a needle (i.e., document or information) in a haystack (i.e., IR system or database) can mean:

1. A *known*[1] needle in a known haystack

2. A *known* needle in an unknown haystack

3. An *unknown* needle in an unknown haystack

4. *Any* needle in a haystack

5. The *sharpest* needle in a haystack

6. *Most* of the sharpest needles in a haystack

7. *All* the needles in a haystack

8. Affirmation of no needles in the haystack

9. Things *like* needles in any haystack

10. Let me know *whenever* a new needle shows up

11. *Where* are the haystacks

12. Needles, haystacks—*whatever*

In the above listing, different possibilities about the "needle" and "haystack" are enumerated but not exhausted. Obviously, searching is a suitable approach for certain cases (e.g., #1) while browsing seems appropriate for other cases (e.g., #12). Similarly, some cases in the list (e.g., #5) may require the combined use of the two retrieval approaches.

6.1 Retrieval by Searching

Searching is the retrieval approach that has long been in use. It is also a topic always being covered in the discussion of information retrieval that might be variously phrased as database searching, online searching, Web searching, or the like. Once the query is represented, the user is ready to conduct the search for retrieving information from the system.

6.1.1 Characteristics of Searching

Searching, first of all, is intended to find out what would match with the terms specified in the query, using different retrieval techniques examined in Chapter 5. Searching can be conducted either via subject or nonsubject access points. Typical subject access points in IR systems include descriptors, identifiers, classification labels, subject headings, cited references in citation searching, and terms from titles, abstracts, or the text itself in full-text searching (Hjørland, 1997). Common nonsubject access points encompass language, publication year, document type, and the like.

Searching can be an effective retrieval method when the query is specific and the user knows explicitly what to look for. If the user, for example, would like to find all of Salton's research published in the 1990s, a search by the author field and publication year field should produce anticipated results. If the user intends to learn about, for instance, all those who made contributions to the field of information retrieval, searching alone is unlikely to meet the need.

In the searching approach, retrieval techniques such as Boolean logic allow the user to combine different facets in a search query wherever needed. With the exception of some Internet retrieval systems, most IR systems support further modification of search queries with the help of appropriate retrieval techniques (e.g., field searching). All these tasks are completed by the system once they are submitted to the system as part of queries. The process is straightforward and does not place a heavy cognitive load on the user.

Searching is a structured activity, however. There is little chance for serendipity—that is to discover something unexpectedly during a search—as the system only presents results that match the query. In addition, searching skills do not come naturally. The user must learn how to search and practice to master them. The cost for learning and practicing can be high if the IR system is fee-based.

6.1.2 Types of Searching

Searching can be categorized into different types according to search objectives. When the user has a particular document in mind, the search is called known item search. Known item search is generally conducted based on a known document attribute such as author and title. A close analogy of the known item search is Koll's "A known needle in a known haystack" (Koll, 2000).

When people select research topics, they perform a literature search to find out if other researchers have done any work in this area. The researchers are not surprised if they do not find anything germane to their query in a search. Rather, they are pleased to know that nothing has been published yet on the topic. This type of search is labeled "negative searching" (Stielow & Tibbo, 1988) or, as Koll (2000) puts it, the "affirmation of no needles in the haystack." Negative searching should be thorough and comprehensive so that the end-user can be confident that no similar research is in existence.

In order to keep abreast of a research front or for other similar reasons, people like to find out what is new in a field by conducting literature searches. This kind of search has been named Selective Dissemination of Information (SDI.) As explained in Chapter 1, Luhn (1959) designed the SDI method that later became widely used especially in the business and scientific communities. For SDI searches, the query remains the same but is submitted to the IR system periodically. SDI searches can also be processed automatically. Koll (2000) portrayed SDI searches as "Let me know whenever a new needle shows up."

Subject or topical search stands for another searching type. The end-user has an information need and would like to search for some relevant results. Subject access points mentioned in §6.1.1 should be used to formulate the search query supplemented by nonsubject attributes (e.g., language and publication year). Different retrieval techniques should be considered in determining the recall and precision of the search. Koll (2000) gave several examples of subject search when making the following analogies from the perspective of recall and precision:

- Any needle in a haystack—The search is low in recall but high in precision.

- The sharpest needle in a haystack—The search is high in precision.

- Most of the sharpest needles in a haystack—The search is high in recall.

- All the needles in a haystack—The search has a perfect recall.

Other possibilities (e.g., searches low in precision but high in recall) apparently exist for measuring retrieval outcome with recall and precision. Compared with other types of searching, subject search seems to be the most complex and complicated partly because the results obtained from the search have to be evaluated using the controversial criteria—recall and precision. As mentioned before, the controversies around precision and recall as retrieval performance measures will be closely examined in Chapter 11, Evaluation of Information Representation and Retrieval.

Passage searching, briefly mentioned in §1.2.1, represents a different kind of search in which only the relevant passage (e.g., a paragraph) in the document rather than the entire document itself will be presented to the user. The filtering function is capitalized in passage searching. Although emerging in recent years, passage searching exhibits a great potential in helping the user reduce information overload and improve retrieval precision.

Known item search, negative search, SDI, subject search, and passage search are the five different search types just depicted. Baeza-Yates and Ribeiro-Neto (1999) classified searches into two kinds: ad hoc and filtering. No matter how a search type is labeled, the objective is to decide which search techniques and search strategies should be adopted to satisfy the user's needs.

6.1.3 Search Strategies

Search strategies are the approaches people take when conducting searches. In the golden age of online searching, the following four types of search strategies were identified and illustrated (Fenichel & Hogan, 1981).

6.1.3.1 The Building Block Approach

The building block approach starts with single concept searches. Single concepts are those that have been identified in concept analysis, e.g., *Web filtering, controversy* listed in Table 5.1. After all the single concept searches are completed, the resulting sets are combined using appropriate Boolean operators.

This strategy can decompose a complex search task into simpler ones. It also allows the user to make corrections or adjustments in a timely fashion during the searches if needed. The user does not have to re-do the entire search because of, for example, a small typo made when entering the search statement. As a result, the building block approach puts less pressure on the user who can then focus more on interacting with the system. For these reasons, this search strategy is highly recommended to users, especially to novice users.

6.1.3.2 The Snowballing Approach

The snowballing approach, also known as the citation pearl-growing approach (Fenichel & Hogan, 1981), implies search results will increase in quantity like making a snowball in the snow. Obviously, this approach aims to improve recall. Using this search strategy, the user first conducts a search, and then modifies the search query based on the results retrieved. The modification process includes going over the results, selecting relevant terms (e.g., title words and descriptors), and incorporating them in a revised version of the query. This process can be repeated until the user is satisfied with the search.

For example, if a search on *electronic book* retrieves documents that contain terms such as *Stephen King* and *e-book*, the user can adopt the snowballing approach by including these two terms in the revised search statement to expand search results. We know that Stephen King is the first popular book writer to publish his book electronically while *e-book* is an abbreviated form of *electronic book*. The snowballing approach in essence is similar to the advanced retrieval technique, query expansion, discussed in §5.1.2.3. Korfhage (1997) named this practice "citation processing." As shown, this snowballing approach is particularly useful when the user would like to identify related terms in order to expand a search.

6.1.3.3 The Successive Fraction Approach

The successive fraction approach appears to be the opposite of the snowballing approach. Starting a search with a broad concept, the successive fraction approach narrows the search by applying various limiting techniques. One type of limiting uses related Boolean and proximity operators when composing a search statement. As discussed previously, the NOT operator narrows down a search by excluding certain terms. The AND operator achieves the same purpose by adding more requirements in a search. The WITH operator also narrows down a search by specifying the position of words in a search query. Another kind of limiting can be done by using nonsubject attributes such as language, document type, and publication year. Limiting by such nonsubject attributes seems more straightforward than that by operators.

Suppose a search was conducted on *filtering*, and the results include everything about *filtering* that is covered in the IR system. If our purpose is to find out information on Web filtering as a controversy but not as an information technology, we can use the successive fraction approach to reach our objective. For example, we would first add the term *Web* to the search statement using the AND operator. The term *controversy* can be added similarly. Then, the NOT operator would be applied to exclude any results containing the term *information technology*. Further limiting can be accomplished by restricting the search only to documents published, for instance, after 1996.

As discussed, the successive fraction approach narrows down a search step by step using limiting techniques available from the IR system. This search strategy requires the user to be familiar with the system's limiting features and to stay interactive with the system during the search. If the successive fraction approach is chosen, cost may be a concern for the user of online IR systems (defined in §8.1) as it requires greater processing time than other search strategies. It is true that Internet retrieval systems (§8.4) do not impose charges to the user; however, the limiting facilities provided by such systems continue to be far from adequate.

6.1.3.4 The Most Specific Facet First Approach

The most specific facet first approach is applied to multiple-concept searches (Fenichel & Hogan, 1981). It assumes that the user knows all the facets or concept groups contained in a search and also is able to identify the most specific one. This search strategy can be very efficient as it begins a search with a term that should take the least amount of time to be processed. In addition, there will be no point to continue the search if the number of results retrieved for the most specific facet seems unacceptable. For example, there are three facets in the statement "treatment and prognosis of neuroendocrine tumors in the lung," namely, *treatment and prognosis*, *neuroendocrine tumors*, and *lung*. Among the three facets, *neuroendocrine tumors* appears to be the most specific one and will be searched first with this approach. If a search on *neuroendocrine tumors* retrieves only two documents, a search including all three facets will not likely produce more outcome than the two already located.

Besides its efficiency, implementation of this approach seems very sophisticated. As concept analysis alone is undeniably a daunting task, it becomes virtually impossible for a novice user to single out the most specific facet in a multiconcept search request. The most specific facet first approach thus is not recommended for neophytes.

One extension of the most specific facet first approach is called "the next most specific facet first" method, which takes the facet coming next in terms of specificity for conducting searches. However, neither approach is often used in the IR community. The lowest posting first approach, described in Fenichel and Hogan (1981), is simply a variation of the most specific facet first approach as the most specific facet usually generates the lowest postings.

6.1.3.5 Toward a "Quick/Convenient" Approach

As pointed out in the beginning of this section, all the aforedescribed search strategies were proposed and developed in the peak time of online searching. The retrieval environment (e.g., the emergence of Internet retrieval systems) and the searchers themselves (e.g., end-users as searchers without the assistance of intermediaries) have significantly changed since then. While the building block approach and the snowballing approach are still favored by some users, many people just type in a single keyword they would like to search on or enter several terms at once by leaving a space in between with little use of the Boolean operators and other search facilities (e.g., Jansen, Spink & Saracevic, 2000; Siegfried, Bates & Wilde, 1993; Wallace, 1993). This approach can be labeled the "quick/convenient" approach. Few searchers would try the successive fraction approach or the most specific facet first approach in today's world of information retrieval. On the other hand, some of the search facilities or devices (e.g., language and Boolean operator) are now incorporated as part of the IR system's interface. The user can simply choose these options from predefined buttons or drop-down menus without actually typing them in a search statement.

6.2 Retrieval by Browsing

Browsing is another major form of retrieval activity. In comparison with searching, browsing did not receive much attention in the IR community until the 1990s. With the development of CD-ROM systems, OPAC systems, and particularly the hyperstructured Web, browsing gained popularity quickly and became economically feasible in information retrieval when the user no longer needed to worry about the connection charge as in the case of professional online IR systems. Today, users can retrieve information by browsing at their leisure.

6.2.1 What Is Browsing?

Browsing is seeking and selecting information by skimming, scanning, and other similar activities. In information retrieval, people like to browse:

- For getting information when a topic is not clearly defined

- For finding information that is hard to be specified explicitly

- For obtaining an overview of the information the IR system offers

- For choosing the right information among a mixture of relevant and irrelevant items

- For discovering and learning new information

- When the IR environment encourages browsing

Additional reasons for browsing can be found in Marchionini (1995) along with thorough explanations. In cases like "Needles, haystacks – whatever" (Koll, 2000), browsing should be a preferred retrieval method.

When browsing, the user does not need to represent a retrieval problem with specific terms as required in the search process. In that sense, browsing is less demanding intellectually than searching. However, people have to stay interactive with the IR system while browsing in order to examine and assess the information they are browsing, and then make rapid relevance judgments (Marchionini, 1995). The cognitive load on the user in the browsing environment would therefore be greater than that if searching is chosen as the retrieval approach.

Unlike searching, browsing can be done without any training and practice as a retrieval approach. According to Marchionini (1995):

> [Browsing] is natural because it coordinates human physical, emotive, and cognitive resources in the same way that humans monitor the physical world and search for physical objects. (p. 100)

People can browse as they are able to breathe. Nevertheless, there are few well-developed techniques to facilitate the browsing process. The user generally has few guidelines to rely on as to when to continue browsing for more information and when to stop browsing.

On the other hand, browsing can be a rewarding exercise as it might lead to serendipity, i.e., finding something useful unexpectedly, because browsing allows the user to look for information randomly and unstructurally. Retrieval by browsing is a method that has strengths as well as weaknesses.

6.2.2 Types of Browsing

Unlike searching, browsing does not appear to be a structured retrieval method. But different types of browsing are identified and discussed in the literature (e.g., Herner, 1970; Kowalski, 1997; Marchionini, 1995). Herner (1970) suggests that browsing could be directed, semi-directed, and undirected by judging if the user seeks a specific entity or not and depending upon the browsing tactics taken. Similarly, Marchionini (1995) puts browsing into three categories: systematic, exploratory, and casual.

Directed or systematic browsing is done when the user knows clearly what to look for, e.g., a particular Web page on a Web site or a specific term in an online glossary. Users doing semi-directed or exploratory browsing have less specific and clear objectives for retrieval. They skim and scan to locate what they are seeking. For instance, it is known that an important idea is discussed in a lengthy report. The user then has to browse the report to locate the right part in it. Undirected and causal browsing has the lowest predictability among the three types of browsing. With no particular information need, the user browses in the IR system. One example could be that a user jumps from one news item to another when scanning a Web-based newspaper, hoping to find something interesting to read.

To examine browsing from a different perspective, Kowalski (1997) lists how people browse over search results they obtained. 1) Browse by ranking. As search results in the digital retrieval environment are normally presented in ranked order based on certain ranking algorithm, users can choose to browse, for example, results ranked high in relevance. 2) Browse by zone. The zone here refers to traditionally defined fields such as title and abstract. Titles and abstracts are some examples of content-rich zones for browsing. 3) Browse by highlighted area. Some IR systems highlight certain terms (e.g., search terms) and their contexts to help people locate what they are looking for efficiently. Those highlighted areas are good candidates for browsing.

In addition to the browsing types Kowalski describes, two other kinds of browsing have become prevalent in Internet retrieval systems. One is to browse by category, and the other is to browse by hyperlinks. Browsing by category is exemplified at the directory-based Internet retrieval systems (e.g., Yahoo!). The information such Internet retrieval systems collect is indexed and classified into categories (e.g., Computers, Education, Entertainment, Sports). If a user intends to find a movie to watch, the person would naturally browse the Entertainment category, for example, at Yahoo!. As for browsing by hyperlinks, the Web with its hyperstructure makes it not only feasible but also very inviting.

Hyperlinks are the nodes and pointers embedded in hypertext, which cleverly mimics the associative thinking of human beings. As Bush (1945) pointed out:

> ... The human mind ... operates by association. With one item in its grasp, it snaps instantly to the next that is suggested by the association of thoughts, in accordance with some intricate web of trails by the cells of the brain. (p. 106)

That kind of association has been vividly and thoroughly reflected on the Web via the implementation of hyperlinks. The entire Web consists of textual as well as multimedia information, intertwined by uncountable hyperlinks. Those links serve as guides for Web users to browse, navigate, and locate digital information (Chu, 1997). Hyperstructured IR systems become one of the best, if not the best, environments for browsing.

Obviously, browsing can be categorized by applying different classification criteria. But the objective for browsing should always be the same in information retrieval: seeking information one intends to find.

6.2.3 Browsing Strategies

Browsing, like searching, can take different strategies. Marchionini (1995) writes that there are four browsing strategies, namely, scan, observe, navigate, and monitor. Choosing the right browsing strategy can help people achieve their objective of browsing more effectively.

According to Marchionini (1995), scanning is a browsing strategy for seeking well-defined objects in a highly organized IR environment. The user knows what to look for and can scan information either linearly or selectively. Linear scan is to browse in the information space sequentially, e.g., going over a list of retrieved results one by one. Selective scan means viewing only certain portions of the information (e.g., headings, hyperlinks, images, and contents of different color at a Web site) out of all those being presented. Scanning seems to be the most basic strategy for systematic browsing.

In comparison, observation is the primary strategy used in exploratory or casual browsing (Marchionini, 1995). The user should be attentive to certain portions of what is being observed while other components in the IR environment (e.g., ads at Web sites) may distract one's attention. In other words, inputs of various kinds are sent to the user from different sources. The user has to stay focused on what is sought after, and ignore noise and other distractions.

Navigation as a browsing strategy balances the influence of the user and the environment in that the environment restricts browsing by providing possible browsing routes while the user exercises some control by selecting which routes to follow (Marchionini, 1995). Navigation, also depending on the feedback of the IR system, can be used either for systematic or casual browsing. Observation is often applied in conjunction with navigation.

Monitoring is similar to scanning except that it tolerates poorly structured environments (Marchionini, 1995). While the user is looking at the results retrieved by the system, for example, the person can also pay some attention to a news report being broadcasted on the radio. Information seeking activities take place in parallel. Monitoring is most often used in exploratory browsing.

In sum, browsing strategies seem subtler than the search strategies discussed previously. There are no concrete criteria for the user to determine whether the browsing should continue or end. There are no guidelines for the user to follow with regard to the change of browsing strategies. Instead, the user has to consider a number of qualitative factors (e.g., satisfaction and cognitive effort) for decision-making purposes. There is also no clear-cut line as to when to choose which strategy and under what circumstance. Does browsing as a retrieval method function better when used in conjunction with searching rather than being used alone? The next section attempts to answer this question.

6.3 Searching and Browsing Integrated in Retrieval

Searching and browsing are two distinctive retrieval methods. Almost a half century ago, Luhn (1958) classified retrieval methods as:

1. Retrieval of information by look-up in an ordered array of stored records

2. Retrieval of information by search in a nonordered array of stored records

3. A combination of 1 and 2

The terminology and structure of the system database have undoubtedly been changed over the years. However, it remains possible to see that the first category Luhn described represents browsing while the second denotes searching. The third type is the theme to be explored: the integration of browsing and searching.

6.3.1 Comparison of the Two Retrieval Approaches

The characteristics of both browsing and searching have been depicted in the previous sections. According to Cox (1992), browsing can be regarded as going from where to what. The idea is that the user knows where he/she is in the database and wants to know what is available there. Conversely, searching can be considered as going from what to where. The idea is that the user knows what he/she wants and wishes to find where in the database it is available. Marchionini (1995) states that searching is the formal and analytical strategy while browsing is the informal and heuristic strategy. Aside from those distinctions, searching and browsing differ from each other in the following aspects.

6.3.1.1 Information Need

Information need is one major criterion that divides searching and browsing as retrieval methods. For a specific and known information need, searching appears the suitable choice as it would help the user obtain the "needle" from the "haystack" efficiently. In comparison, browsing can be used to perform retrieval tasks for users with broad and unspecified information needs. People can use different browsing tactics (e.g., scanning and navigation) to find out if there is any information relevant to the information need in the IR system.

6.3.1.2 Efficiency and Potential for Improvement

Efficiency in retrieval and potential for improvement should be taken into consideration when comparing searching with browsing. Generally speaking, searching is quick, focused, and right to the point whereas browsing could be time-consuming and is not intended as a focused activity. It also appears likely that the user may get distracted in the browsing approach. While various techniques are available for the user to broaden or narrow down a search in searching, browsing has few facilities to help improve its performance. The user also can only get information from the portions of the system being browsed. Theoretically, browsing can go on and on if the user does not end it. Meanwhile the accuracy of browsing is likely diminished in such a prolonged process (Marchionini, 1995).

6.3.1.3 Cognitive Load

The entire search process can be divided into approximately three stages: representing the query, conducting the search, and evaluating results. Cognitive load on the user would be high at the first and third stage, and relatively low if the user does not try to be interactive during the search. Browsing, by contrast, is a highly interactive process throughout between the system and the user. Browsing becomes pointless if the user does not interact with the system and stay attentive to what is presented by the system. It is grueling for people to remain focused in the browsing approach for a long period of time as they have to constantly and rapidly assess the information they are browsing according to certain parameters. However, browsing relies on recognition of relevant information rather than recall from memory (Large, Tedd & Hartley, 1999), which might lighten some cognitive load on the user.

6.3.1.4 Serendipity

The chance for serendipity in searching is virtually nonexistent because the system basically matches the query with what the database contains. It is neither feasible nor possible for the user to scan the whole system to discern additional information. By comparison, browsing provides opportunity for serendipity. The user would not be surprised to find something useful unexpectedly while browsing. This feature of browsing, however, could also easily become the source for distraction and disorientation, a limitation cited by researchers like Marchionini (1995).

6.3.1.5 Efforts

Searching is a structured endeavor that requires people to learn and practice before they can perform it. Browsing by contrast is a retrieval approach natural to the user who does not need to spend time learning it. Moreover, no query representation is involved in the browsing process, which can relieve the user from the highly sophisticated task and let the user simply focus on browsing.

Table 6.1 recapitulates the comparisons made between searching and browsing in five different aspects.

Table 6.1   Comparison of Searching and Browsing

Aspect / Approach	Information Need	Efficiency	Cognitive Load	Serendipity	Efforts
Searching	Specific & known	High	Light	Less	More
Browsing	Broad & uncertain	Low	Heavy	More	Less

6.3.2 The Integrated Approach

The comparison in Table 6.1 shows that both searching and browsing have their own strengths and limitations. Each retrieval approach works well in certain conditions and circumstances. While there are occasions on which one retrieval approach seems more suitable than the other, the integration of the two can lead to better retrieval performance in general. Searching may not be needed for every retrieval task. But browsing seems always necessary in judging the relevance of retrieved results.

Furthermore, IR systems have been designed to promote the integrated approach in the IR community. In IR systems developed earlier, menu and search options are provided simultaneously (e.g., DIALOG) so that the user can choose browsing or searching as needed. For Internet retrieval systems developed in the late 1990s, the norm is to have both a directory and search mechanism side by side. Unlike in the days when Internet retrieval systems were just introduced to the public, these systems offered either a directory (e.g., Yahoo!) or a search mechanism (e.g., AltaVista), but not both. Fortunately, many Internet retrieval systems quickly realized the advantage of supporting both browsing and searching within one IR system, and subsequently changed their old practices. Today, there are hardly any Internet retrieval systems that provide only one retrieval option for the user.

Users benefit from the integrated approach because they not only have the right apparatus for the right retrieval task but also get more out of the same IR systems. For example, Yahoo! supports searching within its browsable categories (e.g., Arts). Searching within a browsable category is therefore similar to searching a database that is specialized in an area the browsable category represents. That is to say, searching at Yahoo! within its Arts category is like conducting searches in an art database. Browsing and searching become integrated activities in this environment.

One plus one could be more than two if the combination is done wisely. This is true for the integrated retrieval approach covered here.

Endnote

1. Italics are in the original text.

References

Baeza-Yates, Ricardo, and Ribeiro-Neto, Berthier. (1999). *Modern information retrieval.* New York: ACM Book Press.

Bush, Vannevar. (1945). As we may think. *Atlantic Monthly, 176(1),* 101–108.

Chu, Heting. (1997). Hyperlinks: How well do they represent the intellectual content of digital collections? *Proceedings of the 60th Annual Meeting of the American Society for Information Science, 34,* 361–369.

Cox, K., (1992). Information retrieval by browsing. In Ching-Chih Chen (Ed.), *NIT'92: Proceedings of the Fifth International Conference on New Information Technology* (pp. 69–79). West Newton, MA: MicroUse Information.

Fenichel, Carol H., and Hogan, Thomas H. (1981). *Online searching: A primer.* Marlton, NJ: Learned Information.

Herner, S. (1970). Browsing. In Allen Kent, Horald Lancour, and William Z. Nasri (Eds.), *Encyclopedia of Library and Information Science* (Vol. 3, pp. 408–415). New York. Marcel Dekker.

Hjørland, Birger. (1997). *Information seeking and subject representation.* London: Greenwood Press.

Jansen, B.J., Spink, A., and Saracevic, T. (2000). Real life, real users, and real needs: A study and analysis of user queries on the Web. *Information Processing and Management, 36(2),* 207–227.

Koll, Matthew. (2000). Track 3: Information Retrieval. *Bulletin of the American Society for Information Science, 26(2)*, 16–18.

Korfhage, Robert R. (1997). *Information storage and retrieval.* New York: John Wiley & Sons.

Kowalski, Gerald. (1997). *Information retrieval systems: Theory and implementation.* Boston: Kluwer Academic Publishers.

Large, Andrew, Tedd, Lucy A., and Hartley, R.J. (1999). *Information seeking in the online age: Principles and practice.* London: Bowker-Saur.

Luhn, H.P. (1958). Review of information retrieval methods. In Claire K. Schultz (Ed.), (1968). *H.P. Luhn: Pioneer of information science: Selected works* (pp. 140–144). New York: Spartan Books.

Luhn, H.P. (1959). Selective dissemination of new scientific information with the aid of electronic processing equipment. In Claire K. Schultz (Ed.), (1968). *H.P. Luhn: Pioneer of information science. Selected works* (pp. 246–254). New York: Spartan Books.

Marchionini, Gary. (1995). *Information seeking in electronic environments.* New York: Cambridge University Press. (Cambridge Series on Human-Computer Interaction 9).

Siegfried, S., Bates, M., and Wilde, D. (1993). A profile of end user searching behavior by humanities scholars: The Getty online searching project report no. 2. *Journal of the American Society for Information Science, 44(5),* 273–291.

Stielow, F., and Tibbo, H. (Spring 1988). The negative search, online reference, and the humanities: A critical essay in library literature. *RQ, 27(3),* 358–365.

Wallace, P. (1993). How do patrons search the online catalog when no one's looking? Transaction log analysis and implications for bibliographic instruction and system design. *RQ, 33(3),* 239–252.

CHAPTER 7

Information Retrieval Models

A model is defined as "a tentative description of a theory or system that accounts for all of its known properties" (Soukhanov, et al., 1984). Various models have been developed in information retrieval over the years. This chapter is devoted to the presentation and exploration of some common IR models in order to facilitate the understanding and appreciation of the foundation of IR practices.

There are many levels at which IR procedures can be modeled. Theories and notions from other disciplines (e.g., Boolean logic, vector space, and probability) are drawn to form the bases for modeling IR activities. Different schemes have been suggested for classifying all the IR models developed so far (e.g., Baeza-Yates & Ribeiro-Neto, 1999; Belkin & Croft, 1987; Sparck Jones & Willett, 1997). This chapter will focus on discussing system-oriented models such as Boolean logic, vector space, and probability. Other IR models, for example, the user-oriented cognitive model and the language-based natural language model, will be examined respectively in other parts of the book where they fit more logically with regard to the subject content.

7.1 Foundation of All IR Models: Matching

Matching is not a model in information retrieval, but it lays the foundation for IR activities. As stated in §1.4.1, matching is the fundamental mechanism in information retrieval. Matching can be made between terms or between similarity measurements such as distance and term frequency. Term matching is performed directly on terms derived from or assigned to queries, documents, or their representations while similarity measurement matching is conducted indirectly on measurements obtained by calculating, for example, distance between vectors as in the vector space model. The following two subsections will focus on discussing these two kinds of matching respectively.

7.1.1 Term Matching

As explained in §2.1.1, terms used in IRR can be keywords, descriptors, or identifiers. Terms also include words, phrases, or other kinds of expressions. In addition, term matching can be done in one of the following four ways: exact match, partial match, positional match, and range match.

Exact match means that the query representation matches exactly with the document representation in the IR system. Case sensitivity search and phrase search are examples of the exact matching. For example, *Web filtering* is a term in a query and the same phrase also appears in the system to be searched. Then an exact match is obtained as a result of searching.

Unlike exact matching, partial match only has part of the term being matched with the document representation in the IR system. Truncation in searching is a typical example of partial matching. For instance, a search query of *information technolog** (where * is the truncation symbol) would retrieve documents containing *information technology, information technologies,* and *information technologists* as a result of the partial matching.

Positional match is done by taking into consideration the positional information of what is being matched in the process. Proximity searching is a case in point. If a search query reads *used* 1WITH *store*, the retrieved results would include documents containing phrases such as *used book store, used cloth store, used furniture store.* Here the matching is only done with the first and last words given between the query and document representation while the word in the middle position is ignored during the matching process.

Range match is applicable to numeric expressions (e.g., sales amount) or expressions with a natural order (e.g., January, February, ... December). What is being matched in range matching is the upper limit of the range (publications before year 2002), lower limit of the range (e.g., publications after 1992), or both (e.g., publications between 1993 and 2001). Numeric databases and publication dates are conventional examples of range searching.

All these four different types of term matching deal with the original queries and document representations without any further calculation or conversion. Term matching is most often seen in the Boolean logic model. In other IR models (e.g., vector space and probability), terms in query and document representations are not directly matched. Rather, they would be transformed as some similarity measurements before being matched.

7.1.2 Similarity Measurement Matching

Similarity measurement matching is done in a number of different ways. For example, matching is based on the distance between vectors or degree of vector angle in the vector space model: the smaller the vector angle, the higher degree of similarities between queries and documents. In the probabilistic model, similarity can be calculated based on term frequency to determine the probability of relevance between queries and documents.

In matching of this kind, a similarity measure other than terms themselves must be chosen. It is on this measurement that the matching is finally made. On one hand, the similarity measurement matching provides additional approaches to accomplishing the retrieval task. On the other hand, such practice can introduce mistakes and noises, particularly in the process of obtaining similarity measurements.

Regardless of the matching type, matching is the essential mechanism in information retrieval. The IR models discussed here demonstrate how matching is done in different circumstances, along with their respective features, advantages, and limitations.

7.2 The Boolean Logic Model

The Boolean logic model is named after George Boole who proposed Boolean logic in the mid-19th century. Boolean logic covers three logical operations: the logical product (x), the logical sum (+), and the logical difference (-). Three corresponding operators AND, OR, NOT are used to express the logical operations in information retrieval. In the early versions of some Internet retrieval systems, the plus sign (+) was used to represent the AND operator, which might have caused some confusion to the user because it actually stands for the OR operator in Boolean logic.

The logical product, or AND operator, combines two or more terms in a search statement and requires all the terms be present in the documents to be retrieved. The logic sum, or OR operator, links two or more synonyms or related terms in a search statement. Documents that contain any one of the terms specified in the search statement would be regarded as hits or anticipated results. The logical difference, or NOT operator, limits searches by excluding terms listed after the NOT operator in queries. Specific examples of Boolean operator usage were already given in §5.1.1.1 when the Boolean search technique was presented.

As indicated in §1.1.2.1, Mortimer Taube introduced the Boolean logic to information retrieval. With the rapid development of computerized IR systems, Boolean logic has been increasingly adopted and used. As we are moving into the digital age, few IR systems do not support the Boolean model of searching. In fact, the Boolean logic model has become a widely applied mechanism in information retrieval (Sparck Jones & Willett, 1997). This does not mean, however, that Boolean logic is an IR model without limitations. To the contrary, discussions about the strengths and weaknesses of the Boolean logic model can be found in many publications (e.g., Chowdhury, 1999; Cooper, 1988; Frants, et al., 1999; Korfhage, 1997; Sparck Jones & Willett, 1997).

7.2.1 Strengths of the Boolean Logic Model

The extensive application of the Boolean logic model in information retrieval proves the value of the model. First, it supports the manipulation of different facets obtained by decomposing a query or document. The AND operator can combine two simple facets to form a complex one, thus narrowing down a search. The OR operator allows the specification of alternative facets of a query or document, thus broadening a search. The NOT operator can separate complex facets into individual simple ones, thus excluding unwanted facets from appearing in final search results. Such manipulations, if applied appropriately, can bring flexibility and effectiveness to information retrieval at a level with which no other existing IR models can compete.

Second, Boolean logic IR systems are cost-effective and already indispensable to the user (Frants, et al., 1999). Thousands of Boolean logic IR systems are operational. The end-user can make use of the Boolean operators to broaden, narrow, or eliminate certain results from a search. In that sense, the Boolean logic model is well established although some researchers (e.g., Belkin & Croft, 1987) commented that the model became established more through practice than theory.

Third, the Boolean logic model is well understood (Sparck Jones & Willett, 1997) even though there is much less discussion about what the model can accomplish than what the model is unable to do, which might be a result of two factors. One is that the Boolean logic model is the oldest among all IR models. It is assumed that its strengths have been well appreciated so no further elaboration is needed. The other factor is that Boolean logic, as the oldest IR model, will have to be criticized whenever a new IR model is presented. It is natural for people to state that a new IR model is built to overcome the limitations of the old one. The system designer and user alike would prefer to work with a model that is well understood.

Fourth, Boolean IR systems are relatively easy to build, as the algorithms involved appear simpler to implement than those based on other IR models. That may also contribute in part to the wide implementation of Boolean IR systems. Because of the aforementioned strengths (e.g., the manipulation mechanism and wide usage), the Boolean logic model always receives a lot of attention whenever IR retrieval models are scrutinized in detail.

7.2.2 Limitations of the Boolean Logic Model

The limitations of the Boolean logic model, as indicated before, are thoroughly examined and explored in many publications (e.g., Chowdhury, 1999; Cooper, 1988; Frants, et al., 1999; Korfhage, 1997; Sparck Jones & Willett, 1997). The following discussion is a recapitulation of the shortcomings of the model.

First, it is difficult for the user to conduct Boolean searches without a fair degree of training and practice. The difficulty lies in the following two aspects: 1) It is difficult for the user to choose the right Boolean operator. There usually exists confusion about the AND and OR operators among users as these two words have different meanings in conventional sense or common semantics.

The word *and* traditionally means "plus" as in, for example, "They will search for this topic at AltaVista *and* Google," while the word *or* implies "either one" as in, for instance, "They will search for this topic at AltaVista *or* Google." Literally, more sites will be searched in the former case than in the latter one. Some users customarily think the same when they form Boolean queries, i.e., use the AND operator when they want more results, and use the OR operator when they want less. Boolean logic obviously does not work that way. That difference would likely lead the user to choose the wrong operators, namely, using AND and OR operators in wrong places. 2) It is difficult for the user to correctly employ the order of processing in compound Boolean searching. As described in §5.1.1.1, compound Boolean searching involves more than one type of Boolean operator whose natural order of processing is defined as: the NOT operator first, the AND operator second, and the OR operator last. However, the natural order of processing for compound Boolean searching can be altered by applying parentheses when needed. Such alteration is, nevertheless, complicated and demanding especially for novices. The user would not be able to become comfortable with the artificial rules (e.g., the most inner parentheses being processed first) for changing the natural order of processing for compound Boolean searches until given adequate training and practice.

Second, it is difficult to express relationships other than the Boolean among terms (e.g., causal relationship) because such mechanism is simply not provided in the model. Suppose a user would like to find some information about "the application of computers in education." A search query is then formed using the Boolean operator as *computers* AND *education*. The term *application* is not included in the query because this relationship is supposed to be expressed via Boolean operators. But none of the Boolean operators has this function. Consequently, the user would get information on not only "the use of computers in education" but also "education about computers" by conducting the search. Boolean search statements can certainly get very complicated. But there are still only three operators available to the user to link the concepts involved. It is generally true that the more complicated a search statement is, the more likely it would cause misinterpretations due to the inability of the Boolean logic model to express relationships other than the Boolean logic among terms.

Third, no weighting mechanism is available in the Boolean logic model to indicate the relative importance of different concepts in a search query. All the terms or concepts in Boolean queries are assumed to have the same degree of significance, which is not always true in information retrieval. For example, a search query is *information access* AND *security* and the user would like to place more emphasis on the term *security*. In other words, the user would like to get some information about the security issue in information access, rather than treating both terms as equal in importance. Within a Boolean IR system, however, the user's expectation would not be met because no weights can be assigned to the query terms.

Fourth, it is impossible to express a partial relevance of search results in the Boolean logic model because it simply divides all the data in a system as either relevant when there is a match between the query and document representations or irrelevant when there is no match. Nothing is left in between. Therefore, Boolean logic systems cannot present results in the order of decreasing relevance. Since there is no ranked output, the user cannot specify, for instance, to have the 15 top-ranked documents retrieved. The user has to sift through all the results, sometimes numbered in thousands or more, that the Boolean system presents in no particular order of relevance. In that sense, the user has no control over the size of output in Boolean searches.

Fifth, the user may get null output or output overload when doing Boolean searching. Null output is possible if the search query is very restrictive when, for example, several terms are linked together by the AND operator. Meanwhile, output overload may occur if the search query is broad when, for instance, several terms are linked together by the OR operator. The user can modify the search query for increasing or reducing search output. However, the outcome then will not be what the user was initially looking for but the output of the modified query.

In order to cope with the limitations of the Boolean model, Cooper (1988) suggested some possible solutions, such as formulating queries free of Boolean operators to manage the unfriendliness of Boolean queries. A good number of algorithms and methods, including IR models, have also been developed for providing ranked outputs, weighted inputs, and the like. However, "other retrieval models that may be more interesting theoretically have not, in practice, achieved results that are distinctly superior to those of Boolean retrieval systems" (Korfhage, 1997).

7.3 Vector Space Model

The vector space model, also known variously as vector processing or vector product retrieval, has been developed by Salton and his colleagues who built the SMART system to serve as the base for conducting extended series of IR experiments (e.g., Salton, 1968). A series of IR techniques (e.g., term weighting, ranked output, and relevance feedback) have also been devised in the process of building the model. Apart from Boolean logic, the vector space model has had the most influence on the development of IR and of operational IR systems (Sparck Jones & Willett, 1997).

In the vector space model, each term is defined as a dimension while each query or document is expressed as a vector. A vector actually consists of a list of term values representing an item (i.e., a query or document). Term values in a vector could be either binary or weighted. The binary values could be one or zero, with one indicating the existence of the term in the item. The weighted values include real positive numbers (e.g., 1.5, 0.3, 2.4, 5.6). The weighted value for each term corresponds to the relative importance of that term in representing the item (Kowalski, 1997). The scheme used for term weighting in the vector space model could be objective (e.g., term frequency) or subjective (e.g., user's perception). The weighting methods discussed in §5.1.2.2 are theoretically applicable in assigning weights to terms in a vector. Each weighting algorithm has its pros and cons. Korfhage (1997) discussed in detail the term frequency-based approach and the user's perception-based method for assigning weights to terms in a vector.

The number of dimensions in a query or document vector is equal to the number of different terms representing the item. All query and document vectors constitute the multidimensional space. The complete set of term values in a vector thus describes the position of the query or document it represents in the space (Sparck Jones & Willett, 1997).

Conducting a search in the vector space IR system means to check the distance, shown as an angle, between the query and document vectors in the space. The vector space model judges the similarity between a document and a query (or between any two documents) by comparing their corresponding dimensions and by calculating such similarity measurements as cosine coefficient. If a query and a document are on a similar topic, the angle between their vectors should be small. If a query and a document are on different topics, the angle between their vectors should be large (Lesk, 1997). Similarity between documents can be measured likewise.

7.3.1 Strengths of the Vector Space Model

The vector space model, according to Sparck Jones and Willett (1997), provides a unifying basis for a wide range of retrieval operations, including indexing, relevance feedback, and document classification. The strengths of the model become quite obvious when contrasted with the limitations of the Boolean logic model.

First, the user is no longer required to understand and apply Boolean logic when conducting searches in a vector space IR system. Rather, what the user needs to do is simply select several terms based on his or her information need.

Second, the terms or concepts chosen to represent the query or document can be weighted to indicate their relative importance in the vector. For example, if a query or document is mainly concerned with the security issue in networking, a higher weight can be assigned to the term *security* and a lower weight to the term *networking*. In that way, these two terms will not be treated as having equal importance in the vector, and a more appropriate representation of the query or document can be made.

Third, the output of vector space searches are ranked in decreasing relevance as the model expresses the similarity or relevance between documents or between the query and document on a scale (e.g., from 0.0 to 1.0 with 1.0 being the most relevant) instead of a binary division (i.e., relevant or irrelevant) as done in the Boolean logic model. Therefore, the user can go over, for example, the top 10 ranked documents only and still be assured that the remaining results unexamined would not be more relevant to his/her query than the 10 documents being viewed. The fact that the user can limit the size of retrieval output is an improvement over the Boolean logic model. Ranked output saves the user's time and energy in the information retrieval process as the user does not have to view all the documents, often in the thousands, before deciding which ones are the most relevant. The system is able to choose and present the most relevant documents to the user automatically.

Fourth, relevance feedback is a mechanism implemented in the vector space model for improving retrieval performance. Based on the relevant outcome previously retrieved, the vector space IR system would be able to automatically modify the query vector and present the user with more relevant results. Relevance feedback can be completed without the involvement of the user, and the process can be repeated for as many times as necessary. The user can activate the process by simply choosing the option labeled as, for instance, "More like this" or "More similar results" in Internet retrieval systems.

As seen in this discussion, the vector space model has overcome some limitations associated with the Boolean logic model. However, the vector space model itself also introduced some new problems to the field of information retrieval.

7.3.2 Limitations of the Vector Space Model

The first limitation of the vector space model refers to the assumption of independence between terms selected for describing a vector. When the Boolean logic model is examined, it is pointed out that the model cannot express other kinds of relationships except the Boolean logic. However, the vector space model is unable to convey any relationship, including the Boolean relationship, existing between the terms. Rather, it requires the assumption that terms forming the basis for the vector space are orthogonal or independent of each other. The assumption is apparently incorrect. If the following terms are selected to describe a document vector: *automobiles, export*, and *import*, how can we assume that there is no relationship at all between the terms listed? This limitation has been criticized the most among all those that pertain to the model.

The second limitation of the vector space model is the difficulty in specifying explicitly synonymous or phrasal relationships due to the absence of the Boolean and proximity operators. To be more specific, the model does not support Boolean and proximity operators. Consequently, the OR operator cannot be used to indicate synonyms (e.g., *cars, automobiles*) and the WITH operator cannot be employed to form phrases (e.g., *information* WITH *retrieval*) in a vector. Yet in actual searches, there are always occasions when synonyms or phrases are needed to represent queries or documents. It is therefore hard for the user to conduct searches without the Boolean and proximity facilities in the vector space IR system when synonymous or phrasal relationships have to be represented.

The third limitation of the vector space model relates to its weighting mechanism, which can be subjective and complex. The weighting process is subjective when the user is asked to assign weights to terms, particularly query terms, based on his/her own perception and judgment. The user is supposed to estimate the relative importance the term would have in the search, and then assign a weight to it. Subjectivity is inevitable during that process. On the other hand, weighting can be complex in that no weighting algorithm works without a flaw and finding the best algorithm for a particular retrieval environment is not an easy task. In addition, databases in IR systems are dynamic, as they need constant updating. Term weights should thus be changed accordingly because the parameters (e.g., term frequency) on which a weighting scheme is based have changed. Kowalski (1997) outlines a number of approaches to deal with the dynamically changing databases and the impact on weighting algorithms. But, as pointed out by Kowalski himself, none of the approaches can be implemented without some concerns (e.g., cost).

Apart from the three limitations just described, the vector space model also needs several terms to represent a query or document so the vector would be discriminating enough for good retrieval performance. In comparison, "only two or three AND'ed terms may suffice in a Boolean environment to obtain a high-quality output" (Sparck Jones & Willett, 1997). Assigning more terms in the vector space model would result in more expense. In addition, the model lacks theoretical justification for some of the vector manipulation operations. For example, the choice of a particular measure for computing vector similarity in using the IR model is not prescribed by any theoretical considerations. Instead, it is left to the user (Salton, 1989).

Ideally, the vector space model should place document vectors in such a way that those documents jointly relevant to certain queries are clustered together and those never wanted simultaneously would appear well separated in the space (Salton, Wong & Yang, 1975). However, matching a query against clusters of documents, coined as the cluster hypothesis, has not been possible (Sparck Jones & Willett, 1997).

The vector space model has not been applied in many operational IR systems until the advent of Internet retrieval systems. The SMART system, serving as its test-bed, enables the model to grow and mature. The creation of the vector space model has greatly enriched the research and development of the IR field.

7.4 Probability Model

The probability model was introduced by Maron and Kuhns (1960) and further developed by Robertson and other researchers (e.g., Robertson & Sparck Jones, 1976). According to Sparck Jones and Willett (1997):

> The rationale for introducing probabilistic concepts is obvious: IR systems deal with natural language, and this is far too imprecise to enable a system to state with certainty which documents will be relevant to a particular query (a situation that is in marked contrast to the unambiguous retrieval operations that are required for searching in numeric database management systems). (p. 259)

The model applies the theory of probability, e.g., an event has a possibility from 0 percent to 100 percent (0.0–1.0) of occurring, to information retrieval. It takes into consideration the uncertainty element in the IR process, i.e., uncertainty about whether documents retrieved by the system are relevant to a given query (Bookstein, 1985). The model intends to estimate and calculate the probability that a document will be relevant to a given query based on some methods. The "event" in this context of information retrieval refers to the probability of relevance between a query and document. Unlike other IR models, the probability model does not treat relevance as an exact miss-or-match measurement. Rather, relevance is expressed in terms of probability. For example, Document D has a 35 percent probability of being relevant to Query Q.

The model adopts various methods to determine the probability of relevance between queries and documents. Relevance in the probability model is judged according to the similarity between queries and documents. The similarity judgment is further dependent on term frequency. Generally speaking, the more similarity exists between queries and the documents, the higher probability that those documents are relevant to the queries. In a probabilistic IR system, the results obtained for any query are supposed to consist of documents that satisfy that query with a probability higher than a specified threshold (Korfhage, 1997).

7.4.1 Strengths of the Probability Model

In comparison with the Boolean logic model or vector space model already described, the probability model has the following strengths.

First, the model provides "an important guide for characterizing retrieval processes, as well as theoretical justification for practices used previously on an empirical basis such as the introduction of certain term-weighting systems" (Salton, 1989). The retrieval processes are characterized with a degree of uncertainty when the relevance between queries and documents is judged. It is more realistic to express the probability of relevance rather than pure relevance alone between queries and documents. Furthermore, major operations of the model, e.g., the query–document similarity measurement, are determined by the model itself instead of some arbitrary decision as in the vector space model.

Second, the model includes term dependencies and relationships (i.e., the occurrence of one event will affect the other) in its operations. Users no longer need to, as they have in the vector space model, assume the independence between terms, an assumption not supported in practice. The model also weights query terms and association between queries and documents so that the users can specify the relative importance of the term or association in the retrieval task. Ranked output is also provided since the model assumes that the principle function of an IR system is to rank the documents in a collection in order of decreasing probability of relevance to a user's information need (Sparck Jones & Willett, 1997). This assumption is called the probability ranking principle. Under the probability ranking principle, the user can have some control over the size of retrieval output. Both the weighting and ranking are expressed in probability.

Third, the model is able to take advantage of feedback information to develop well-founded methods (Bookstein, 1985). Similarly, Kowalski (1997) pointed out that this model could accurately identify its weak assumptions and work to strengthen them. The self-improving feature adds another positive element to the probability model.

Fourth, the probability model in its original form does not employ the Boolean logic facility that many users find hard to apply. In that sense, IR systems based on the probability model are more user-friendly than Boolean-based IR systems.

7.4.2 Limitations of the Probability Model

The limitations of the probability model have also been scrutinized from different perspectives since its creation. A brief summary of them follows.

First, although the relevance value in this model is continuous instead of the dichotomous zero or one as in the Boolean model, the probability model assumes that relevance has a binary property:

$$Pr_{(nonrel)} = 1 - Pr_{(rel)}$$

where $Pr_{(rel)}$ is the probability of relevance, and $Pr_{(nonrel)}$ is the probability of nonrelevance. In other words, the value for the probability of irrelevance is fixed once the probability of relevance is computed, thus eliminating the intrinsic uncertainty factor from the IR process. Just as Robertson (1977) noted, the assumption of dichotomy is a strong one and almost certainly not generally valid.

Second, the probability model cannot greatly improve retrieval effectiveness. Results obtained using the probability model, although good, have not been sufficiently better than those retrieved from the Boolean logic or vector space systems. A question would naturally arise regarding the necessity of having an additional IR model when it would do only as well as the existing ones.

Aside from the two limitations just discussed, the model has other weaknesses. For example, sophistication in mathematics is required to understand and use the probability theory, which could affect the accessibility of the model. Moreover, the model has many variations. There are disagreements on which methods are the best and on how to resolve various technical questions even though a consensus exists for the general model (Bookstein, 1985). Similar to the vector space model, the probability model has been tried more for experimental purposes than applied in operational IR systems until the emergence of Internet retrieval systems.

7.5 Extensions of Major IR Models

Boolean logic, vector space, and probability are in general regarded as the three major IR models. Each of them has some extensions. For instance, extended Boolean logic is an extension of the Boolean logic model and vector space model in combination. Fuzzy set is also based on the Boolean logic model but additionally introduces the set theory into information retrieval. Latent semantic indexing is a derivation of the vector space model. It is designed to find a smaller set of dimensions and values that can be used as a substitute for the original matrix (Lesk, 1997). Inference network, an extension of the probability model, ranks documents in order of decreasing probability so that they satisfy the user's information need rather than the probability that they are relevant, as in the basic probability model previously discussed (Sparck Jones & Willett, 1997).

Additional extensions of the major IR models can be found in the taxonomy of information retrieval models presented by Baeza-Yates and Ribeiro-Neto (1999). Two of the better-known extensions, extended Boolean logic and fuzzy set, will be further examined in the following two sections.

7.5.1 Extended Boolean Logic Model

As shown in earlier discussions, the Boolean logic model has the disadvantage of not incorporating term weights and the vector space model has the weakness of not being capable of expressing Boolean logical relationship. The extended Boolean logic model is therefore developed to have weighted terms while keeping the Boolean structure. Although Bookstein and others have also conducted research on this topic (e.g., Bookstein, 1978), it was Harry Wu who under the supervision of Gerard Salton formally introduced the extended Boolean logic model when he was writing his dissertation (Salton, Fox & Wu, 1983; Wu, 1981).

In the extended Boolean logic model, term weights are assigned based on any combination of the following parameters: proximity, location, frequency, and perceived relevance. Thanks to the term weighting feature, the model can also provide ranked output and thus control the number of retrieved documents. Meanwhile, the advantages of the structured Boolean query formation are preserved.

But, the extended Boolean logic model has not been widely implemented in information retrieval due to the following reasons. First, it is hard to assign term weights effectively and accurately because of the issues outlined in §7.3.2 when we discussed the limitations of the vector space model. Second, logically equivalent queries may fail to produce the same results when different weights are assigned to query terms (Korfhage, 1997). Normally, more documents will be retrieved for the term with a larger weight. Nevertheless, the model attempts to cope with the limitations of the Boolean logic and vector space models by combining their respective strengths. Some Internet retrieval systems (e.g., AltaVista) support the extended Boolean logic searching.

7.5.2 Fuzzy Set Model

The fuzzy set model, initially proposed by Zadeh (1965), aims to overcome one limitation of the Boolean logic model (i.e., inability to express a partial relevance of search results) by generalizing the traditional set theory. In a traditional set, an object is either in the set or not in the set. Similarly, a document is either relevant or not relevant to a given query in the Boolean system.

This sharp boundary separates members of a set from nonmembers, or relevant documents from irrelevant ones. But such a clear-cut line virtually is nonexistent in information retrieval because the system and often the user cannot accurately tell whether a document is relevant to a particular query (Korfhage, 1997). Rather, a partial relevance should be a more precise reflection of the judgment.

The concept of partial membership, in correspondence to the notion of partial relevance needed to improve the Boolean logic model, is introduced as fuzzy set theory. The model assumes that fuzzy documents and queries do not exist but fuzzy judgment can be made. For fuzzy sets, degrees of membership are identified in the range of zero (0.0) to one (1.0) with one indicating a full membership. An object can belong to a set partially by having a membership grade between zero and one. The boundary that divides members and nonmembers of a set thus becomes fuzzy.

For example, a set of top students are to be selected to form an honors class. The selection can be done in two ways. One is to use the traditional set theory by exactly defining "top students" as those who hold a GPA of 3.9 and above. Any student who meets the specification will become a member of the honors class. All other students whose GPAs are below 3.9 will not be admitted into or become a member of the class even though some of them may have a GPA of 3.89. In contrast, the other method for selecting top students for an honors class employs the fuzzy set theory by assigning a membership grade to each student. Top students are therefore defined by the membership grades they receive. Those who have a GPA of 3.9 should be given a membership grade of 1.0 while students whose GPAs are, for instance, 3.5 or below will get a membership grade close to 0.0. Students with a GPA in between, say 3.8, will receive a membership grade of 0.8, for example. In that way, students who did not get a GPA of 3.9 can still be included in the set of top students with their membership grades showing their connection with the set.

In application of the fuzzy set theory to information retrieval, the relevance of documents should not be judged as relevant or irrelevant only, as done in the Boolean logic system. Instead, a membership grade can be assigned to a document to indicate how close it belongs to the set of relevant documents. Membership grades for the fuzzy set of documents are determined by the indexer during the indexing process (Bookstein, 1985).

The strengths of the fuzzy set model include the relaxation of the restriction in the Boolean logic model, namely, documents are either relevant or irrelevant to a query and no partial relevance is allowed. In assigning the membership grade, the fuzzy set IR system can provide ranked output in decreasing order of relevance so the user can choose to view the top-ranked results. In addition, the Boolean query structure is preserved in the model for expressing logical relationships. Systems based on the fuzzy set model are good for exploratory retrieval.

The fuzzy set IR system is not as flexible as desired, however, because it does not assign weights to query terms as opposed to document terms. The retrieval values of the documents therefore depend only on the values of document terms (Salton, 1989). This statement is about the consequence of keeping the Boolean framework in the fuzzy set model. In such Boolean searches using the OR operator (e.g., A OR B OR C), a document D_1 with only one query term (i.e., A) is assumed to be as important as document D_2 containing all query terms (i.e., A, B, C). Obviously, the value or relevance for document D_1 is judged only on one term (i.e., A) in this case, due to the fact that query terms are not weighted. As for queries using the AND operator (e.g., A AND B AND C), document D_1 containing all query terms but one (i.e., A, B) is considered as useless or irrelevant as document D_2 having no query term at all.

In addition, the fuzzy set model provides no mechanism for query expansion if compared with the vector space model. In contrast to the probability model, the fuzzy set model is less robust at least theoretically. The model is only applied sporadically in the field of information retrieval.

7.6 IR Models: A Further Look

As indicated at the beginning of this chapter, the IR models and extensions illustrated up to this point are primarily system-based. Other IR models are built on different parameters. For example, the cognitive model takes into consideration the user factor in information retrieval, and thus will be discussed in Chapter 10. The natural language model concerns the language issue in information retrieval by relying heavily on research in natural language processing, a topic covered in Chapter 12 as one AI application.

7.6.1 A Review of the Major IR Models

Verbatim descriptions of the three major IR models, i.e., Boolean logic, vector space, and probability, have been given in the previous sections. Table 7.1 is intended to summarize some important characteristics of these models.

The three IR models listed in Table 7.1 are reviewed from five different aspects: 1) Is Boolean logic supported? 2) Is term weighting provided? 3) Is output ranked? 4) Which matching criterion is used to determine similarity between queries and documents? 5) Any unique feature? These five aspects, to a large extent, determine the strengths and limitations of the IR models. For example, the availability of the Boolean search facility enables the user to compose structured queries. On the other hand, the same feature (i.e.,

Table 7.1   Features of Three IR Models

Model / Feature	Boolean Logic	Vector Space	Probability
Boolean Logic	Yes		
Weighting		Yes	Yes
Ranking		Yes	Yes
Matching Criterion	Term presence	Vector distance	Term frequency
Unique Feature		Relevance feedback	

Boolean logic) would also make an IR system user unfriendly because of the difficulty involved in conducting Boolean searches.

The Boolean logic model seems to be the weakest among the three listed in Table 7.1. It only supports Boolean searching and matching is made based on the presence of a term in the system. But, the model is heavily used and applied widely in information retrieval. The other two models appear similar on the surface in that they both, in their original form, do not include Boolean logic but provide the weighting and ranking mechanism. The criteria used by the vector space and probability models for weighting terms, ranking outputs, and measuring similarity are nevertheless dissimilar. In addition, relevance feedback is introduced as a unique retrieval capability in the vector space model. Efforts have been made to develop better IR systems in using the vector space or probability model. Such systems, however, have not been able to markedly outperform systems based on the Boolean logic model (Korfhage, 1997).

7.6.2 IR Models vs. Retrieval Techniques

In Chapter 5 various retrieval techniques were presented and discussed. What is the relationship then between IR models and retrieval techniques? While there is no exact or explicit one-to-one association between the two, some of the retrieval techniques are clearly connected with the IR models from which they are derived. For instance, Boolean searching is no doubt an application of the Boolean logic model. Query expansion, particularly relevance feedback, is supported by the vector space model. Weighted searching can be based on algorithms developed in the probability model or other IR models such as the extended Boolean. Fuzzy searching comes from the fuzzy set model.

Aside from those retrieval techniques whose origins are evidently marked, the remaining ones are also backed by IR models. For example, proximity searching has its root in the extended Boolean model. Moreover, retrieval techniques do not have to come from the same IR model in order to be used together during the searching process. They could be applied side by side regardless of their sources of origin if an IR system is so designed. In fact, the building of multimodel IR systems should be encouraged, as is discussed in §7.6.3.

Knowledge about the relationship between the IR models and retrieval techniques can help in choosing the right systems for retrieval tasks. One obvious example is that a Boolean system must be chosen if the user wants to do Boolean searches. If weighted searching is to be conducted, the user must choose an IR system based on, for instance, the vector space model.

7.6.3 Toward Multimodel IR Systems

IR models, as demonstrated in this chapter, have their pros and cons. IR systems applying these models consequently can only perform certain retrieval functions as defined. In order to take advantage of the strengths different IR models possess, IR systems should be constructed by incorporating features from multiple IR models. A similar idea is expressed by Frants and others (Frants, et al., 1999), although they call systems using many IR principles "multiversion systems."

The current practices in the field of information retrieval indicate that Boolean logic is the only model used in almost every IR system while other models are gradually implemented in systems such as Internet retrieval systems. Information queries can be very rudimentary as well as extremely sophisticated. IR systems for processing these queries should be designed accordingly by adopting a multimodel approach. Multimodel IR systems are increasingly seen on the Internet, which is becoming a major platform for IR systems.

The remaining question about multimodel IR systems is how the various IR models should be integrated. Projects like TREC can provide some guidance. The target user community of an IR system should also be surveyed to better understand their information needs in this digital age.

References

Baeza-Yates, Ricardo, and Ribeiro-Neto, Berthier. (1999). *Modern information retrieval*. New York: ACM Book Press.

Belkin, Nicholas J., and Croft, W. Bruce. (1987). Retrieval techniques. *Annual Review of Information Science and Technology, 22*, 109–145.

Bookstein, Abraham. (1978). On the perils of merging Boolean and weighted retrieval systems. *Journal of the American Society for Information Science, 29(3),* 156–158.

Bookstein, Abraham. (1985). Probability and fuzzy-set applications to information retrieval. *Annual Review of Information Science and Technology, 20,* 117–151.

Chowdhury, Gobinda G. (1999). *Introduction to modern information retrieval.* London: Library Association Publishing.

Cooper, W.S. (1988). Getting beyond Boole. *Information Processing and Management, 24,* 243–248.

Frants, Valery I., et al. (1999). Boolean search: Current state and perspectives. *Journal of the American Society for Information Science, 50(1),* 86–95.

Korfhage, Robert R. (1997). *Information storage and retrieval.* New York: John Wiley & Sons.

Kowalski, Gerald. (1997). *Information retrieval systems: Theory and implementation.* Boston: Kluwer Academic Publishers.

Lesk, Michael. (1997). *Practical digital libraries: Books, bytes and bucks.* San Francisco: Morgan Kaufmann.

Maron, M.E., and Kuhns, J.L. (1960). On relevance, probabilistic indexing and information retrieval. *Journal of the ACM, 7,* 216–244.

Robertson, S.E. (1977). The probability ranking principle in IR. *Journal of Documentation, 33,* 294–304.

Robertson, S.E., and Sparck Jones, K. (1976). Relevance weighting of search terms. *Journal of the American Society for Information Science, 27,* 129–146.

Salton, Gerard. (1968). *Automatic information organization and retrieval.* New York: McGraw Hill.

Salton, Gerard. (1989). *Automatic text processing: The transformation, analysis, and retrieval of information by computer.* New York: Addison-Wesley.

Salton, G., Fox, E.A., and Wu, H. (1983). Extended Boolean information retrieval. *Communications of the ACM, 26*, 1022–1036.

Salton, G., Wong, A., and Yang, C.S. (1975). A vector space model for automatic indexing. *Communications of the ACM, 18*, 613–620.

Soukhanov, Anne H., et al. (Eds.). (1984). *Webster's II new Riverside university dictionary*. Boston: The Riverside Publishing Co.

Sparck Jones, Karen, and Willett, Peter. (Eds.). (1997). *Readings in information retrieval*. San Francisco: Morgan Kaufmann.

Wu, Harry. (1981). *On query formulation in information retrieval*. Unpublished doctoral dissertation, Cornell University, Ithaca, NY.

Zadeh, L.A. (1965). Fuzzy sets. *Information and Control, 8*, 338–353.

CHAPTER 8

Information Retrieval Systems

Tasks of information retrieval are accomplished in IR systems. Different types of information retrieval systems have been developed since the 1950s to meet different kinds of information needs. Online systems, CD-ROM systems, OPACs, and Internet retrieval systems are the four major categories of IR systems that have served users in various capacities to satisfy their information requests. In this chapter, each of the system types will be examined to show conceptually their features, functions, and capabilities in information retrieval.

8.1 Online Systems—Pioneer IR Systems

Online IR systems, also referred to as professional online systems, are often abbreviated as online systems or online databases. The word *database* is treated as a synonym for *system* in the latter case. They are the first kinds of IR systems that have applied computer technology. DIALOG and MEDLINE are two examples of online IR systems.

Online systems allow the user to search databases located remotely with the help of the computer and telecommunication technology. The systems initially only supported batch mode (i.e., an individual search request is not processed immediately after its submission but until a certain number of requests have been assembled), and later introduced real-time interaction between the user and system. There are three stages in the development of online systems (Bourne, 1980):

- Feasibility studies and demonstration projects—1950s

- Production with restricted user populations—1960s

- National or multinational IR services—1970s to present

Hahn (1996) presented a detailed account of the pioneers involved in the development of online systems. After the advancement and improvement made since the 1950s, online systems have become a distinct group of IR systems in the digital age with their own characteristics.

8.1.1 Features of Online IR Systems

Online systems collected mainly bibliographic plus some numeric information before the 1980s, and eventually included full-text information.

Multimedia information is not often seen in this type of retrieval system. Information included in online systems is selected and represented by professionals (e.g., indexers). Controlled vocabulary is extensively used for information representation and retrieval although keyword searching is supported at the same time. Command language was the norm for users to interact with online systems until menu selection was introduced in the 1980s. Graphical interface was gradually employed in the 1990s, especially when online systems started adopting the Web as the platform.

A great variety of retrieval techniques and IR models have been applied in online systems. Basic retrieval techniques, e.g., Boolean searching, case sensitivity searching, truncation, proximity searching, and field searching, are universally available in almost every online system. Advanced retrieval techniques such as weighted searching, fuzzy searching, and query expansion, though not supported in all online systems, can be found in some applications. In fact, online systems prior to the mid-1990s served as test-beds for IR research and development. They also functioned as showcases for new IR technologies before the emergence of Internet retrieval systems. For example, DIALOG implemented ranked output by introducing the RANK command in 1993 (Basch, 1993).

In addition, online systems can be regarded as a laboratory for acquiring information retrieval skills for several reasons. First, the system is constructed to allow structured practice and manipulation. Some online systems even set up special facilities (e.g., DIALOG's ONTAP files and workshops) to help train users. Second, online systems represented the only computerized IR systems at that time. Third, a wide range of retrieval skills can be tried and practiced in online systems. The fourth reason is nevertheless on the negative side: It is assumed that online system users must receive training before using it. The system is not intuitive and cannot be used simply by trial and error. As a result, end-users in online searching are generally information professionals who take up the role of search intermediaries between the system and the user with information needs.

8.1.2 Online Systems and Information Retrieval

Among the four types of IR systems identified in this chapter, online systems have the longest history and greatest influence in information retrieval. They implicitly set standards for others to follow. Whenever a new kind of IR system emerges, people always compare it with online systems to see how well the newcomer can do in the field. For example, Nahl-Jakobovits and Tenopir (1992) investigated the factors of response time, coverage, content, and cost in both the CD-ROM and online versions of Psychological Abstracts and Sociological Abstracts. Hildreth (1988) contrasted OPACs with online IR systems, and explored the incorporation of online system features in OPACs.

Chu (1998) compared Internet retrieval systems against online systems in aspects such as database structure, search capability, retrieval performance, output option, and user effort.

Online systems have apparently established themselves as the benchmarking systems in information retrieval. As mentioned previously, however, online systems are by no means perfect. High cost and user unfriendliness are attributes frequently ascribed to online systems. On the other hand, the pioneer role online systems have played in information retrieval is also well acknowledged.

8.2 CD-ROM Systems—A New Medium for IR Systems

CD-ROM systems emerged from the application of CD-ROM technology in information retrieval. CD-ROM systems are usually searched locally and do not rely on telecommunication for access if the systems are not networked. PsycLIT from SilverPlatter is one example of a CD-ROM system.

CD-ROM systems can be approximately regarded as online systems in the CD-ROM medium because these two kinds of IR systems share many features and because CD-ROM systems are modeled after online systems in many ways. Furthermore, CD-ROM systems were not implemented on a large scale until the 1980s when online systems had already become very influential in the field.

There seem to be no obvious phases in the development of CD-ROM systems. One main reason for this phenomenon is that CD-ROM systems were not an endeavor starting from scratch but rather a marriage between CD-ROMs and the mature online systems, using the former as a new storage medium. Therefore, the unique features of CD-ROM systems to a large extent are determined by the characteristics of the CD-ROM medium.

8.2.1 Features of CD-ROM Systems

Bibliographic, numeric, and full-text information remain the dominant information source processed in CD-ROM systems. But an increase in multimedia information storage occurred as CD-ROM technology became more capable of handling such types of information than online systems. Controlled vocabulary is used for information representation and retrieval in conjunction with natural language. Human involvement continues to be heavy in CD-ROM retrieval. Command language is seen less often in CD-ROM systems whereas menu selection is implemented more often. Graphic interface made its debut in the CD-ROM environment, and some systems even applied the hyperstructure in their implementations.

Basic retrieval techniques (e.g., Boolean searching and proximity searching) are supported in CD-ROM systems while advanced search facilities (e.g., weighted searching and output ranking) are applied in a limited scope. It is not uncommon to see that one single system is stored on several CD-ROMs, which may restrict the application of some advanced retrieval technologies in the system.

Thanks to their high storage capacity and relatively small physical size, CD-ROM systems are theoretically portable because several disks can hold all the information needed in a database. However, the database alone cannot function as an IR system. Special equipment is required to run the system. On the other hand, it is more convenient for the user to search in CD-ROM systems, as they are not dependent on telecommunication technology to be functional. It is cheaper to conduct CD-ROM searches since they do not incur connection or other charges once the systems are purchased and installed. Users therefore can conduct searches without worrying if the clock is ticking and can concentrate more on the search itself.

The end-user, rather than the intermediary, does most of the searching in the CD-ROM environment. One reason is that CD-ROM systems usually impose no extra charges to the end-user according to the policy of fixed fee and unlimited access. Second, the interface of CD-ROM systems is friendlier than that of online systems as a result of the implementation of menu selection and graphic interfaces. Third, CD-ROM systems encourage browsing since online cost is not a concern to the end-user in this case. As discussed in Chapter 6, browsing and searching are the two major retrieval approaches while the former is favored in some circumstances. By comparison, browsing in an online retrieval session is costly.

CD-ROM systems, however, have limitations in updating. Each update means the replacement of existing CD-ROM disks, which significantly limits the updating frequency. Typical update frequency for CD-ROM systems is quarterly or bi-annually. Yet, the online counterparts of CD-ROM systems can be updated weekly, daily, or even continuously (e.g., Bridge World Markets News on DIALOG). Speed in searching CD-ROM systems can also be a problem, particularly when one system is spread over several CD-ROMs. CD-ROM systems also do not allow remote access if they are not networked.

8.2.2 CD-ROM Systems and Information Retrieval

CD-ROM systems have filled some voids that are not covered by online systems in information retrieval by reaching out to the end-user and by providing retrieval services to more people for whom online systems might be too expensive or difficult to use. A large percentage of CD-ROM systems have corresponding online versions although their coverage and features may not be exactly the same.

CD-ROM as a storage medium is gradually being replaced by Digital Versatile Disk (DVD), a more recent optical disk technology. With two layers on each of its two sides, a DVD holds up to 17 gigabytes of video, audio, or other information. In comparison, a current CD-ROM disk of the same physical size holds less than 700 megabytes of information (Whatis.com, 2000). Although the replacement of CD-ROMs with DVDs has yet to take place in the field of information retrieval, the fact that DVDs represent a more advanced technology is likely to make CD-ROM an obsolete application. Will CD-ROM systems become extinct? Will CD-ROM IR systems be replaced by systems based on DVD or another emerging technology while the Web is used more and more often as the platform for information retrieval? Answers to these questions are yet to be found.

8.3 OPACs—Computerized Library Catalogs as IR Systems

Online Public Access Catalogs (OPACs) are traditional catalogs executed in a different medium (Malinconico, 1984). There were only some pioneering efforts, such as the Library Control System at the State University of Ohio, before 1980. Since 1980, however, prototype and operational OPACs have been installed in a steadily growing number of libraries (Hildreth, 1985). Few libraries nowadays do not have an OPAC in their systems.

OPACs, either stand-alone or as part of an integrated library automation system such as Horizon from AmeriTech, are an outcome of library automation. OPACs were first developed by both vendors and in-house teams. The latter option ceased to exist when library automation system vendors became more experienced and established. OPAC interfaces have been changed from command language to menu selection, form fill-in, and graphical presentations.

Hildreth (1984) classified OPACs into three generations to chart their recent history and predict their possible future design at that time. The first generation of OPACs emulates more or less the card catalog approach to file content, organization, and access for mainly known-item searching. The second generation of OPACs adds enhancements in subject access points, search capabilities, and other aspects. OPACs of this generation resemble online systems in many ways. The third generation of OPACs, becoming a reality nowadays, makes the division between OPACs and online/CD-ROM systems less visible by having expanded access. The user can search online databases or CD-ROM resources via the OPAC of one's local library. Some other enhancements (e.g., integration of free text and controlled vocabulary search approaches) projected by Hildreth in 1984 for this generation of OPACs have also materialized.

8.3.1 Features of OPACs

Changes and developments are made as OPACs evolve from one generation to another. But there are certain features that seem unique to OPACs as one type of IR system. First, OPACs contain bibliographic information about library resources for institutions at various levels (e.g., local, regional, national). Although one OPAC is built for one library most of the time, there are occasions where one OPAC includes resources for multiple libraries. In contrast, the other three types of IR systems do not limit their coverage to bibliographical information at one institution or more.

Second, OPACs can be considered as an extension of MARC (i.e., a cataloging standard) records that are typically prepared by librarians using a set of rules and standards (e.g., classification schemes and cataloging rules) for the user population the library serves. Information representation in other kinds of IR systems cannot be done by using almost identical guidelines and with specific target users in mind. For example, DIALOG alone has hundreds of databases in its system. Each database is likely to be built and maintained using a different controlled vocabulary. While it is possible to define the user community of a library, it seems hard to clearly identify who would use an online system or CD-ROM system let alone the apparently immeasurable and ever-changing Internet retrieval systems.

Third, OPACs presently support at least field searching (e.g., author, title), keyword searching, and Boolean searching although library patrons make little use of the Boolean facility due to the reasons discussed in previous chapters. Known item searching constitutes a significant portion of all OPAC searches in part because OPACs are more likely to cover items "known" to the user than online or CD-ROM systems. Advanced search features (e.g., weighted searching) are usually not provided for OPACs since good retrieval performance is possible to achieve even by using the basic searching facility and thanks to the well-defined library collection.

Fourth, many present generation OPACs provide access to other resources including CD-ROM and online systems. With the help of Z39.50—a standard for retrieving information from different sources using a uniform interface—users can search other OPACs located at different places. Neither online nor CD-ROM systems can offer gateway services similar to OPACs mainly due to their for-profit nature.

Fifth, the design of OPACs encourages browsing in that OPAC users can typically browse by access points such as author and title while other types of IR systems usually present results chronologically or by relevance ranking. Browsing by call number in OPACs is particularly helpful to the user because the presentation order of the results bears a resemblance to the physical shelving order of library items. OPAC users thus are given the opportunity to locate more related items shelved next to each other before going to the shelves in person.

However, OPACs are still hard to use despite the fact that most of the OPACs now belong to the third generation. Borgman (1986; 1996) contributes the negative end result to the design of OPACs, which fails to incorporate lessons learned from information retrieval studies, and to insufficient understanding of searching behavior. The assumption that users without training should be able to use OPACs (Hildreth, 1988) is still not adequately supported today.

8.3.2 OPACs and Information Retrieval

The question about whether OPACs are library catalogs or online information retrieval systems was asked in the past (Hildreth, 1985). The answer to this question today should be that OPACs are information retrieval systems with their own characteristics. OPACs have been helping users locate materials in a library collection with functionalities unheard of when compared to their predecessors—card catalogs. In addition, OPACs also serve as a gateway to other IR systems by making linkages to them. As monographs are usually a major category of library materials, OPACs are the chief, if not the only, retrieval tool for accessing them. Without OPACs, library collections would become inaccessible in this digital age, as other kinds of IR systems are not designed specifically for that purpose.

8.4 Internet Retrieval Systems—The Newest Member in the Family of IR Systems

The exponential growth of the Internet makes it possible for people to access large quantities of digital information regardless of time and geographical locations. Meanwhile, it becomes obvious that additional IR systems are needed for retrieving any particular "needles" from the Internet "haystack." Individuals, companies, and institutions have subsequently developed a great number of Internet retrieval systems, or IR systems for the Internet, to cope with the information explosion on the Internet.

As known, the phrase "Web search engines" seems a more popular name than Internet retrieval systems when people make reference to systems for retrieving information from the Internet. However, this author chooses to use the latter because the former appears too narrow in meaning. First, Web is only one application, although currently the dominant one, of the Internet. Information handled by other applications such as File Transfer Protocol (FTP) is also covered by Internet retrieval systems. Therefore, naming Internet retrieval systems as Web search engines implies that they only deal with information on the Web, excluding information originating from other Internet applications. Second, some Internet applications have their own search facilities (e.g., Archie for FTP information) although many have been phased out or started using the Web as the platform. Third, Internet retrieval tools can be directory-based (e.g., Yahoo!) or search-based (e.g., AltaVista). It would then be inappropriate to refer to directory-based Internet retrieval systems as Web search engines because searching was not supported in their original design. The searching component now available in many directory-based Internet retrieval systems is a result of the union between the two different types of systems, as will be discussed later.

More information will be presented in this book about Internet retrieval systems for two reasons. One is that Internet retrieval systems are newer compared with the other three types of IR systems. Another reason is that the other three types of IR systems have been studied in depth by many researchers over the years (e.g., online systems by Harter, 1986; Large, Tedd & Hartley, 1999; Meadow, Boyce & Kraft, 1999; Walker & Janes, 1999; CD-ROM systems by Chowdhury, 1999; Rowley & Slack, 1997; OPACs by Beaulieu & Borgman, 1996; Hildreth, 1985) while Internet retrieval systems have yet to be examined thoroughly and systematically.

8.4.1 Taxonomy of Internet Retrieval Systems

Internet retrieval systems, though with a short history, come in great numbers as well as varieties. It has been impossible to enumerate how many Internet retrieval systems are available on the Net since these systems began mushrooming in the mid-1990s. However, a categorization of Internet retrieval systems by the following criteria is intended to provide an overview of the newest member in the IR family.

8.4.1.1 By Retrieval Approach

Searching and browsing are the two major retrieval approaches described in Chapter 6. On the Internet, retrieval systems based on searching are called search engines (e.g., AltaVista and Google) whereas IR systems based on browsing are called directories (e.g., Yahoo!). Directories are also often referred to as "catalogs." Search engines let users compose their own search queries. By contrast, directories organize and present network resources under hierarchically structured categories. Users of directory-based Internet retrieval systems can locate information by following a predefined path, i.e., the hierarchy of categories developed for the system.

As discussed in Chapter 6, either searching or browsing as a retrieval approach has its limitations. For instance, search queries are difficult to formulate but required for conducting searches in search-based Internet retrieval systems. Internet users have to compose their own queries as information professionals usually do not act as intermediaries in this environment. Similarly, the number of results retrieved from the Internet for most topics can easily exceed thousands, if not millions. But browsing, as a retrieval approach, has no mechanism for narrowing a retrieval problem. Consequently, Internet retrieval systems attempt to surmount such difficulty by supporting both browsing and searching at the same site. The directory-based Internet retrieval systems license with search engines to provide the search component at their sites. The search-based Internet retrieval systems likewise contract with directory services to offer the browsing option at their sites. For example, Yahoo! used Google as its search engine and AltaVista was listed at its site directories compiled by Open Directory and LookSmart. The partnerships between these two kinds of Internet retrieval systems nevertheless change constantly. It would not be surprising to see, for instance, that Yahoo! changes to a different search engine for itself in the future as it did in the past. More specific information about how various search engines and directories form partnerships with each other for Internet retrieval can be found in the "Search Engine Alliance Chart" compiled by Danny Sullivan (Sullivan, 2001).

The combination of browsing and searching at one site produces the third type of Internet retrieval systems, namely, hybrid Internet retrieval systems. In the hybrid environment, the user can search or browse at the same site without switching to another. Retrieval effectiveness is improved subsequently.

8.4.1.2 By Application

Since the creation of the Internet, many different applications have been developed: Telnet, FTP, Gopher, Wide Area Information Servers (WAIS), and the Web or World Wide Web (WWW), to name some. Each of those applications performs certain functions. For example, Telnet is for remote login from a local system so that resources (e.g., hardware and software) at the remote site can be utilized. FTP is for transferring files between remote systems and local ones seamlessly at high speed. The Web is the largest information repository on the Internet because of its friendly user interface and hypermedia feature. Gopher, an obsolete application today and completely superseded by Web, was designed for storing and retrieving resources on the Internet with hypermenu interface. WAIS, on the other hand, was a Z39.50-complied keyword search tool for Internet resources. Retrieval systems were built at one point or another for these applications except WAIS because it consisted of a retrieval mechanism itself. Table 8.1 lists retrieval systems created for major Internet applications under two different retrieval approaches.

Table 8.1   Major Internet Applications and Corresponding Retrieval Systems

Application	Search-based	Directory-based
Telnet	(Various)	Hytelnet
FTP	Archie	(None)
WWW	AltaVista, etc.	Yahoo!, etc.
Gopher	Veronica, Jughead	Gopher Jewels
WAIS	(Imbedded)	(Via Gopher)

As shown in Table 8.1, Internet retrieval systems comprise more than just Web search engines. Although many of the retrieval systems listed in the table no longer exist today, they did play a distinguished role in retrieving information from the Internet, particularly before the Web-based Internet retrieval systems were developed. To be more specific, Hytelnet provided a list of many Telnetable resources via a hypertext interface. It also allowed automatic logins for the sites listed. Archie, developed by Alan Emtage, a graduate student then at McGill University in Canada, periodically scanned anonymous FTP hosts and compiled information (e.g., host name, directory name, and file size) for files available on those hosts. People were able to search FTPable files by host name, directory name, and file name using Archie. Gopher enjoyed great popularity before the Web became the star application on the Internet. The retrieval systems designed for Gopher information—Veronica, Jughead, and Gopher Jewels—are rarely used as Gopher fades away from the Internet. The life span of WAIS was relatively short in part because of its command language interface and the emergence of Web-based Internet retrieval systems. However, the uniform interface as well as platform independent Z39.50 implemented in WAIS has been carried on in many other retrieval applications (e.g., OPACs).

Portions of the retrieval tasks previously accomplished by non-Web-based systems such as Archie have been transferred to Web-based systems. For example, Tile.net (http://tile.net/ftp) is a Web-based retrieval system devoted to finding FTP and other information. Other non-Web-based retrieval systems (e.g., Veronica) are not available anymore because their retrieval mission is fulfilled. Information from such Internet applications as USENET (for many-to-many discussions about numerous topics) and lists (for one-to-many discussions on selected subjects) is also retrievable via general (e.g., Google at http://groups.google.com for USENET information) or specific Web-based retrieval systems (e.g., Tile.net at http://tile.net/lists for list information).

In sum, Internet retrieval systems are at present all Web-based or use the Web as the platform. These retrieval systems include information coming from the Web and other applications (e.g., FTP and USENET) even though the Web is currently the largest information repository on the Internet.

8.4.1.3 By Content

Internet retrieval systems can also be categorized by the content of information they cover. Some of them maintain comprehensive coverage (e.g., AltaVista) by gathering information from various sources and subject areas. By contrast, others may be built for only one particular field. One such example is Gateway for Educational Materials (GEM at http://www. geminfo. org) for education.

Some Internet retrieval systems have evolved into portals by expanding the content coverage beyond searchable information. But search remains as the core in portals. Vortals, by comparison, are portals restricted to a vertical market (e.g., healthcare, insurance, automobiles, or food manufacturing). The market is vertical because it focuses on a relatively narrow range of goods and services, whereas a horizontal market is one that aims to produce a wide range of products and services (Whatis.com, 2001). Roughly speaking, portals can be regarded as generic Internet retrieval systems. Vortals, on the other hand, are specialized in retrieving information targeted for one vertical market. Both portals and vortals are hybrid Internet retrieval systems that support browsing and searching.

In addition, there are retrieval systems devoted to retrieving special types of information on the Internet. For instance, SWITCHBOARD (http://www. switchboard.com) and FOUR11 (http://www.four11.com) of Yahoo! can be used for obtaining addresses and phone numbers. WHOWHERE (http:// www.whowhere.com) of Lycos are created for locating e-mail addresses. MapBlast (http://www.mapblast.com) lets users type in an address and retrieve, for example, a detailed interactive map for that address.

This taxonomy of Internet retrieval systems illustrates the variety and capacity of IR systems developed over the years for the Internet. Internet retrieval systems, as a group, apparently have evolved and become the newest yet eminent member in the IR family.

8.4.2 Features of Internet Retrieval Systems

Internet retrieval systems, particularly Web search engines and directories, were not initially designed as part of the Internet development with the exception of WAIS. Instead, they were created as an afterthought when Internet users faced with an enormous amount of unprocessed information were without any tools for retrieval purposes. For example, Archie was developed when FTP users wanted to find out whether any anonymous FTP sites hosted the information they needed. Web search engines and directories were built after Web users found it increasingly difficult to locate what they wanted by just following hyperlinks imbedded at Web sites. If the entire Web had been treated as a library, we would have had the library collection before creating a library catalog for it. Besides, Internet retrieval systems differ from the other three types of IR systems in several aspects as discussed in the following sections.

8.4.2.1 Coverage and Source Information

Any information, before getting into online systems, CD-ROM systems, or OPACs, must go through editing, peer review, or similar checking procedures to ensure its quality. However, there are few quality control mechanisms in the information production process on the Internet. Anyone can put any information onto the Internet without its being checked for quality and suitability. Information of this kind would become the source information for Internet retrieval systems.

Internet retrieval systems rely primarily on automatic harvesting devices such as robots, spiders, or crawlers for gathering information from the Internet. These systems also allow people to submit information about their own sites although self-submission accounts for only a small percentage of all the information collected. Except for directory-based Internet retrieval systems, it appears rare to have human beings manually select information from the Internet. By comparison, information professionals are responsible for the data collection process in other kinds of retrieval environments.

When robots, spiders, or the like are dispatched for data collection, they are not all designed to copy the full content of a site. For example, Archie only copied the directory information of FTP sites. Some harvesting devices get the first 200 words or 20 lines of each site they visit. Others just obtain certain information (e.g., title, headings, and hyperlinks) from them. Furthermore, Web sites as the largest information storage on the Internet have the networked hyperstructure. Few Internet retrieval systems have the intent and resources to collect information from every hyperlinked document. For example, some may decide to copy the documents by following one level of hyperlinks, leaving information at other levels untouched. As a result, most sites only have part of their full information included in Internet retrieval systems.

Besides the two factors just described, there is also the so-called "invisible Web" that affects the coverage of Internet retrieval systems. Invisible Web refers to those components that are not accessible by common Internet retrieval systems because of file formats (e.g., CGI scripts) or structures (e.g., databases mounted onto the Web). Portable Document Format (PDF) files on the Internet were not covered by any Internet retrieval system until Google changed its practice in early 2001.

According to studies conducted by Lawrence and Giles (1998; 1999), Internet retrieval system coverage relative to the estimated size of the publicly indexable Web (i.e., 800 million pages as of February 1999) has decreased substantially since December 1997, with no system indexing more than about 16 percent of the estimated size of the publicly indexable Web. In 1997, the coverage figure was about 33 percent. The conclusions were made after they examined six and 11 Internet retrieval systems respectively in the two studies using real queries performed by NEC Research Institute employees. Others (e.g., Smith, 2000) estimate that the top Internet retrieval systems fail to index 70–75 percent of the pages on the Web.

No matter what the actual coverage is, one thing becoming clear is that Internet retrieval systems are only able to process a decreasing portion of Internet information as the Net itself grows exponentially. The incomplete coverage of information and unselective practice of source information distinguish Internet retrieval systems from their counterparts in other IR environments.

8.4.2.2 Indexing Mechanism

Automatic indexing algorithms based on word frequency and similar criteria dominate the indexing practice in the creation of Internet retrieval systems. Limited human involvement is required in the indexing process even though some systems (e.g., Yahoo!) choose to manually categorize the information to be included in their databases. Controlled vocabulary is seldom adopted in indexing Internet materials in consideration of factors like cost, effectiveness, and the nature of information on the Net.

There are some projects (e.g., NetFirst at http://www.oclc.org/oclc/netfirst/index.htm) that apply controlled vocabularies for organizing

Internet resources. A list of similar projects can be found at CYBERSTACKS, a Web-based virtual directory of many undertakings germane to library and information science (McKiernan, 2001). But these projects, strictly speaking, function more as OPACs for Internet resources than as Internet retrieval systems. In addition, NetFirst is fee-based while the Internet retrieval systems under discussion are basically free.

Fields (e.g., author, title, and publication year) are identified and indexed when databases for online, CD-ROM, and OPAC systems are constructed. By comparison, Internet retrieval systems consist of no field data in the traditional sense in their databases other than the field-less index files for keywords and their corresponding locations in the system. Tagged information such as <title> ... </title> in HyperText Markup Language (HTML) or <price> ... </price> in eXtensible Markup Language (XML) can be treated at most as quasi-fields because they are not uniformly assigned during the indexing process.

In short, the indexing mechanism for Internet retrieval systems differs from that of other types of IR systems in that the former adopts the automatic approach based on keywords and does not index Internet resources by fields.

8.4.2.3 Searching Facilities

As one type of IR system, Internet retrieval systems provide virtually all the search facilities available in other retrieval environments. But there exist some points unique to Internet retrieval systems, which are discussed here.

Boolean searching, being taken for granted in non-Internet retrieval systems, is not supported in every Internet retrieval system. For example, the AND operator is not provided at Google as it is supposed to be since the order in which the terms are typed will affect the search results (Google, 2002; Rousseau, 2001). On the other hand, the plus (+) sign was used widely as a surrogate for the AND operator in the early years of Internet retrieval, which appears, however, misleading because the + sign represents the notation for the OR operator or the logical sum as explained in §7.2. Although that practice has been discontinued and the + sign now becomes the weighting symbol for weighted searching, it causes confusion to the end-user especially when the person has not done Boolean searching before.

Proximity searching is essential in retrieving phrases (if database information is not phrase indexed) and specifying the relative positions of search terms. Online systems are particularly strong in supporting proximity searches. By contrast, proximity searching has not yet become a universal feature for Internet retrieval systems. Among those systems that do support proximity searching on the Internet, few provide the full range of proximity operators that are typically available to online and other kinds of IR systems.

As for truncation, field searching, and case sensitive searching, Internet retrieval systems support them on a limited scale and with limited capabilities. Take truncation as an example, other IR systems can get very specific by, for instance, limiting the number of characters to be truncated. But most Internet retrieval systems can only go as far as unlimited right-hand truncation. Yet, automatic truncation is the default in some cases, generating more noise in search results. As mentioned in §8.4.2.2, there are only a few quasi-fields (e.g., title and URL) in Internet retrieval systems because such systems in effect are field-less. There are not many opportunities for the user to limit a search by field in Internet retrieval systems.

Weighted searching, not often seen in other kinds of retrieval systems, appears in the search facility repertoire of many Internet retrieval systems. The plus (+) sign is used consistently among Internet retrieval systems as the weighting symbol, meaning more weights for the term signaled. Based on the writer's current experience, weighted searching overrides Boolean searching on the Net. For example, in a query on *tax* AND *penalty* with a weight assigned to *penalty*, the results might contain only the term *penalty* while *tax* is totally ignored in the search.

Fuzzy searching, although not a common feature for other types of IR systems, does get implemented in some Internet retrieval systems. For instance, if one intends to search *Roosevelt Avenue* from Mapblast, an Internet retrieval system specialized in map information, a misspelled phrase of *Roosvelt Avenue* would still lead the searcher to the right location when other parts of the address (e.g., zip code) are correctly given. Google's "Did you mean: ..." feature, shown after a typo is made when entering a search query, is also an implementation of fuzzy searching.

Multiple database searching is not new, for example, to online systems. Databases suitable for performing such types of searching are usually set up or managed in one single system. For example, DIALOG is able to support multiple database searching by having several hundreds of databases that are similar structure-wise. In the case of Internet retrieval systems, cross database searching would be a more appropriate term to be used in this context because each singular retrieval system is constructed independently and different from others. They are not designed as subdivisions of a larger entity. Systems that can provide cross database searching on the Internet are called metasearch engines (e.g., Dogpile) or metaretrieval systems to be consistent with the terminology used in this book. The number of individual retrieval systems each metasearch engine covers varies from one system to another, normally in the range of half a dozen to two dozen. Usually single keyword searching works the best in cross database searching as there are more differences than similarities in terms of search syntax and semantics among those individual IR systems. Some Internet metaretrieval systems remove duplicates before presenting results to the user.

Concept or meaning-based searching, rather than keyword matching, is particularly desirable on the Internet because it is crucial in improving retrieval performance. Yet, controlled vocabularies are not commonly used in Internet retrieval systems. Some attempts have been made in this respect. For example, SimpliFind (http://www.simpli.com) utilizes SimpliNet, a product of linguistics and cognitive science research, to automatically generate a list of concepts based on input query terms from which the user can choose. When a query is *book a flight*, for instance, SimpliFind would present a pull-down menu listing concepts such as *air travel*, *trip*, and *trajectory*. Then the user can choose a corresponding concept (e.g., *air travel*) to proceed with the actual search. Another example related to concept searching on the Net can be found at Oingo (http://www.oingo.com). Calling it a "meaning-based" searching engine, Oingo claims that it goes beyond searching for just simple text characters by allowing the user to refine a search based on the actual meaning of the query terms. Searches are conducted in Oingo's semantic space, bringing up categories and documents that are close in meaning to the concepts the user is interested in. A particular word (e.g., *subway*) absent in a document would not exclude the possibility that the document is indeed conceptually relevant to the query on, for example, *public transportation*. Both SimpliFind and Oingo, strictly speaking, can only be considered as quasi-concept searching because their indexing does not appear concept-based—a prerequisite for concept searching. Rather, concepts are mapped onto keywords during searches using certain devices (e.g., SimpliNet). In the other three kinds of IR systems, controlled vocabulary is almost universally applied and concept searching is generally supported. SimpliFind and Oingo have now both changed from free to fee-based services.

Peer-to-peer (P2P) searching is a feature new in the IR field, which relates closely with the collaborative filtering approach used in commercial marketing. Search histories and bookmarks of previous users are examined when a new query is received to detect relevant information. When one joins a P2P network, that person's query will be searched against the sites visited and bookmarked by other people belonging to the same initial network. This process can be repeated by expanding the search scope to additional P2P networks of which those people are also members. Festa (2001) describes P2P using Pandango, a project carried out by i5 Digital, as an example:

> Pandango ... would determine relevance by examining a radiat-ing network of "referrers." Once someone downloaded Pandango and joined its peer-to-peer network, that person's keyword search would examine the Web histories and bookmarks of an

initial network of 100 referrers. From there, the application would search the Web histories of those 100 referrers' combined 10,000 referrers, and once again – so that the query would canvass the Web pages visited and bookmarked by 1 million people. (p. 1)

P2P searching is distributed, making use of search information generated by previous users instead of searching in a centralized database. Certain issues (e.g., privacy and security) would inevitably arise as a result of P2P searching on the Internet. But they are beyond the scope of this book. P2P is also referred to as "bonding" in some publications (e.g., Schwartz, 2000). By comparison, neither online nor CD-ROM systems nor OPACs have the mechanism built in for conducting P2P searching.

8.4.2.4 Ranking Techniques

Ranking mechanism has been introduced to Internet retrieval as an effort to help the user locate "needles" in the huge "haystack" more effectively. Algorithms commonly employed for ranking search results in all IR environments include, as depicted in §5.1.2.2, term frequency, term proximity, term location, and inverse document frequency. While these algorithms rank search results according to the intrinsic attributes of documents (e.g., term frequency), the following three ranking methods focus on the extrinsic features generated by people when they access target Web documents or when they create their own sites.

The first new ranking technique, spearheaded by Google, is based on backlinks, i.e., links pointing to a site to be retrieved (Vidmar, 1999). Google assumes that the more times a site is pointed to by other sites, the more important it becomes. This practice appears very similar to citation analysis—an established method used for, among other things, evaluating the quality of scholarly publications. Borrowing some terminology from citation analysis, we can call the site being pointed to as the "cited site" while the site referring to the cited site becomes the "citing site." In other words, Google has developed a mechanism for analyzing and ranking the links pointing to a cited site using PageRank, an algorithm named after one of its creators—Lawrence Page. Other parameters such as title, fonts, term proximity, and the importance of citing sites are also considered in the rank computation (Brin & Page, n.d.).

The second new ranking algorithm, known as the popularity approach, was developed by Direct Hit (http://www.directhit.com), which later became a part of Teoma (http://www.teoma.com). It ranks a site by the number of times users actually visit (thus the word "hit"). If we regard AltaVista and similar search engines as author-controlled IR systems (i.e., the relevance of search results is determined by how well keywords match with document content), if we call Yahoo! and similar directories editor-controlled IR systems (i.e., editors locate and catalog sites by examining them one by one), Direct Hit represents a third kind of search mechanism: user-controlled IR systems in which search rankings depend on the choices made by users (Frauenfelder, 1998). The more times a site is visited by others, the more popular that site becomes, and the better ranking it receives.

The third ranking algorithm involves two steps. First, sites are ranked by using the traditional ranking methods such as frequency and proximity for analyzing hyperlinks contained within and the text around them. Second, these hyperlinks are further scrutinized using the backlink method Google employs. This ranking method, called "hypersearching" by its developers, is implemented in the Clever project at http://www.almaden.ibm.com/cs/k53/clever.html (Chakrabarti et al., 1999). Clever aims to identify the following two kinds of Web sites by hypersearching: 1) authorities – the best sources of information on a particular topic, and 2) hubs – collections of links to those locations. The reiteration of the above two steps locates and fine-tunes search results, which are eventually presented as pages of relevant links, separated into hubs and authorities. Hubs and authorities would receive higher ranking than regular sites. Clever is officially an IBM research project. So far it has offered only demo searches and research reports.

While traditional ranking methods may cause problems such as word stuffing (i.e., repeating some keywords deliberately in order to get a better ranking) or make little sense in situations like "pay for placement" (i.e., ranking search results based on the amount of fees paid), the three techniques described here open up a new dimension for ranking and evaluating Web sites. However, they may bring further biases into the ranking process as new and unlinked sites would have an increasingly difficult time becoming visible in those retrieval systems (Lawrence & Giles, 1999).

The backlink method adopted by Google is not novel in the online retrieval environment. The Institute of Scientific Information (ISI) has built a series of databases (e.g., Science Citation Index) since the 1960s according to the citation principle. But citation frequency was not implemented as a criterion for ranking search results in citation databases until the introduction of the RANK command by DIALOG in 1993. Direct Hit's popularity method and Clever's hypersearching algorithm, on the other hand, do not have counterparts in other retrieval environments where the ranking mechanism is still not widely available.

8.4.2.5 Search Modification

Modification of search queries or statements in online retrieval systems is well supported. The user can broaden or narrow down a search with various facilities (e.g., truncation or field searching) available in the system. CD-ROM systems operate in a manner similar to online systems because the former can be treated to a certain extent as online systems in CD-ROM medium. OPACs, compared with online and CD-ROM systems, are less flexible in search modification. Since known item searching makes up a significant portion of all OPAC searches, the need for modifying searches is relatively small.

By contrast, Internet searches usually require modification because of the large amount of results each search produces and the difficulty in letting the end-user compose a precise query. Yet, it does not seem easy for users to modify their searches. First, no sets are created and stored for each search while this is a common feature in online and CD-ROM systems. Second, little modification mechanism is provided for refining searches. Lycos, for example, does permit users to conduct further searches within the results just retrieved by selecting the "Search these results" option. That is basically what the user can get in current Internet retrieval systems with regard to search modification. The flexibility and diversification of search modification supported in other retrieval environments are still absent on the Internet.

As controlled vocabularies are not commonly applied in processing network information, some systems (e.g., AltaVista) try to suggest a list of terms based on the query a user enters for modifying searches. For example, when a query on *tulips* is made, AltaVista provides the following terms for further refining the search: *Holland, plant, spring, tulip bulbs*, and more. The user can choose and decide which of the terms in the listing to be included in the search. Even with such features for search modification, it remains extremely hard for Internet users to narrow down a search to a desired level. Relevance feedback, the automatic approach for expanding a search, is, however, available in systems such as Google. The user can do relevance feedback by simply clicking on hyperlinks labeled as "Similar pages" or "More like this," for example. The concern is how useful this approach is when the user seems already overwhelmed by the number of search results the system retrieved even without using the relevance feedback option.

8.4.2.6 Interface

Command language and menu selection are used as the interface in a large percentage of online, CD-ROM, and OPAC systems. Internet retrieval systems created for applications other than the Web (e.g., Archie and Veronica) had interfaces of similar kinds. As the Web becomes a major Internet application and popular platform for other applications (e.g., USENET), Internet retrieval systems tend to all have the Web interface, which is graphical and hyperstructured. The uniformity in interface contributes to the user friendliness of Internet retrieval systems as a whole, a characteristic hard to attain by other kinds of IR systems.

In summary, Internet retrieval systems have unique features in coverage, source information, indexing, searching facilities, ranking methods, search modification, and interface when compared with online, CD-ROM, and OPAC systems. The searching of multilingual and multimedia information should also differentiate Internet retrieval systems from other types of IR systems. That topic is covered in Chapter 9, Retrieval of Information Unique in Content and Format.

8.4.3 Generations of Internet Retrieval Systems

Internet retrieval systems have grown into a new member of the IR family. A lot of changes and enhancements have been introduced to them since their inception. Although having only a short history of development, Internet retrieval systems can be classified into three different generations based on the attributes presented in Table 8.2.

The first generation of Internet retrieval systems refers to such pioneer systems as Yahoo! and WebCrawler. Text information was the major type of information those systems collected. No particular attention was paid to multimedia information processing when this generation of Internet retrieval systems was built besides displaying the images already embedded on the pages or sites along with the text information retrieved. Directories and search engines were separated, and each system provided one retrieval approach, either browsing or searching. These systems did keyword indexing and supported, as one generation, basic searching capabilities (e.g., Boolean search, truncation, and proximity search). No search modification was possible with this generation of systems. Search outputs were not ranked but users were given the opportunity to choose formats (e.g., title only or title with a brief summary) and the number of results (e.g., 10, 20, or 30) a system would present without refreshing the screen.

Table 8.2   Three Generations of Internet Retrieval Systems

Generation / Attribute	1st Generation	2nd Generation	3rd Generation
Information Covered	Mainly text	Text or nontext	Multimedia
Retrieval Approach	Browsing & searching separated	Browsing & searching combined	Browsing & searching integrated
Indexing	Keyword	Keyword with concept mapping	Keyword & concept
Searching Capability	Basic	Basic & advanced	Precision improving
Search Modification	No	Limited support	More narrow-down features
Output	Not ranked	Ranked	Personalized

The second generation of Internet retrieval systems grows significantly in number. Some systems represent improvements over their initial versions (e.g., Yahoo! and AltaVista) whereas others are new additions (e.g., Google and Teoma). A considerable number of the second-generation systems not only provides text information retrieval services but also helps locating image, video, and MP3 files. The retrieval process is, however, limited to data-bases or files that contain a particular type of multimedia information. In other words, text and multimedia information is processed separately in this generation of Internet retrieval systems. Although powered by different com-panies, both the browsing and searching mechanisms are presented at the same site so that the user can make a choice of retrieval approaches without switching to another site. Indexing is still based on keywords but some efforts have been made to map concepts onto keywords using devices such as SimpliNet from Simpli. While basic searching continues being supported by the second-generation Internet retrieval systems, advanced search facilities (e.g., weighted search) are introduced. Most Internet retrieval systems clas-sify their searching capabilities into two kinds: 1) searches free of symbols or notations (e.g., operators) as simple searching, and 2) queries with symbols and notations as advanced searching. Search forms are normally used for advanced searches. Searches can be broadened and narrowed down in a lim-ited number of ways, such as by date, by language, search within results, or relevance feedback. Search results are ranked most of the time based on a ranking algorithm whose composition is usually kept secret. Choices of out-put number and display format gradually fade away in this generation of Internet retrieval systems due to their diminishing significance to the user. As IR systems, the second generation has made a lot of progress in functionality and performance.

The third generation of Internet retrieval systems should have further enhancements in attributes listed in Table 8.2. First, multimedia will not be treated separately from text information in the new generation of Internet retrieval systems. Rather, techniques for processing and retrieving multime-dia will be integrated with those for text information. Since the Web is noted for its capability in presenting multimedia information and has become the major Internet application, there is no reason why multimedia cannot be represented, processed, and retrieved together with the text information as research in multimedia IR advances. Second, directories and search engines are being integrated rather than simply offered at the same site. The user can search within a browsable category (e.g., Yahoo!) and search results are grouped into categories for browsing (e.g., Teoma). In addition to keyword indexing, concept indexing will be done when further progress has been made in research on natural language processing and representation. Search capabilities supported by previous generations will be improved and enhanced with a focus on improving precision. Additional search facilities (e.g., concept searching, natural language searching) will be brought into the repertoire of retrieval capability the system maintains. The search modification mechanism should be oriented more toward effectively narrowing down searches because the user is usually overwhelmed by the huge numbers of results produced by Internet retrieval systems. Search result presentation will ideally be ranked and customized according to the user's specification instead of the system's predefined options. For instance, Fast (http://www.alltheweb.com) in its advanced search interface allows the user to decide, among other things, if offensive results should be eliminated or if pages whose sizes are larger than certain kilobytes should be presented. The third generation of Internet retrieval systems should be able to show noticeable enhancement of retrieval performance.

As seen from these descriptions, Internet retrieval systems have apparently passed the first generation, and are evolving well into the second generation. The third generation is emerging on the horizon with great potential. In less than a decade of time, we have experienced the change of generations in Internet retrieval systems because of the rapid development of the Internet for which those retrieval tools have been built. Their significance in the IR field and especially in the digital age cannot be overstated.

8.4.4 Internet Retrieval Systems and Information Retrieval

The Internet has become not only a gigantic information warehouse but also a popular platform for accessing other kinds of IR systems. Internet retrieval systems no doubt are the only tools for retrieving information from the Internet. Meanwhile, they also function as gateways to other information sources. As more and more information is put onto the Internet, the importance of Internet retrieval systems in the field will increase in proportion.

In addition, Internet retrieval systems are turning into the lab and showcase for new, advanced, and sophisticated IR techniques, a role that online systems have played in the past. To stay current with the most recent developments in the IR field, one should closely monitor Internet retrieval systems instead of online or other kinds of systems. Changes occur constantly, if not on a daily basis, in Internet retrieval systems. Net-based newsletters and sites (e.g., Notess, 2002; Sullivan, 2002) are created to inform the user of the latest developments about them.

On the other hand, Internet retrieval systems as a group are notorious for their low precision search performance. Information retrieved from the Internet may not be accessible due to factors such as broken and dated links, a consequence much less likely in other IR environments. The user must also be responsible for judging the quality of information since the quality control mechanism for information on the Internet, if available, is at best very loosely structured (e.g., at the time of cataloging Internet resources for directory-based systems).

Searching, according to Brewer (2001), is the most visible and important aspect of the Internet after communication. Internet retrieval systems are designed specifically for retrieval purposes. Moreover, these systems are free of charge to end-users if they already have Internet access. It is therefore not an overstatement to say that Internet retrieval systems hold a prominent place in the field of information retrieval at present and will do so for a long time to come.

8.5 Convergence of Various IR Systems

It can be seen from the descriptions and discussions in this chapter that each kind of IR system has its features, functions, and capabilities in the area of information retrieval. Yet they are all designed and maintained for information retrieval purpose. In order to provide better and more convenient IR services to the user, the convergence of various IR systems has occurred in recent years. Convergence may take any of the following forms.

The first form of convergence, chronologically speaking, is the loading of CD-ROM systems onto OPACs. Since OPACs are generally created for individual libraries that also house CD-ROM systems, many institutions consolidate these two systems. Links are made from the OPAC to CD-ROMs, allowing the user to access two different IR systems at one place. Some institutions also establish links from their OPACs to online systems so that the connection procedure can be eliminated when the user conducts any online searches. This form of convergence takes place basically at the system connection level.

The second form of convergence occurs at the system database content level between OPACs and online systems. For example, an OPAC search reveals that a particular item is not in the library collection. The query for that item can then be submitted to the online system that the OPAC is linked with to see if the item is in the online system. Document delivery systems (e.g., ProQuest or UnCover) would very likely be used to obtain a physical copy of the item. But it is the linkage between OPACs and online systems that truly facilitates the retrieval process.

The third type of convergence happens when the hyperstructured Web has increasingly been used as the platform for Internet retrieval systems as well as online, CD-ROM, and OPAC systems. These IR systems become so interrelated that the boundaries among them are getting fuzzy. For example,

Field 856 of MARC, a cataloging standard, is allocated for recording URLs of Internet resources. The end products of this practice by nature would be, as indicated in §8.4.2.2, OPACs for Internet resources. In addition, more and more books and journals are being published electronically on the Web, integrated into the library collection, and represented in the OPACs. Therefore, information on the Internet, previously the unquestionable target of Internet retrieval systems, is included in OPACs that have been reserved exclusively for representing and retrieving library collections in the past. This practice has brought about the convergence of OPACs and Internet retrieval systems. Another example of such convergence can be found where Web documents list references or citations that are covered by online systems. Assuming a Web document along with its references is located with the help of an Internet retrieval system, the user can further search in the online system containing the hyperlinked references. The association between online systems and Internet retrieval systems is seamlessly established.

From a broader perspective, the Web is becoming the platform for using all four different types of IR systems. From a narrower viewpoint, it is not unthinkable for a user to have access to a Web-based library information system that includes all four kinds of IR systems, namely, the library's OPAC, online and CD-ROM systems the library subscribes to, and some Internet retrieval systems the library chooses to present. Will the Web become the only platform for IR systems in the future? Will a common platform catalyze further convergence among the IR systems? What will the impact of the convergence be on the user? We do not yet know the answers.

References

Basch, Reva. (1993). Dialog's Rank command: Building and mining the data mountain. *Online, 17(4),* 28–35.

Beaulieu, Micheline, and Borgman, Christine L. (Guest editors). (1996). Special topic issue: Current research in Online Public Access Systems. *Journal of the American Society for Information Science, 47(7),* 491–583.

Borgman, Christine L. (1986). Why are online catalogs hard to use? Lessons learned from information retrieval studies. *Journal of the American Society for Information Science, 37,* 387–397.

Borgman, Christine L. (1996). Why are online catalogs still hard to use? *Journal of the American Society for Information Science, 47(7),* 493–503.

Bourne, Charles P. (1980). On-line systems: History, technology, and economics. *Journal of the American Society for Information Science, 31(3)*, 155–160.

Brewer, Eric A. (2001). When everything is searchable. *Communications of the ACM, 44(3)*, 53–55.

Brin, Sergey, and Page, Lawrence. [No publication year]. The anatomy of a large-scale hypertextual Web search engine. http://www7.scu.edu.au/programme/fullpapers/1921/com1921.htm. (March 18, 2001)

Chakrabarti, Soumen, et al. (June 1999). Hypersearching the Web. *Scientific American.* http://www.sciam.com/1999/0699issue/0699raghavan.html. (May 26, 1999)

Chowdhury, Gobinda G. (1999). *Introduction to Modern Information Retrieval.* London: Library Association Publishing.

Chu, Heting. (1998). Internet search services vs. online database services. In Martha E. Williams (Ed.), *Proceedings of the 19th National Online Meeting,* (pp. 69–75). Medford, NJ: Information Today.

Festa, Paul. (February 26, 2001). Search project prepares to challenge Google. *CNET News.com.* http://news.cnet.com/news/0-1005-202-4950537.html. (February 26, 2001)

Frauenfelder, Mark. (September 25, 1998). The future of search engines. *The Industry Standard: The Newsmagazine of the Internet Economy.* http://www.thestandard.com/articles/article_print/0,1454,1826,00.html. (May 26, 1999)

Google. (2002). The basics of Google search: Automatic "and" queries. http://www.google.com/help/basics.html. (August 29, 2002)

Hahn, Trudi Bellardo. (1996). Pioneers of the online age. *Information Processing & Management. 32(1)*, 33–48.

Harter, Stephen P. (1986). *Online information retrieval: Concepts, principles, and techniques.* New York: Academic Press.

Hildreth, Charles R. (1984). Pursuing the ideal: Generations of online catalogs. In B. Aveney, and B. Butler (Eds.), Online catalogs, online reference:

Converging trends. *Proceedings of a Library and Information Technology Association Preconference Institute* (pp. 31–56). Chicago: American Library Association.

Hildreth, Charles R. (1985). Online public access catalogs. *Annual Review of Information Science and Technology, 20,* 233–285.

Hildreth, Charles R. (1988). Online library catalogues as information retrieval systems: What can we learn from research? In P.A. Yates-Mercer (Ed.), Future trends in information science and technology. *Proceedings of the Silver Jubilee Conference of the City University's Department of Information Science* (pp. 9–25). London: Taylor Graham.

Large, Andrew, Tedd, Lucy A., and Hartley, R.J. (1999). *Information seeking in the online age: Principles and practice.* London: Bowker-Saur.

Lawrence, Steve, and Giles, C. Lee. (April 3, 1998). Searching the World Wide Web. *Science, 280(5360),* 98–100.

Lawrence, Steve, and Giles, C. Lee. (July 8, 1999). Accessibility of information on the Web. *Nature, 400,* 107–109.

Malinconico, S. Michael. (1984). Catalogs & cataloging: Innocent pleasures and enduring controversies. *Library Journal, 109(11),* 1210–1213.

McKiernan, Gerry. (2001). Beyond bookmarks: Schemes for organizing the Web. http://www.public.iastate.edu/~CYBERSTACKS/CTW.htm. (8/14/02)

Meadow, Charles T., Boyce, Bert R., and Kraft, Donald H. (1999). *Text information retrieval systems.* Orlando, FL: Academic Press.

Nahl-Jakobovits, Diane, and Tenopir, Carol. (1992). Databases online and on CD-ROMs: How do they differ? Let us count the ways. *Database, 15(1),* 42–50.

Notess, Greg R. (2002). Search Engine Showdown: The Users' Guide to Web Searching. http://www.notess.com. (August 21, 2002)

Rousseau, Ronald. (2001). Google search. [List messages]. sigmetrics@listserv.utk.edu. (January 7, 2001 & January 9, 2001)

Rowley, Jennifer, and Slack, Frances. (1997). The evaluation of interface design on CD-ROMs. *Online and CDROM Review, 21(1)*, 3–11.

Schwartz, Candy. (2000). Meeting review: Notes from the Boston 2000 Search Engine Meeting. *Bulletin of the American Society for Information Science, 26(6)*, 26–28.

Smith, Ian. (2000). The invisible Web: Where search engines fear to go. http://www.powerhomebiz.com/vol25/invisible.htm. (December 12, 2000)

Sullivan, Danny. (2001). Search engine alliance chart. http://searchengine watch.com/reports/alliances.html. (August 29, 2002)

Sullivan, Danny. (2002). Search Engine Watch. http://searchenginewatch. com. (August 29, 2002)

Vidmar, Dale J. (1999). Darwin on the Web: The evolution of search tools. *Computers in Libraries, 19(5)*, 22–28.

Walker, Geraldene, and Janes, Joseph. (1999). *Online retrieval: A dialogue of theory and practice.* 2nd ed. Englewood, CO: Libraries Unlimited.

Whatis.com. (2000). Digital versatile disk. Entry updated on August 20, 2000. (March 4, 2001)

Whatis.com. (2001). Vortal. Entry updated on January 26, 2001. (February 25, 2001)

CHAPTER 9

Retrieval of Information Unique in Content or Format

Up to this point, the theme of information retrieval is explored assuming that the information is mainly text, in English, and taking the linear structure. This chapter focuses on the retrieval of information unique in content or format, i.e., multilingual information, multimedia information, and hypertext/hypermedia information.

9.1 Multilingual Information

There are approximately 6,703 different living languages all over the world, of which 2,000 are used in Africa, 1,000 in the Americas, 2,200 in Asia, 200 in Europe, and 1,300 in the Pacific (Sands, 2000). According to the estimation made in February 1999, the top three first languages in the world are Mandarin Chinese (885,000,000 people), Spanish (332,000,000 people), and English (322,000,000 people) (Sands, 2000). Although English has become the major language for recording scholarly information since World War II, other languages do get used in various contexts and environments. The same holds true in information retrieval.

9.1.1 Multilingual Information Retrieval in the Past

Before the advent of the Internet and Internet retrieval systems, multilingual information was included in online, CD-ROM, and OPAC systems but on a selective basis. These systems usually adopt a selection policy with regard to the collection of multilingual information. For example, either translation or transliteration would be provided if information in a certain language is to be included. In multilingual information retrieval, locating information using the same language in which the information is recorded (e.g., search Chinese information using queries in Chinese) does not seem widely supported although there are some exceptions. Generally speaking, foreign language information is transliterated for retrieval purpose in OPACs. Online and CD-ROM systems often use a first language to represent (e.g., indexing and abstracting) foreign language information, which can be later retrieved with the same first language.

There are systems designed for retrieving multilingual information directly instead of via translation and transliteration. For example, OPACs in China normally support two language modes: one for the Chinese language and the other for the so-called Western languages such as English and French. People can use, for example, Chinese to retrieve Chinese information, and English for retrieving information in English. Multilingual IR systems of this kind should presumably produce better results than those based on translation and transliteration because the former can avoid introducing further discrepancy, which may be caused by translation or transliteration, into the retrieval process.

9.1.2 Multilingual Information Retrieval on the Internet

Although online, CD-ROM, and OPAC systems do collect multilingual information, the need for multilingual information retrieval in those environments does not appear as strong as that on the Internet due to the following factors. First, the coverage of multilingual information in those systems is highly selective and restricted to quality information. Second, the Internet is a global network of networks, naturally carrying much more multilingual information than the other three kinds of IR systems. Third, the absence of a quality control mechanism, as discussed in §8.4.2.1, also contributes to the boom of multilingual information on the Internet.

Based on international polls and year 2000 census information, Global Reach, a technology research firm in San Francisco, estimates that 128 million of the almost 280 million people who use the Internet speak languages other than English. Jupiter Communications, a technology research group in New York City, estimated that the number of non-English speakers would surpass English speakers in 2001 (Kushner, 2000). Other studies show that about 20–30 percent of the information on the Web is in languages other than English (Baeza-Yates & Ribeiro-Neto, 1999), and the percentage of multilingual Web information appears to be on the rise.

Internet retrieval systems address the issue of multilingual information retrieval by either supporting multilingual searches or providing translation facilities developed by companies such as SYSTRAN (http://www.systran soft.com). AltaVista took the lead in both areas by collaborating with SYSTRAN while many other Internet IR systems (e.g., Google) followed suit especially in the domain of multilingual searching.

When Internet retrieval systems were initially developed, English was the only language that people could use for retrieval. At present, people can search the Internet using more than two dozen different languages (e.g.,

English, Chinese, French, German, Spanish, and Russian). Multilingual searching on the Internet can be accomplished in one of the following two ways. One is to conduct the search using an Internet retrieval system specifically built for a particular language (e.g., AltaVista in France) with search queries in that language. The other type of multilingual searching is to restrict the search results to a specific language by selecting the chosen language listed on the home page of an Internet retrieval system. The search query remains in English, for example, but the results will be in the language specified (e.g., Spanish). Retrieval of this kind should, in a strict sense, be considered as cross language information retrieval, which is discussed in §9.1.3.

In addition to multilingual searching, multilingual information on the Internet can also be obtained by means of translation thanks to the joint efforts made by Internet retrieval systems and automatic translation software companies. The collaboration between AltaVista and SYSTRAN is one such example. For instance, any results retrieved by AltaVista can be translated from English to Chinese, French, German, Italian, Japanese, Korean, Spanish, or Portuguese and vice versa using the SYSTRAN software although the translation quality is not quite satisfactory due to the inherent limitation of automatic translation (Balkin, 1999).

9.1.3 Research on Multilingual Information Retrieval

The retrieval of multilingual information has attracted researchers' attention in recent years, and become a track (i.e., a particular retrieval subproblem) in TREC-4 through TREC-6. The multilingual track investigated issues of information retrieval in languages other than English. Spanish and Chinese, the two most widely used non-English languages (Sands, 2000), were examined by more than 20 research teams from 1995 through 1997. Researchers found (Sparck Jones, 2000):

> The extension to Multilingual Spanish is relatively modest, but to Chinese is more demanding in covering a radically different script system. It therefore clearly raises the question of whether in practice, as opposed to broad principle, indexing and searching methods developed for English, e.g., those using statistical techniques, are readily transferred to and are effectively for others, very different languages. (p. 46)

Indeed, different languages require IR systems with different capabilities for handling their distinctive features. For example, it is a very challenging task to automatically segment Chinese text into meaningful query terms because there is no space between words in Chinese writing until the end of a sentence. Therefore, the majority of research teams participating in the TREC-6 Multilingual Chinese track compared different segmentation methods (Voorhees & Harman, 2000). Case sensitive searching, a basic retrieval technique for information in English, is not applicable to Chinese as there are no upper or lower cases in Chinese text.

An area related to multilingual retrieval is cross language searching in which documents covering several languages (e.g., English, German, French, or Italian) and queries are in each language. The Cross Language Information Retrieval (CLIR) track has been added into the TREC series since TREC-6 in 1997. The focus of the CLIR track is to retrieve documents in one target language using queries written in a different language. In TREC-6, 13 groups participating in the CLIR track tried three major approaches to cross language retrieval: 1) automatic translation where either the queries or the documents were translated into the target language; 2) the use of machine-readable bilingual dictionaries or other existing linguistic resources; and 3) the use of corpus resources to train or otherwise enable the cross language retrieval mechanism (Voorhees & Harman, 2000). Artificial intelligence seems to play a role in those approaches.

In brief, multilingual searching means that target information and queries are in the same language whereas cross language retrieval implies that target information and queries are in different languages. Limiting Internet search results to one particular language, as mentioned in §9.1.2, is actually cross language retrieval because the query has to be translated from one language into the language the target information is in before the search is physically conducted. No matter if the retrieval is multilingual or cross language, people should always pay attention to the features of the language in which the information is recorded because each language is unique. Only from this perspective can people successfully perform multilingual or cross language retrieval.

9.2 Multimedia Information

According to a study reported by the School of Information Management and Systems, University of California at Berkeley (Lyman et al., 2000), the world produces between 1 and 2 exabytes (1 exabytes = 1 billion gigabytes) of unique information per year. Although the report did not specify the percentage of multimedia information out of the total, the amount of multimedia information (e.g., broadcast news, video conferences, reconnaissance data, audiovisual recordings of corporate meetings, and classroom lectures) no doubt grows drastically nowadays because the Web is able to store, transfer, and present multimedia information. For example, the publicly indexable Web alone contained an estimated 180 million images or 3 terabytes of image data in February 1999 (Lawrence & Giles, 1999). As the Web develops rapidly and carries more multimedia information, the need for locating and obtaining such information is also steadily increasing.

Multimedia is defined as any combination of sound, image, and text information in Chapter 3, where Figure 3.1 also presents a taxonomy of multimedia information. It should be noted that the term "image" sometimes is used loosely to refer to all kinds of multimedia since both still and moving images can contain textual information while moving images can also include sound information. Since textual information has been the subject of discussion in most parts of the book, the focus in this section is on nontextual information that consists of still images, sound, and moving images.

Numerous methods and algorithms have been developed for retrieving multimedia information. But these methods and algorithms basically fall into two broad categories: the description-based approach and content-based approach. Simply , the description-based approach manually employs captions, keywords, and other descriptions (e.g., artist and work size) of multimedia information for retrieval purpose. Human beings are directly involved in the retrieval process when using this approach. The content-based approach, on the other hand, refers to the techniques of retrieving multimedia based on automatic processing of multimedia information itself.

The description-based and content-based approaches are used respectively by two distinctive research groups (Cawkell, 1992; Chu, 2001; Persson, 2000). It appears that people in the computer science field focus on the content-based approach while the information science community, including library science, concentrates on the description-based method (Cawkell, 1992; Rasmussen, 1997). This division occurs because of two factors. First, the academic background and training of the two groups of researchers are different: one in computer science and the other in information science. Second, the processing methods adopted for retrieving multimedia by the two approaches are dissimilar: one is automatic while the other is manual.

In the following sections, we examine how each approach has been applied in retrieving the three types of multimedia information: still images, sound, and moving images.

9.2.1 Still Image Retrieval

As indicated in §3.3.1, images include both still and moving images. Still images comprise pictures, photos, posters, document images (e.g., PDF – Portable Document Format files), and the like. Moving images, containing still images plus the moving attribute, can be subdivided into two categories: moving images with sound constitute videos or movies whereas moving images without sound are animations or silent movies. For clarity purposes, only still images are covered in this subsection, and moving images will be discussed separately in §9.2.3.

Still images have their own meaning and properties that form the bases for people to perform retrieval tasks. In reference to Renaissance art, Panofsky (1955) identified three strata of meaning for images. The first stratum is pre-iconography, describing primary or natural meaning of images, which is further divided into factual and expressional facets (e.g., a picture of a city appearing very bustling where *city* being the factual facet and *bustling* the expressional aspect). Pre-iconographic descriptions of images require practical experience. For example, the object of a city and a bustling scene are readily recognizable to those who have seen such entities before. The second stratum is iconography, identifying the secondary or conventional meaning depicted in the image (e.g., a picture of Rome as opposed to any other city). Iconographic identification requires knowledge of literary sources, for instance, familiarity with the features of Rome as a city. The third stratum is iconology, representing the intrinsic meaning or symbolic values of the image. The identification and interpretation of the intrinsic meaning of images, often unknown to the artist and maybe even emphatically different from what the artist consciously intended to express, require "synthetic intuition conditioned by personal psychology" (Panofsky, 1955). Such meaning "is apprehended by ascertaining those underlying principles which reveal the basic attitude of a nation, a period, a class, a religious or philosophical persuasion" (Panofsky, 1955). For example, Rome could mean a city with a rich history to some people, and to others it may denote a place in which the Vatican is located. The intrinsic meaning of images is apparently the most difficult to be interpreted. The interpretation would be highly subjective to one's experience and background.

Almost half a century later, Eakins and Graham (1999) classified image attributes into three levels of increasing complexity. Level 1 image attributes are primitive features such as color, texture, and shape. An example of retrieval queries based on Level 1 image attributes is *red triangle*, where *red* indicates color and *triangle* suggests shape. Level 2 image attributes are logical features concerning the identity of objects depicted in the image. The objects could be general (e.g., an office building) or specific (e.g., the Sears Tower in Chicago). Level 2 image attributes are more complex than Level 1 features in that the former makes a logical reference about the identity of objects in the image or contains information beyond the primitive Level 1. For example, the image object is an office building rather than a particular shape or texture. Level 3 image attributes are abstract, involving a significant amount of high-level reasoning about the meaning and purpose of the objects or scenes depicted in the image (Eakins & Graham, 1999). These attributes concern the aboutness of images, for instance, the festivity atmosphere described in a party scene.

Similarities can be found between Panofsky's three strata of meaning for images and the three levels of image attributes presented by Eakins and Graham (1999). The first layer in both cases deals with the ofness or physical attributes of images except that Panofsky included the expressional facet of images in this stratum and did not analyze images down to pixels, a measurement created later only for digital images. The second and third layers in both schemes cover the aboutness or subject attributes of images, dealing with their semantic contents. Some of the subject attributes can be objectively identified (e.g., differentiating Rome from other cities) while some can only be ascertained subjectively (e.g., Rome as a historical city or religious place). No matter how image attributes are categorized, they form the bases for retrieving still image information in both image retrieval approaches to be discussed in §9.2.1.1.

9.2.1.1 Description-Based Retrieval of Still Images

The description-based approach, also known as the concept-based or text-based approach, has to rely on descriptions provided by information professionals for retrieving still images. Still images can be described by their ofness or physical attributes (e.g., a picture of pandas) as well as aboutness or subject attributes (e.g., about endangered animals). If the descriptions concern only aboutness, we can name the image retrieval approach as concept-based (Rasmussen, 1997). If the descriptions are prepared with texts accompanying images, we can refer to the image retrieval approach as text-based (Goodrum, 2000). These descriptions then become the foundations for retrieving still images.

Both keywords and controlled vocabularies are adopted in retrieving still images. Keywords are mostly derived from captions or other textual information accompanying still images (e.g., an introduction to a photo exhibition). Users can also choose query terms themselves at the time of retrieval. Controlled vocabularies used in image retrieval include Art & Architecture Thesaurus, ICONCLASS, and Thesaurus for Graphic Materials. Further descriptions about these controlled vocabularies can be found in Rasmussen (1997). Visual thesauri, using visual surrogates in addition to verbal expressions for image retrieval purpose, have also been tried in some cases (Mostafa, 1994; Rasmussen, 1997). This method appears similar to "query by example," a retrieval technique briefly discussed in §5.1.2.3, Query Expansion.

Aside from retrieving images according to their aboutness or subject attributes, many ofness attributes are available for accessing still images using the description-based approach. Date, size, and type of the image are just a few examples. Searches of this kind do not differ much from field searching in text information retrieval. Techniques developed for retrieving text information (e.g., Boolean searching and truncation) remain applicable in retrieving still images with the description-based approach. The major difference between text and image retrieval lies in the definition of fields. Fields in still image retrieval are defined in accordance with image attributes rather than features of text information.

However, the description-based approach to image retrieval inherits all the problems associated with human involvement in the process, for example, inconsistency and high cost. Furthermore, the subjectivity in interpreting the aboutness of images is inevitable and of a higher degree than that in text retrieval because the interpretation of the aboutness or subject content of images depends heavily on one's personal experience and background. For example, a glass of wine in a picture may be an indication of celebration to one person but a sign of drunkenness to another. Images themselves may not contain explicit cues for interpretation. The content-based approach was introduced to the area of image retrieval in part to cope with this problem of using the description-based method. Other factors that contribute to the emergence of the content-based approach include the development of technology and the growth of image information in the digital age.

matching (e.g., a particular shape of roof on a building) that can be easily done in content-based image retrieval would be an impracticable task for the description-based method. Each approach obviously holds its own place and has its own strengths in image retrieval (Chu, 2001).

Research in image retrieval is growing and expanding, especially in the content-based domain. The content-based approach appears to be used currently more often and extensively than the description-based approach in research projects although the former was introduced more recently (Chu, 2001). Nevertheless, the description-based approach remains the primary choice for operational systems (e.g., Graham, 1999).

The need for the integration of the two approaches becomes increasingly apparent as time passes and before automatic means for processing the semantic content of images are found (Cawkell, 1992). Eakins and Graham (1999), naming the description-based approach as the keyword method, believe that the use of keywords and image features in combination would prove to be desirable. They listed several reasons to support their proposition. First, keywords can be used to capture the semantic content of images while primitive feature match can usefully complement this by identifying image attributes (e.g., color or texture) that are hard to name using the description approach. Second, higher precision and recall scores can be achieved when, for example, text and color similarity are used in combination than when either is used separately. Third, retrieval by a combination of methods using different cognitive structures is likely to be more effective than by any single method (Ingwersen, 1996).

Indeed, some researchers from the content-based community did try to incorporate textual and semantic information with visual attributes of images into their research, signifying a promising start of the integration of the two methods (Chu, 2001). Reports linking the two distinct research approaches (e.g., Chang et al., 1997B) were also published in recent years. In addition, Eakins and Graham (1999) note in their study that the barriers between different research communities of the field are gradually coming down. The integration of both approaches would bring about better and more efficient access to still images as well as other types of multimedia information.

9.2.2 Sound Retrieval

Sound, also referred to as audio, includes nonverbal music and verbal speech in addition to other natural or artificial sounds (e.g., birds chirping and traffic noise). Music and speech are the two major types of information explored in sound retrieval.

Music has its own semantics, and a melody can convey meaning that words may or may not be able to describe. Speech is in many ways a richer form of communication than written text because of the additional sound component. For example, the sound of voice can help determine the speaker's identity (Oard, 2000). Speech is often referred to as spoken documents. Broadcast news, conference talks, and telephone conversations are some examples of spoken documents. But sound information cannot be skimmed or scanned during the retrieval process. People have to listen to it from the beginning to the end when attempting to locate a particular segment from it. In general, listening to speech takes far more time than scanning text. Sound information obviously needs retrieval methods different from the ones for text retrieval.

9.2.2.1 Description-Based Retrieval of Sound Information

The description-based approach was the only method for sound information retrieval before the emergence of the content-based approach. People can search music, for example, by composer, style, instruments that are playing, or even by music theme being played (Lesk, 1997). Speech information can be retrieved by, among other access points, speaker, location, date, media that record the speech, and speech topic. The main problems in using the description-based approach for sound retrieval are time and accuracy. Since sound information is not browsable, it is extremely time-consuming to prepare descriptions about sound information for retrieval purposes. If sound information attributes are categorized into two kinds: ofness and aboutness, the aboutness of sound information, like any other type of information, is hard to be judged accurately by human beings. This seems especially true for nonverbal sound information such as music that may not be intended for verbalization.

9.2.2.2 Content-Based Retrieval of Sound Information

Various musical attributes, e.g., pitch, harmony, rhythm, and timbre, have been used as access points for content-based music retrieval. For example, Downie (2000) proposed the retrieval of music information by the n-gram intervals (i.e., distance between notes) contained within melodies. N-grams (see also §5.1.2.1) form discrete units of melodic information much the same way as words are discrete units of language. There seem to be as many automatic algorithms for music retrieval as there are users (Downie, 2000). But research on music retrieval is scarce even though annual conferences (e.g., International Symposium on Music Information Retrieval) have been organized in recent years particularly for music retrieval.

By comparison, a lot more research on content-based speech retrieval has been reported (e.g., Goodrum & Rasmussen, 2000; Sparck Jones et al., 1996) and one track has been created for spoken document retrieval (the SDR track) in the TREC series since TREC-6 (Voorhees & Garofolo, 2000). The first step in speech retrieval is to separate nonspeech segments from speech segments. Nonspeech segments or speech constraints include nonspeech events (e.g., loud breath and tongue clicks), disfluencies (e.g., partially spoken words, pauses, and hesitations), functional events or components (e.g., *and* and *in addition*), and music or noise overlaid on speech. After these nonspeech segments are removed, the speech segments can be further analyzed by various speech attributes.

Speech segmentation is a challenging but necessary step in speech retrieval. While it is possible to directly transcribe the continuous stream of speech information without any prior segmentation, partitioning offers several advantages over the straightforward solution. First, interesting information can be extracted (e.g., the division between speakers, and speaker identities) during the segmentation. Second, prior segmentation can avoid problems caused by linguistic discontinuity as the speaker changes. Third, eliminating nonspeech segments and dividing the data into shorter segments substantially reduces the computation time and simplifies decoding at a later stage (Gauvain, Lamel & Adda, 2000).

A variety of algorithms have been developed for speech recognition and speech understanding. Recognizing who is talking is a slightly different problem from recognizing what is being said (Lesk, 1997). Speech recognition depends on speech understanding, which relies further on natural language processing (NLP). Pitch, speed, and intensity (i.e., longer pause between sentences than between words) are among the attributes commonly used for sound retrieval. In addition, the speaker's gender, word usage statistics, and keywords characterizing each segment are employed in conjunction with a vocabulary specially created for speech recognition and understanding (Kubala et al., 2000; The SRI MAESTRO Team, 2000; Wactlar et al., 2000). Established retrieval techniques such as weighting are also applied in speech retrieval (Sparck Jones et al., 1996). The speech is automatically transcribed by creating corresponding text that will be used for matching during the retrieval process. Queries can be issued in the form of speech if a speech recognition mechanism is provided at the search end.

According to Lesk (1997), there are four parameters that strongly affect the difficulty of speech recognition: 1) Speech continuity—Continuous speech is more difficult to be understood than speech with pauses between words and sentences. 2) Number of speakers—If all the speakers involved in a speech should be recognized, the task would be more difficult than the case in which only one speaker is the subject of analysis. 3) Content of the speech—The content of a speech could range from anything without a fixed topic to a specific theme with a well-defined vocabulary. It is much easier to perform speech recognition in the latter case than in the former one. 4) Speech environment – Many possibilities exist for speech environment: At one extreme the speaker could use a quality microphone in a quiet room (e.g., a conference speech) and at the other the speaker talks in a noisy street without a good microphone (e.g., an on-site interview). The former environment is apparently the ideal one for speech recognition while the latter is not. Besides the four factors, the speaker's accent could add to the complexity of speech recognition as well.

9.2.3 Moving Image Retrieval

Retrieval of moving images is built upon still image and sound retrieval just discussed because of their compositions. Moving images, comprising still images plus the moving attribute, can be with sound or without sound. Videos, movies, or TV programs are examples of moving images with sound whereas animations or silent movies represent moving images without sound.

The description-based approach has been exploited in retrieving moving images. Typical descriptions for moving images include such aspects as movie director and year of production that are traditionally selected for reflecting their ofness and aboutness. Moving image retrieval using this approach is, however, prone to the same problems (e.g., high cost and low efficiency) that are often present in retrieving other types of multimedia information.

Moving image retrieval using the content-based approach essentially involves three major tasks although the retrieval may be conducted with some variations. One task is to separate the sound component, if there is one, from moving images and process the sound information. The other task is to segment moving images into still images by events or scenes. The third task is to process the still images extracted. In other words, moving image retrieval ultimately can be boiled down to sound and still image retrieval. What really differentiates moving image retrieval from sound and still image retrieval lies in the segmentation of moving images. Since sound and still image retrieval has been considered in the previous subsections, the following discussion will concentrate on the segmentation of moving images for retrieval purposes.

Moving images have to be segmented or decomposed before they become retrievable. Scenes or events are commonly used semantic units for segmenting moving images. They are identified by automatically detecting changes in such parameters as color distribution, texture, cuts, fades, dissolves, and camera flashes. For example, a scene comprises multiple shots that can be further decomposed into several frames each. So the breakdown can be done by scene, shot, or frame. The frame that is representative of each shot is called the keyframe. A group of keyframes can then be put together to form a storyboard of annotated still images for representing each scene. In addition to the keyframe method, video skimming is also used to produce a series of short video clips, each capturing the essential details of a single sequence or a series of semantically meaningful shots (Eakins & Graham, 1999). Those entities form the bases for moving image retrieval. A sequence of moving images generally provides more information than keyframes for retrieval purpose. Moving images themselves could serve as queries if short video clips are extracted and available in the IR system. Query-by-motion-example is one case in point (Chang et al., 1997A). Sometimes, the speech information contained within moving images can be employed to resolve the ambiguities in the segmentation and interpretation of moving images. The reverse also holds true (Wactlar et al., 2000).

From this brief description, it can be seen that automatic segmentation of moving images is obviously not an easy task. Rather, the segmentation is a complex and multistep process. For example, a video can first be composed by story, then by event, shot, and frame (Boykin & Merlino, 2000). While the breakdown by shot and frame appears straightforward, the segmentation by story and event requires human efforts or artificial intelligence. This is another reason why the content-based approach should be combined with the description-based method in multimedia retrieval given the current status of retrieval technology.

9.2.4 Multimedia Retrieval on the Internet

The Web of the Internet is well known for its capability of handling multimedia information. Consequently, a good number of Internet retrieval systems (e.g., AltaVista and Fast at http://www.alltheweb.com) support multimedia searching either alone or in collaboration with companies specialized in multimedia information management, allowing the end-user to have access to the wealth of multimedia on the Web.

Three different description-based methods are available to end-users to retrieve multimedia information from the Web. 1) By keyword. Users can retrieve multimedia information by keyword just as they do in search of text information. This method works particularly well at sites that are designated, for example, for searching images at Amazing Picture Machine (http://www. ncrtec.org/picture.htm) and for searching music at Lycos Music Search (http://music.lycos.com). 2) By multimedia type. Multimedia is a collective name for various kinds of nontext information such as image, MP3, and video. These multimedia types can serve as access points in the retrieval process. Some Internet retrieval systems (e.g., HotBot) implement radio buttons or other similar mechanisms for people to choose the type of multimedia they would like to retrieve. 3) By filename extension. Filenames in the digital environment normally have up to three letters in file extension to specify a file type. In the case of multimedia files, for example, *gif* and *jpg* are typical file extensions for still images. Sound files usually end with *au*, *wav*, *mp3*, or the like. File extensions for moving images include *mpg* and *mov*. These file extensions can be included in the query to retrieve the type of multimedia information specified (e.g., *greatwall.gif* as a search query).

The content-based approach is also available on the Internet for retrieving multimedia information. Some Internet retrieval systems support both approaches. For example, users can begin a search with the description-based keyword approach and then expand it with content-based attributes such as color and shape. Other systems are designed to deal only with content-based retrieval of multimedia information. Convera's Visual RetrievalWare (http://vrw.convera.com:8015/cst/) and SpeechBot (http://speechbot. research.compaq.com) are two such examples for the latter case.

Multimedia information retrieval on the Internet becomes easier than before thanks to technology developments and researchers' efforts. But, multimedia retrieval on the whole still has a long way to go before satisfactory performance can be achieved. Lesk (1997) once summarized the state-of-the-art in multimedia retrieval as follows:

> We can classify pictures very roughly by color, texture and shape; this is not enough to deal with collections of millions of photographs. We can do speech recognition well enough to be of some use in analysis of voice recordings; we have little technology for searching music. We have various tricks for compressing and browsing video but only limited technology for searching it. (p. 97–98)

9.3 Hypertext and Hypermedia Information

The word *hyper* in hypertext means "extension into other dimensions" (Cornejo, 1994). In that sense, hypertext consists of nodes of information and links between them in a multidimensional space. Hypermedia is conceptually and structurally the same as hypertext except that hypermedia contains not only text but also sound and image information.

Nevertheless, both hypertext and hypermedia are different from text and multimedia in the following aspects. First, hypertext and hypermedia take a network structure rather than the linear and flat formation of text and multimedia. Second, linkages among hypertext and hypermedia exist physically while connections among non-hyperstructured documents are merely conceptual. Third, linkages among hyperstructured documents are established for the user whereas the same user has to make connections among non-hyperstructured documents whenever necessary. The unique features of hypertext and hypermedia lead to new ways of information retrieval in the hyperstructured environment.

Browsing, rather than searching, should be the major approach used in retrieving hypertext and hypermedia because, as discussed in §6.2.2, the hyperstructure environment encourages browsing activities. Access points or query terms are provided as hyperlink names in this retrieval process, eliminating the need for the user to choose them. Query term selection may sound easy to the trained information professional. To the end-user, however, it is a complicated and demanding task that involves concept analysis and considering term variations. Moreover, the user is able to move automatically in this multidimensional IR space by just clicking on hyperlinks that connect various nodes of information. When searching is chosen as the retrieval approach, link names are evaluated as more important than regular terms in weighting and ranking if such a mechanism is available. For example, many Internet retrieval systems would rank a particular retrieved item higher than others if the query term matches a link name contained within the document.

On the other hand, retrieving hypertext and hypermedia by browsing has potential problems due to the hyperstructure. First, users may get lost in the hyperspace when browsing by simply following hyperlinks. Second, users may find it difficult to gain an overview of the information they are looking for as their attention can be sidetracked easily by so many other linked documents. Third, users may have difficulty finding specific information even if they know the information is present in the system. Site maps created at certain Web sites could be helpful in this respect. But they are not available in all hyperstructured IR systems, and if available, may not be as detailed as desired.

Introducing the search approach in the hyperstructured environment facilitates the retrieval of hypertext and hypermedia. In fact, searching appears to be able to overcome all the three problems enumerated for hypertext and hypermedia retrieval by browsing. While hyperstructured documents encourage browsing, searching would surmount any retrieval problems associated with browsing in a hyperspace. The integration of searching and browsing approaches, therefore, seem to be the best way of retrieving hypertext and hypermedia.

References

Baeza-Yates, Ricardo, and Ribeiro-Neto, Berthier. (1999). *Modern information retrieval*. New York: ACM Book Press.

Balkin, Ruth. (1999). AltaVista's automatic translation program. *Database, 22(2)*, 56–57.

Boykin, Stanley, and Merlino, Andrew. (2000). Machine learning of event segmentation for news on demand. *Communications of the ACM, 43(2)*, 35–41.

Cawkell, A.E. (1992). Selected aspects of image processing and management: Review and future prospects. *Journal of Information Science, 18*, 179–192.

Chang, Shih-Fu, et al. (1997A). VideoQ: An automated content based video search system using visual cues. *Proceedings of ACM Multimedia, Seattle, WA*, 313–324.

Chang, Shih-Fu, et al. (1997B). Visual information retrieval from large distributed online repositories. *Communications of the ACM, 40(12)*, 63–71.

Chu, Heting. (2001). Research in image indexing and retrieval as reflected in the literature. *Journal of the American Society for Information Science and Technology, 52(12)*, 1011–1018.

Cornejo, J.G. (1994). *Hypertext: Its use in the documentary treatment of data*. Santiago, Chile, REDUCE-CIDE.

Downie, J. Stephen. (2000). Access to music information: The state of the art. *Bulletin of the American Society for Information Science, 26(5)*, 23–25.

Eakins, John P., and Graham, Margaret E. (January 1999). Content-based image retrieval: A report to the JISC Technology Applications Programme. http://www.unn.ac.uk/iidr/research/cbir/report.html. (October 6, 1999)

Faloutsos, C., et al. (1994). Efficient and effective query by image content. *Journal of Intelligent Information Systems, 3*, 231–262.

Flickner, Maron, et al. (1995). Query by image and video content: The QBIC system. *IEEE Computer, 28(9)*, 23–32.

Gauvain, Jean-Luc, Lamel, Lori, and Adda, Gilles. (2000). Transcribing broadcast news for audio and video indexing. *Communications of the ACM, 43(2)*, 64–70.

Goodrum, Abby. (2000). Image information retrieval: An overview of current research. *Informing Science, 3(2)*. http://inform.nu/Articles/Vol3/indexv3n2.htm. (March 27, 2000)

Goodrum, Abby, and Rasmussen, Edie. (2000) Sound and speech in information retrieval: An introduction. *Bulletin of the American Society for Information Science, 26(5)*, 16–18.

Graham, Margaret E. (May 1999). The description and indexing of images: Report of a survey of ARLIS members, 1998/99. http://www.unn.ac.uk/iidr/ARLIS. (February 1, 2000)

Ingwersen, Peter. (1996). Cognitive perspectives of information retrieval interaction: Elements of a cognitive IR theory. *Journal of Documentation, 52(1)*, 3–50.

Kubala, Francis, et al. (2000). Integrated technologies for indexing spoken languages. *Communications of the ACM, 43(2)*, 48–56.

Kushner, David. (April 20, 2000). Untangling the Web's languages. *New York Times*, http://www.nytimes.com/library/tech/00/04/circuits/articles/20tran.html. (April 21, 2000)

Lawrence, Steve, and Giles, C. Lee. (July 8, 1999). Accessibility of information on the Web. *Nature, 400,* 107–109.

Lesk, Michael. (1997). *Practical digital libraries: Books, bytes and bucks.* San Francisco: Morgan Kaufmann.

Lyman, Peter, et al. (2000). How much information? Berkeley, CA: School of Information Management and Systems, University of California at Berkeley. http://www.sims.berkeley.edu/how-much-info/summary.html. (No-vember 4, 2000)

Mostafa, Javed. (1994). Digital image representation and access. *Annual Review of Information Science and Technology, 29,* 91–135.

Oard, Douglas W. (2000). User interface design for speech-based retrieval. *Bulletin of the American Society for Information Science, 26(5),* 20–22.

Panofsky, Erwin. (1955). *Meaning in the visual arts: Papers in and on art history.* New York: Doubleday Anchor Books.

Persson, Olle. (2000). Image indexing – A first author co-citation map. http://www.umu.se/inforsk/Imageindexing/imageindex.htm. (March 2, 2001)

Rasmussen, Edie M. (1997). Indexing images. *Annual Review of Information Science and Technology, 32,* 169–196.

Sands, Stella. (Ed.). (2000). Languages. *Kids Discover, 10(3),* 3.

Sparck Jones, Karen. (2000). Further reflections on TREC. *Information Processing & Management, 36(1),* 37–85.

Sparck Jones, Karen, et al. (1996). Experiments in spoken document retrieval. *Information Processing & Management, 32,* 399–419.

The SRI MAESTRO Team. (2000). MAESTRO: Conductor of multimedia analysis technology. *Communications of the ACM, 43(2),* 57–63.

Voorhees, Ellen, and Garofolo, John. (2000). The TREC Spoken Document Retrieval Track. *Bulletin of the American Society for Information Science, 26(5),* 18–19.

Voorhees, Ellen, and Harman, Donna. (2000). Overview of the Sixth Text REtrieval Conference (TREC-6). *Information Processing & Management, 36(1),* 3–35.

Wactlar, Howard D., et al. (2000). Complementary video and audio analysis for broadcast news archives. *Communications of the ACM, 43(2),* 42–47.

CHAPTER 10

The User Dimension in Information Representation and Retrieval

The user is a crucial factor that must be taken into consideration in all activities and efforts of information representation and retrieval since the ultimate objective of IRR is to satisfy the user's information need. For example, information is represented so that users can retrieve it when needed. Various retrieval approaches and techniques have been developed so that users can choose appropriate ones based on their specific information needs.

The user dimension in information representation and retrieval is vital regardless of the perspective one may take. From the system designer's viewpoint, for example, it is for the users to satisfy their information needs that IRR systems are constructed. Although users in information representation are most likely information professionals, different from those end-users in information retrieval, they share many similarities as users in IRR activities. In this chapter, users and their information needs will be first examined, followed by an exploration of the user-oriented cognitive approach in information representation and retrieval. Finally, the interaction between the user and the IRR system is discussed along with some related issues.

10.1 Users and Their Information Needs

Users are individuals, each with distinctive characteristics. However, it is obviously impractical to study every single user for IRR purposes. Rather, we group users by applying common criteria such as gender, age, occupation, economic status, culture, personality, and educational background. It is based on these general features that we get to know the needs of various user groups better, even though we understand that user needs are affected by many other factors as well (e.g., information sources).

Taking age as an example, users of different ages have different information needs. On the whole, users of school age or at work normally have needs for education- or work-related information while other age groups tend to need general information most of the time. Occupation is another criterion that determines user needs. For instance, scientists usually form the so-called invisible colleges to exchange information (e.g., Crane, 1972; Price, 1963) while engineers in R&D labs rely on "gatekeepers" to communicate with the outside world (e.g., Allen, 1970). Chowdhury (1999) enumerated the information needs of users in different areas of activity (e.g., business and enterprises).

Understanding users and their needs facilitates IRR activities. A great many studies (e.g., for searchers, Borgman, 1989; Fenichel, 1981; Marchionini et al., 1993; Zhang & Chignell, 2001; for indexers, Jacoby & Slamecka, 1962; Leonard, 1975) have been conducted to explore the impact of user attributes on information representation and retrieval. Our knowledge about the user in information representation and retrieval has undoubtedly increased thanks to research of this kind.

Information need, however, is a vague concept in that it is not well structured but messy and disorganized. For this reason, Belkin and his colleagues named it ASK, or anomalous state of knowledge (Belkin, Oddy & Brooks, 1982). In addition, information needs have other features that include changing over time, varying from user to user, and depending on environment. Moreover, information need often remains unexpressed or poorly expressed (Chowdhury, 1999). Indeed, users often have difficulty in articulating their information needs, let alone expressing them accurately. It is not uncommon to get the following statement from users when asked what they are looking for: "I'll know when I see it." Information professionals often conduct reference interviews, a step in assisted searching, to help ease this problem.

Aside from user characteristics, Paisley (1968) identified four other factors affecting users' information needs. 1) Information sources—The array of information sources available to users has some effect on their needs. Users have different expectations when they are provided with, for example, information from a localized system as opposed to that from a system with national coverage. 2) What for—For what purpose do users need the information? If users want information only for answering some factual question (e.g., What is the world's tallest building?), their information needs are simple and straightforward. If users want information for a research project, their information needs clearly fit into another category. 3) External factors—Social, political, economic and other external factors can powerfully affect users and their information needs. 4) Outcome—What consequences do users get as a result of information use? For instance, positive outcomes (e.g., an increase in productivity) serve as rewards to the users and will encourage them to do more in that regard. In short, users themselves along with information sources, purpose, external factors, and outcome constitute the five factors that influence their information needs. Although Paisley's work on information needs was published in 1968, it remains relevant today when we discuss the topic in the context of digital information representation and retrieval.

As information needs are affected by so many factors, it is anticipated that there are different types of information needs. One common classification is to divide information needs into two categories: known-item need and subject need (Lancaster & Warner, 1993) or concrete information need or problem-oriented information need (Frants & Brush, 1988). Though with two different names, known-item need and concrete information need are similar concepts. The same holds true for subject need and problem-oriented information need. Of the two types of information needs, one is specific and concrete while the other is not. It generally takes much more effort to meet subject need or problem-oriented information need. Other criteria (e.g., timeliness of information) for classifying information needs are applied less often. For example, users in hard sciences usually need current information whereas users from soft sciences are more interested in retrospective and comprehensive information.

As pointed out earlier, information representation and retrieval activities should totally be dictated by the information needs of users. Since it is the user who has information needs, the importance of the user dimension in information representation and retrieval is manifest. Because of this reason, researchers try to develop a user-centered approach for information retrieval: the cognitive model.

10.2 The Cognitive Model

Cognition is the mental faculty or process by which knowledge is acquired, or knowledge gained, as through perception, reasoning, and intuition (Soukhanov et al., 1984). The cognitive model, different from other IR models, concentrates on users' cognitive activities during the IR process. For example, how is a user's information need formed? How does a user judge the relevance of results retrieved? These questions are obviously difficult ones, and researchers have been working on them over the years.

The IR models described in previous chapters focus on the information and system aspects of IR. For instance, how shall information or queries be represented? What IR techniques are supported? Which IR technique works better than others? However, these models are still significantly limited in that little or no consideration is given to the social and cognitive contexts in which representation and retrieval tasks are carried out (Ingwersen, 1992). According to the cognitive model of IR interaction Ingwersen (1996) presented, there are three major elements (i.e., information objectives, IR system setting, and social/organizational environment) in addition to the user's cognitive space, which further includes current cognitive state, problem/goal, uncertainty, information need, and information behavior. It is the user's cognitive process that is emphasized in the cognitive model.

The cognitive model has many different implementations. For example, Belkin, Oddy, and Brooks (1982) designed an interactive IR system (e.g., question-answer) to find out the user's information need. The analysis of thinking-aloud protocols is another technique applied in understanding the cognitive activities of users when they search for information (Ingwersen, 1982).

10.2.1 Strengths of the Cognitive Model

The most prominent strength of the cognitive model lies in its focus on the user's cognition, which is a determinant for the IR process. How is an information need formed? How is it transformed into a search query? How are retrieved results evaluated? All these questions relate to the user's cognition and the cognitive model is designed to provide answers to such questions.

The cognitive model is user oriented, distinguishing itself from other IR models that emphasize the information or system components of the IR process. Users are dynamic. So are their information needs. Different users have different information needs. The same user's information need will be different at different times and locations, and may change even during the interaction with the system. Again, only the cognitive model is able to deal with the dynamics of the user with regard to their cognitive activities in information retrieval. Information retrieval should be user-centered. Therefore, the orientation toward the user in the cognitive model can help build flexible and friendly IR systems.

10.2.2 Limitations of the Cognitive Model

Although the cognitive model appears very promising for improving IR performance, people's understanding of cognitive activities remains limited. As Ingwersen (1996) pointed out:

> Computers (or books for that matter) hold predefined and fixed presuppositions, whilst those of human beings are individually unpredictable, formed as they are by episodic, semantic and emotional experiences. (p. 6)

Users' cognitive activities in IR are unpredictable due to the nature of cognition and because we are yet to fully comprehend the cognitive process. Ingwersen (1996) suggests the poly-representation of the user's cognitive space and information space of IR systems (e.g., providing cognitively overlapping access points such as keywords, descriptors, and citations for retrieval purpose) as one method of tackling the uncertainty and unpredictability problem of cognition.

In addition, cognition has some internal restrictions. For example, the capacity of people's short-term memory is seven chunks plus or minus two (Miller, 1956). A chunk is a measurement for the smallest unit of meaningful information. A telephone number within a country, for example, consists of three chunks of information: area code (e.g., 212), region code (e.g., 333) and last four digits (e.g., 1819). The immediate implication of Miller's finding on users in the IR process is their limited capability to process information. If an IR system presents a dozen different choices simultaneously, users will have difficulty because the amount of information presented exceeds the capacity of their short-term memory. Therefore, IR systems should not have, for example, a menu with more than nine selections. On the other hand, a user may also feel tired, bored, or anxious when presented with many possibilities. All these factors can affect the user's cognitive ability. The cognitive model in IR must take such factors into consideration.

Human beings are the most complex creatures in the world. The least understood aspect of human beings is their cognition. Yet, the cognitive model tries to attack the IR problem from the cognitive perspective. The approach is significant, and right on the target, but faces great challenges as well.

10.3 User and System Interaction

User interface is a term created to specifically take account of the user dimension in information representation and retrieval. Interface is what the user sees, hears, and touches in interacting with the system (Shaw, 1991). The term *interface*, however, sounds static and focuses on just one point of the user-system interaction. For this reason, the term *user-system interaction* or simply *interaction* will also be used in this book to refer to the dynamic activities going on between the user and IRR system. Another terminology that receives some clarification in this chapter is *human-computer interaction (HCI)* or *computer-human interaction (CHI)*. Neither term will be used here because both *computer* and *human* are broader in meaning than the *system* and *user* dimensions in information representation and retrieval that this book aims to cover.

10.3.1 Modes of User-System Interaction

User and system interaction in information representation and retrieval can take place in any of the following modes: command language, menu selection, graphical operation, form fill-in, hyperlinks, and natural language dialog. These individual modes can also be applied simultaneously or in parallel for information representation and retrieval.

10.3.1.1 Command Language

Chronologically speaking, command language is the first form developed for user-system interaction and dominated IR systems, particularly online systems such as DIALOG, in the early times of IRR. In this mode, command language (i.e., an artificial language specifically designed for retrieval purpose) is keyed in by the user to instruct the system to perform certain functions (e.g., starting a search). Command languages are short and brief, for instance, *logoff* for ending a search and quitting the retrieval system. Other advantages that have been identified for command language include speed of interaction (Large, Tedd, & Hartley, 1999). Compared with other interaction forms, command language is much faster at getting responses from the system because there are no extra steps (e.g., translating the menu selection into an instruction for the system) to be taken. In that sense, the interaction between the user and system is direct. The speed is also valuable in an environment where charges for information retrieval depend largely on connection time. In addition, users have the flexibility in choosing which commands to use, not limited by the choices listed, for example, in a menu. As a result, users have direct control over the interaction.

Command language as a mode of interaction, however, is not friendly to the user. The user has to learn, practice, and employ it on a regular basis due to its artificiality. The meaning of a command is sometimes not obvious and explicit to the user. For example, *select* stands for *search for* in DIALOG's vocabulary. Moreover, there is little uniformity among different command languages in terms of syntax and semantics. The command language for ending a search session in one system could be, for example, *exit*, and in another *logoff*. Interaction based on command language by and large offers little help and guidance to the user regarding what to do. The system may prompt, for example, "Enter a command," but gives no hint as to which command to enter. Because of these difficulties, command language is mostly an interaction mode between the IR system and intermediaries (e.g., librarians and professional searchers) rather than between the IR system and end-users.

10.3.1.2 Menu Selection

Menu selection is an interaction mode created, in part, to overcome the limitations of command language. CD-ROM systems (e.g., ERIC from SilverPlatter) and OPACs are the first two kinds of IR systems that employ the menu selection mode of interaction. The user interacts with the system by choosing from available options listed on the menu, taking advantage of the fact that people are more capable of recognition than recall from memory.

Therefore, in the menu selection mode the user no longer needs to memorize commands and practice with them as in the command language mode. Menus are also specific to the retrieval process. The menu choices shown, for example, during a search session and at the time of viewing search results are different. By contrast, the user has to figure out when to use which command in the command language mode. Furthermore, help in the form of a menu choice appears readily available to the user in the menu selection mode of interaction.

As an interaction mode, menu selection is more user friendly than command language. However, menu selection does not have the speed of the latter in that the user has to interact with the system via the menu. Making a menu selection takes more time than typing in a command, especially when several levels of menus are provided in the system. Memory overload on the user is likely to occur if the number of menu choices exceeds the capacity of people's short-term memory (i.e., Miller's magic number 7, plus or minus 2). The user also loses flexibility in directly interacting with the system because the user's selection is limited to what the system can supply. For novice users, however, menu selection is a preferred mode when interacting with IR systems.

10.3.1.3 Graphical Mode of Interaction

Graphical operation for user-system interaction is implemented by means of icons, buttons (including radio buttons), windows, and clickable maps. The user interacts with the system by operating (e.g., pointing and clicking) on such visual representations. The graphical mode of interaction is symbolized in Internet retrieval systems. This mode of interaction utilizes representations of real word objects (e.g., a printer icon for printing, and a disc icon for saving files) and concept labels (e.g., a button labeled accordingly for searching) as the interface between the user and system. Windows can be opened, resized, and closed depending on the need of interaction. Clickable maps allow the user to retrieve information by just clicking on the point that represents it. For example, a click at New York City on a national map of the United States would lead to the display of the city's map. The zoom in or zoom out features, if supported, are extremely helpful in using clickable maps.

Graphical mode of interaction, as explained, can take different forms. But this mode collectively puts users at ease when they interact with IR systems. The visualization of activities involved in retrieval tasks avoids overburdening the user with cognitive loads (e.g., choosing from a long list of menu items). The user may find enjoyment in the vivid and often colorful graphical mode of interaction. The multiplicity embedded in this mode enables the user to complete the retrieval task more efficiently. For instance, the user can choose icons for dealing with concrete objects in information retrieval (e.g., print) while selecting buttons for abstract entities (e.g., Boolean searching).

The difficulty involved in developing the graphical mode of interaction should not be underestimated. Some operations in information retrieval (e.g., go to the top of a document) cannot be appropriately represented by icons. In addition, graphical interaction may be unnecessary for certain IR activities (e.g., enter a query). The meaning of graphical representations, if not chosen properly, can be misleading or misunderstood. Graphical designs of interaction occupy more screen space and thus force valuable information off-screen (Shneiderman, 1998). The time needed for interaction in the graphical mode is much longer than that in the command language or menu selection mode because of the graphics. Information retrieval in this mode can thus be slow and cumbersome, which may not concern the user since the connection time accounts for little in computing the retrieval cost in such IR systems (e.g., Internet retrieval systems).

10.3.1.4 Other Modes of User-System Interaction

Form fill-in is another mode of user-system interaction, in which the user fills in such contents as search terms and sets up search limits on a form the system provides. The form fill-in mode actually incorporates features of pull-down menus and buttons. OPACs and Internet retrieval systems are two kinds of IR systems that often support this interaction mode. The user conducts a search by going over and filling out the form. There is no hard decision for the user to make. Rather, the system guides the user through the process of query formation and submission. The obvious limitation of this mode is its inflexibility in user-system interaction because the user is restricted to whatever is listed on the form.

Hyperlinks represent another form of interaction. There is some similarity between hyperlinks and menu selection as both function the same, i.e., clicking on the menu item or link will lead to another entity (e.g., another menu or a document). But hyperlinks do not have to be presented in groups as in the case of menu selection. Hyperlinks can be created wherever they are needed, alone or with other hyperlinks. As discussed in Chapter 6, the hyperlink structure encourages browsing. Hyperlinks therefore are widely implemented in IR systems focusing on browsing. Yahoo!, the directory-based Internet retrieval system, is an excellent example of hyperlink mode of interaction. The user performs retrieval tasks by browsing through the hyperlinked categories Yahoo! develops. The main drawback of hyperlinks as an interaction mode lies in their networked structure. The user may get lost easily when interacting with the system by following the links because hyperlinks take up the network structure. The internal structure of hyperlinks often resembles a maze rather than a well-organized collection of links.

Undoubtedly, the more hyperlinks there are in a retrieval system, the more confusing it becomes for the user to interact with it.

Natural language is beginning to be applied in user-system interaction. Submitting a query in natural language to an IR system seems to be one of the major efforts in this respect. For instance, Ask Jeeves (http://www.aj.com) allows the user to enter queries using complete sentences (e.g., What is natural language processing?). The biggest advantage in using natural language for user-system interaction is its directness as any query representation would inevitably introduce distortion and alteration in meaning. The user in this mode would then have no need to interpret the meaning of the representations created for interaction purpose (e.g., command language, icons, and menu items).

Closely related to the natural language mode of interaction is voice activation in IR systems. The user in this circumstance interacts with the system via spoken language rather than by written language. This mode of interaction relies heavily on voice recognition technology, which is still in the development stage.

10.3.1.5 The Hybrid Mode of Interaction

Recent years have witnessed an emergence of the hybrid mode of interaction, particularly in Internet retrieval systems. Any combination of the interaction modes described previously could form a hybrid interface, although command language is often not incorporated due to its shortcomings. Take AltaVista as an example; it supports menu selection, form fill-in, hyperlinks, command language (for Boolean and proximity operators), and graphical interface. The hybrid mode of interaction can eliminate the limitations of a single mode, and enhance its efficiency and user friendliness. In fact, uni-mode user-system interaction is rarely seen in newly developed IR systems as any single interaction mode has its limitations.

10.3.2 Other Dimensions of User-System Interaction

In addition to interaction mode, there are other aspects that a user should consider when interacting with an IR system. They include display features, output options, and help facilities.

10.3.2.1 Display Features

The user and IR system interact via a certain kind of display but physical devices for interaction (e.g., keyboard or mouse) are beyond the scope of this book. The interaction is then further defined by such display features as color, font, density, and screen layout.

Screen layout marks out how information for interaction purpose is displayed on an interface (usually a computer screen). Are there any overlaying, frames, or multiple windows? Does the user need to scroll up and down in order to view all the information presented? Excessive use of the overlaying feature or putting too many frames or windows on one display can affect the user's ability to interact with the system efficiently. Likewise, most users (and novices in particular), are not deft with scrolling techniques. It is always better to display all the information on one screen, if possible, rather than on multiple screens.

Font type, style, and size determine the display quality of textual information. The minimal standard for displaying texts is clarity and readability. Galitz (1997) suggests that no more than two font types (e.g., Times New Roman or Courier), two styles (e.g., regular and italic), and three sizes should be used for one display. Illegible font type or font size that is too small should be avoided. Font style, if appropriately used, can facilitate the interaction process.

Color, contrast, and brightness decide another display dimension, namely, the comfort level when the user interacts with the system. The number of colors and combination of colors impact whether or not the final display looks pleasant to the user. The right degree of contrast and brightness should also be tested, as extremes in either measure can cause discomfort to users' eyes. Background color and background image fall into this category of display features. Experience shows that black on white is generally a good combination for display. Caution should be exercised when images are used as background because images may overshadow other important information that needs to be displayed. It may also take longer time to load such a display. For these reasons, some Internet retrieval systems that utilized an image background in earlier days soon discontinued the practice.

Density of display is another factor that can influence the friendliness of user-system interaction. For example, how much information should be displayed on one screen? While a detailed specification about density seems unlikely because parameters such as fonts also have an impact on density, an optimal degree of density should be sought in a given setting. Generally, neither a crowded screen nor too much blank space will appear welcoming to the user.

Special effects like highlighting, blinking, and inverse video can all help achieve particular results in user-system interaction if utilized properly. Inconsistent use or overuse of any special effect can cause confusion or even discomfort to the user. Among all the major types of IR systems, Internet retrieval systems seem most likely prone to busy screens, a consequence of overusing special effects and other display features.

10.3.2.2 Output Options

Retrieval results can be presented differently depending on such parameters as formats and quantities. Output formats in online systems are most versatile. The user can choose from predefined formats (e.g., bibliographic information only or bibliographic information plus abstract) or specify particular fields (e.g., author and title) for output. OPAC systems usually support three output formats: short, long, and MARC records. Output format diversity for CD-ROM systems falls in between that for online and OPAC systems. As for Internet retrieval systems, they have limited choices of output formats because of their indexing mechanism. Retrieval results from the Internet usually consist of titles and an extract (i.e., first few lines of a site). Incomplete sentences are the norm rather than an exception in such extracts.

IR systems commonly provide the user with different means for obtaining results: download, print, e-mail, or screen display. Output quantity refers to the number of results to be presented each time when the user makes a request. Online retrieval systems generally allow the user to specify any number of the results retrieved for outputs. CD-ROM and OPAC systems in comparison require users to indicate their choices by first marking or selecting individual records. It is well known that Internet retrieval systems can easily generate thousands, if not millions, of search results. But the user normally can only get 10, 20, or 30 results each time a request for outputs is made. There is no mechanism for the user to have all the outputs at once. However, the limitation in obtaining Internet search results is not a major concern to the user because outputs from Internet retrieval systems are usually ranked in decreasing order of relevance and few users really want to go over all the search results.

Output options are not a crucial factor in user-system interaction. However, flexibility in presenting retrieval results can enhance user friendliness.

10.3.2.3 Help Facilities

Help facilities (e.g., manual, tutorial, or cue cards), to a great extent, determine the user friendliness of IR systems. Help facilities should truly help users find answers to the questions they may ask when interacting with IR systems. Trenner (1989) identified six such questions in a study of comparing the online help facilities in 16 IR systems:

1. What have I done wrong or why have I received this error message?

2. Am I doing the right thing?

3. Where am I and what can I do next?

4. How do I do something?

5. How do I get some information?

6. Why has the system failed?

The first question deals with the situation in which the user did something wrong or received an error message. Ideally, the help facility will not only indicate what was done wrong but also specify what can be done to correct the mistake. However, most help facilities of IR systems are able to do the former but fail to carry out the latter. As a result, the user is left in the dark, bewildered and baffled. As for the rest of the questions Trenner (1989) listed, most help facilities can answer the fourth and fifth questions reasonably well but are weak in handling the other three questions, i.e., the second, third, and sixth questions. At present, help facilities are generally good at listing procedural information for retrieval activities. When it comes to questions that require an explanation, most help facilities in IR systems show their incompetence.

Researchers (e.g., Trenner, 1989; Shneiderman, 1998) have proposed guidelines for designing help facilities for computerized systems including IR systems. From the user's viewpoint, a good help facility should be able to provide answers to users' questions rather than simply present some data the system has pre-prepared. It should also be free of jargon and threatening language (e.g., "an illegal operation is performed") and be available all the time and for users at different levels. Users seek help from IR systems when they need to. If the help facility cannot satisfy their needs, even the function of IR systems may not be fulfilled, let alone the issue of user friendliness.

10.3.3 Evaluation of User-System Interaction

User friendliness is a broad criterion for evaluating user-system interaction. More specific measures have been developed (e.g., Shneiderman, 1998) for the same purpose.

10.3.3.1 Time Needed for the User to Learn Specific IR Functions

Learning takes place when the user interacts with an IR system. That is, users need to learn how to use an IR system before actually conducting searches. The ease of learning is reflected in the time needed for the user to acquire a particular retrieval skill (e.g., Boolean searching). The shorter the learning time, the better the IR system becomes with regard to its user friendliness. A hostile system does not present a relaxing environment for the user to do the learning.

10.3.3.2 Speed of Interaction

How long will it take for the user to receive feedback from the IR system during the interaction? The longer time the process takes, the less user friendly the system becomes. According to Shneiderman (1998), response time for common tasks should be between two and four seconds, and a waiting time longer than 15 seconds will be disruptive. Although these response-time guidelines are for interaction in general, they are certainly applicable to the IR environment. This criterion is decided basically by the IR system's processing capability. Powerful processors usually provide fast speed of interaction.

10.3.3.3 Rate of Errors by the User

If an IR system is intuitive and self-explanatory, users commit few errors in interacting with it. Otherwise, errors are inevitable (e.g., making a wrong choice). The number of errors the user makes during the retrieval process becomes another measurement for judging the user friendliness of an IR system. The help facility discussed previously can play an important role in reducing error rate. Users naturally make fewer mistakes if help is available to them when needed and if the interaction process is transparent to them.

10.3.3.4 Retention Over Time

Interaction techniques, especially in the command mode, need to be learned and practiced in order to be mastered. Retaining these skills over a period of time assesses the user friendliness of IR systems from a different perspective. For example, a command language can be easy to remember if the commands are mnemonic and consistent, just as a print command should use the word *print* instead of *prt, type,* or anything else. A friendly interface will, because of the positive reinforcement, enable users to retain what they know about the system longer than a hostile one.

10.3.3.5 The User's Satisfaction

This measurement for user friendliness is subjective as it is hard to evaluate satisfaction objectively even though satisfaction can be quantified in some way (e.g., number of results retrieved). Nevertheless, this criterion should be considered in the evaluation of the qualitative part in user-system interaction. For instance, how does the user feel about the interaction? Some researchers (e.g., Hildreth, 2001) categorize user satisfaction into material satisfaction (i.e., results obtained from the IR interaction) and emotional satisfaction (i.e., a sense of achievement as a result of the interaction). In general, the friendlier a user-system interaction is, the more satisfied the user becomes.

There are, however, forced tradeoffs among the five criteria just described (Shneiderman, 1998). It is hard for any user-system interaction to achieve top performance in all the aspects. Consideration should always be given to the user since all the IR activities are centered on the user rather than the system.

Despite the fact that there is still much more left to be desired in user-system interaction, this process has definitely improved as more experience has been gained in meeting user requirements (Large, Tedd & Hartley, 1999). From command language mode to hybrid mode of interaction, from monochrome display to artistic application of various features, from help messages loaded with technical terms to cue cards free of jargon, user-system interaction is friendlier today than in the past.

10.4 The User and Information Retrieval in the Digital Age

Digital technology indeed improves the efficiency of information retrieval activities. Meanwhile, it also brings about some concerns and issues to the user, especially the neophyte. For instance, information retrieval in the digital age depends on digital technology that might cause anxiety and alienation to the user. Not everyone is comfortable conducting searches in a computerized system. Due to the imperfection of current IR systems, the user may feel disoriented when trying to retrieve information in the digital environment. In addition, necessary equipment is needed to retrieve information digitally. The pencil-and-paper approach for searching information manually in the print world no longer works effectively in the digital age.

Furthermore, IR systems in the digital age are constantly upgraded or new ones are introduced. The user may have to learn or be trained on a regular basis to keep up with the changes, which adds extra work to the user's already demanding schedule. In other words, information retrieval in the digital age can have side effects on the user because of the technology factor.

In addition to the technology factor, users of different IR systems should be treated differently as they tend to have different IR experiences. For instance, online system users are either information professionals as intermediaries or end-users who have received proper training. In contrast, users of Internet retrieval systems are less likely to have training in information retrieval. The user dimension thus becomes increasingly diversified for information retrieval in the digital age.

Although information representation in the digital age does not have as direct an impact on the user as does information retrieval, the influence of digital technology in this area is by no means negligible. What makes the influence less visible is the fact that people who do information representation are usually information professionals who have adapted to the rhythm and tempo of the digital age through their training and work.

References

Allen, Thomas. (1970). Communication networks in R & D laboratories. *R & D Management, 1*. Reprinted in Belver C. Griffith. (Ed.). *Key papers in information science* (pp. 66–73). White Plains, NY: Knowledge Industry Publications.

Belkin, Nicholas J., Oddy, Robert N., and Brooks, Helen M. (1982). ASK for information retrieval. Part I. Background and theory. *Journal of Documentation, 38(2)*, 61–71.

Borgman, Christine L. (1989). All users of information retrieval systems are not created equal: An exploration into individual differences. *Information Processing & Management, 25(3)*, 237–251.

Chowdhury, Gobinda G. (1999). *Introduction to modern information retrieval.* London: Library Association Publishing.

Crane, Diane. (1972). *Invisible colleges: Diffusion of knowledge in scientific communities.* Chicago: University of Chicago Press.

Fenichel, Carol H. (1981). Online searching: Measures that discriminate among users with different types of experiences. *Journal of the American Society for Information Science, 32*, 23–32.

Frants, Valery I., and Brush, Craig B. (1988). The need for information and some aspects of information retrieval systems construction. *Journal of the American Society for Information Science, 39(2)*, 86–91.

Galitz, Wilbert O. (1997). *Essential guide to user interface design: An introduction to GUI design: Principles and techniques.* New York: John Wiley & Sons.

Hildreth, Charles. (2001). Accounting for users' inflated assessments of online catalog search performance and usefulness: An experimental study. *Information Research, 6(2)*, http://www.shef.ac.uk/~is/publications/infres/ircont.html. (May 21, 2001)

Ingwersen, Peter. (1982). Search procedures in the library analyzed from the cognitive point of view. *Journal of Documentation, 38,* 165–191.

Ingwersen, Peter. (1992). *Information retrieval interaction.* London: Taylor Graham.

Ingwersen, Peter. (1996). Cognitive perspectives of information retrieval interaction: Elements of a cognitive IR theory. *Journal of Documentation, 52(1),* 3–50.

Jacoby, J., and Slamecka, V. (1962). *Indexer consistency under minimal conditions.* Bethesda, MD: Documentation Inc. RADC-TDR-62-426.

Lancaster, F.W., and Warner, Amy J. (1993). *Information retrieval today.* Arlington, VA: Information Resources Press.

Large, Andrew, Tedd, Lucy A., and Hartley, R.J. (1999). *Information seeking in the online age: Principles and practice.* London: Bowker-Saur.

Leonard, L.E. (1975). *Inter-indexer consistency and retrieval effectiveness: Measurement of relationships.* Doctoral thesis. Urbana-Champaign, IL: University of Illinois, Graduate School of Library Science.

Marchionini, Gary, et al. (1993). Information seeking in full-text end-user-oriented search systems: The roles of domain and search expertise. *Library and Information Science Research, 15,* 35–69.

Miller, George A. (1956). The magical number seven plus or minus two: Some limits on our capacity for processing information. *Psychological Review, 63,* 81–97.

Paisley, William J. (1968). Information needs and uses. *Annual Review of Information Science and Technology, 3,* 1–30.

Price, Derek J. de Solla. (1963). *Little science, big science.* New York: Columbia University Press.

Shaw, Debora. (1991). The human-computer interface for information retrieval. *Annual Review of Information Science and Technology, 26,* 155–195.

Shneiderman, Ben. (1998). *Designing the user interface: Strategies for effective human-computer interaction.* 3rd ed. Reading, MA: Addison-Wesley.

Soukhanov, Anne H., et al. (Eds.). (1984). *Webster's II new Riverside university dictionary.* Boston: The Riverside Publishing Co.

Trenner, L. (1989). A comparative survey of the friendliness of online 'help' in interactive information retrieval systems. *Information Processing & Management, 25(2),* 119–136.

Zhang, Xiangmin, and Chignell, Mark. (2001). Assessment of the effects of user characteristics on mental models of information retrieval systems. *Journal of the American Society for Information Science and Technology, 52(6),* 445–459.

CHAPTER 11

Evaluation of Information Representation and Retrieval

After the various aspects and components of information representation and retrieval are discussed, it is time to evaluate these interrelated activities. Many researchers (e.g., Keen, 1971; Large, Tedd & Hartley, 1999; Swanson, R.W., 1978) have elaborated on the need for evaluating information representation and retrieval. It is hoped that information representation and retrieval will be improved when the weaknesses of IRR systems are identified and eventually eliminated as a result of the evaluation process.

Evaluation of information representation and retrieval is a subject that has been of interest to many great minds in the field for more than 40 years. Nevertheless, there exists much controversy about evaluation measures and methodologies. In this chapter, three major topics will be discussed: 1) evaluation measures (e.g., precision and recall) for representation and retrieval performance, 2) evaluation criteria for different types of IR systems, and 3) two major IRR evaluation projects: the Cranfield tests and TREC series. The issue of evaluation methodology is to be examined along with the major experiments in the field.

11.1 Evaluation Measures for Information Representation and Retrieval

Many measures have been developed for evaluating information representation and retrieval. For clarity purposes, evaluation measures will be discussed separately for information representation and information retrieval.

11.1.1 Evaluation Measures for Information Representation

As depicted in Chapters 2 and 3, information can be represented in a variety of ways. Indexing, categorization, and summarization are some major forms of information representation. Although each form of information representation has its unique features, collectively they are intended to bring out the essence in information and make it retrievable at a later time. Therefore, a common set of evaluation criteria (e.g., accuracy, brevity, consistency, and objectivity) is applicable to all kinds of information representation.

11.1.1.1 Accuracy

Accuracy is the most important measure in evaluating the quality of information representation because a distorted representation of original documents would lose the entire point of doing so. Accuracy means that the representation accurately represents the content of original documents. Reduction in representation would happen in terms of magnitude but not in terms of content. Consideration should also be given to accuracy in, for example, citation and spelling.

Specificity is a concept closely related to accuracy, and commonly used to measure indexing quality. By definition, specificity means the extent to which a concept or topic in a document is identified by a precise term in the hierarchy of its genus-species relations (Wellisch, 1995). For example, in the hierarchy of *information retrieval – multimedia retrieval – video retrieval*, the term *video retrieval* will be assigned to a document dealing with the topic to ensure the highest indexing specificity. The other two terms in the hierarchy would have lower specificity by comparison. Specificity is determined by the indexing language (i.e., controlled vocabulary or natural language) used. Natural language generally enables one to achieve high indexing specificity.

11.1.1.2 Brevity

One of the objectives for representing information is to help users save time and effort to get the information they need. Information explosion is one phrase coined to describe the enormous amount of information that users have to deal with. On the other hand, it is an acknowledged fact that it takes much less time for the user to go over a representation (e.g., abstracts, summaries, and indexing terms) than read an original document. Brevity thus becomes a principal measure for judging if the objective of saving time and effort is achieved.

Specific criteria have been set up for different formats of information representation (e.g., Lancaster, 1998) with regard to brevity. Take journal articles as an example: usually 5-10 indexing terms are assigned and an abstract of 250 words or fewer is prepared. If a representation takes a lengthy format, it offers little help to users in reducing their time in information retrieval. Exhaustivity in indexing can be treated as a related term to brevity. Wellisch (1995) defines exhaustivity as the extent to which concepts and topics are made retrievable by means of index terms. Exhaustivity is decided by the indexing policy adopted in the practice.

11.1.1.3 Consistency

The same document may be represented in multiple formats (e.g., indexing and abstract) and by different people. It is also common to see one publication (e.g., a journal) indexed by different indexing services. For example,

Journal of the American Society for Information Science & Technology is indexed in *Chemical Abstracts, Computer Literature Index,* and 10 other abstracting and indexing service products. While this practice implements the poly-representation of information Ingwersen (1996) suggested, the end products may be inconsistent in coverage and style. Studies in indexing have found that a high level of consistency is very difficult to obtain, and indexing consistency ranges from 10-80 percent (e.g., Hooper, 1965). Cleverdon (1984) reported that when two experienced indexers indexed the same document, using the same controlled vocabulary, they only assigned 30 percent terms in common. Information representation in the digital age, thanks to the auto-mated and automatic techniques, can theoretically attain better consistency, but empirical research in this area has yet to be conducted.

Consistency does not just imply word-by-word matches. Rather, it refers to a uniform representation (e.g., vocabulary, depth of coverage) of the essence of original documents regardless of format and the person who does the representation. Inconsistency can affect the quality of representation and eventually retrieval performance as well.

11.1.1.4 Objectivity

Objectivity constitutes another evaluation criterion for information repre-sentation as subjectivity and personal interpretations are likely to be brought in during the representation process. Information representation should be an authentic description of the original document without any alteration of its content. It is also important not to project one's personal preferences into the representation. More specifically, any reinforcement of the opinions of the author, deliberate interpolation of the attitudes of the indexer, selection of terminology implying attitudes, or suppression of ideas from the docu-ment in the index impair the objectivity of information representation (Bell, 1991). A subjective representation will not be able to reflect the true image of the original document.

11.1.1.5 Clarity, Readability, and Usability

In addition to the measures just described, other criteria have been put forward for evaluating information representation. Clarity, readability, and usability are among them. These measures all attempt to show user friendli-ness and make users more at ease when they deal with information repre-sentation.

Evaluation measures for information representation are fewer than those for information retrieval, and this kind of evaluation also does not distinguish the representation process from representation performance. Strictly speak-ing, the quality of representation cannot be truly evaluated unless it is used in information retrieval. Meanwhile, the quality of information retrieval depends on the quality of information representation. Good information representation plays an essential role in ensuring good retrieval performance. It is only through information retrieval that the quality of information representation can be ultimately judged.

11.1.2 Evaluation Measures for Information Retrieval

Compared with information representation, researchers have put much more time in exploring evaluation measures for information retrieval partly because the former is merely a prerequisite for the latter. As previously mentioned, the quality of representation cannot be truly assessed until the representation is used in retrieval. Information retrieval is both performance-oriented and process-oriented, although people, especially end-users, are typically more interested in what has been retrieved than what has been done during the process. A better understanding of the retrieval process would, however, help improve retrieval performance. For this reason, evaluation measures developed for information retrieval can be approximately categorized into two kinds, one concentrating on performance and the other on process. The former kind of measure is discussed in §11.1.2 whereas measures for evaluating retrieval process or the entire IR system are covered in §11.2. Among the measures for evaluating retrieval performance, recall and precision are the two most well known and widely adopted criteria (Salton, 1992).

11.1.2.1 Recall and Precision

Table 11.1 presents all the possible outcomes for a retrieval task, using the notation and terminology commonly seen in IR publications. For instance, "hits" mean retrieved documents that are relevant. "Misses" are defined as documents that are relevant but not retrieved. Based on these possible retrieval outcomes, a variety of evaluation measures are derived. Recall and precision, initially proposed by Kent and his colleagues (1955) as "pertinency factor" and "recall factor," are two such measures.

Table 11.1 Possible Retrieval Outcomes

Result \ Judgment	Relevant	Not Relevant	Total
Retrieved	a (hits)	b (noise)	a + b (all retrieved)
Not retrieved	c (misses)	d (rejects)	c + d (all nonretrieved)
Total	a + c (all relevant)	b + d (all nonrelevant)	a + b + c + d (total in the system)

As discussed in Chapter 5, recall (or R) is defined as the ratio between the number of relevant documents retrieved and the total number of relevant documents in a system. Using the notation given in Table 11.1:

$$R = a/(a+c)$$

Accordingly, precision (or P) is the ratio between the number of relevant documents retrieved and the total number of documents retrieved from a system. Thus,

$$P = a/(a+b)$$

The relationship between recall and precision tends to be inverse (e.g., Lancaster & Warner, 1993) although Fugmann (1993) challenged the statement with several examples. Fugmann found that an increase in precision is not always accompanied by a corresponding decrease in recall, and an increase in recall is by no means observed to have always in its wake a decrease in precision. A partial explanation to Fugmann's finding is that retrieval of relevant documents affects both recall and precision while retrieval of nonrelevant documents affects only precision (Korfhage, 1997).

Recall is supposed to measure the retrievability of an IR system whereas precision should assess the ability of an IR system in separating the nonrelevant from the relevant. But there are two major stumbling blocks in the calculation of these two measures. First, how can relevance be defined and measured? Second, how can the total number of relevant documents in a system be known?

11.1.2.1.1 The Notion of Relevance

The discussion, or more precisely, the debate on the meaning of relevance has been long and heated. Mizzaro (1997) presented a history of relevance by reviewing about 160 papers written on the topic since before the 1950s through the mid-1990s. Even though so much attention has been given, no agreement is reached on how relevance should be defined and how it can be measured simply because relevance is essentially a subjective judgment dictated by many interrelated factors. Relevance, in a sense, like love, is in the eye of the beholder. It is not a concept that can be explicitly described and easily quantified.

Nevertheless, a great number of definitions have been suggested for relevance. Saracevic (1975) traced, analyzed, and summarized many existing definitions of relevance. He concluded that our understanding of relevance is much better, clearer, deeper, and broader than it was shortly after WWII. But there is still a long way to go. Schamber, Eisenberg, and Nilan (1990) reexamined the issue of defining relevance 15 years later and indicated that people still had not reached a consensus with regard to a definition. They believe that relevance is a multidimensional concept, dependent on both internal and external factors. It is also based on a dynamic human judgment process. Specifically, 80 factors affecting relevance judgment are identified and grouped under six categories: judges, requests, documents, information systems, judgment conditions, and choice of scale (Schamber, 1994). Furthermore, the learning factor and sequence of presentation also affect relevance judgment (Froehlich, 1994). The judge will be able to learn during the process of relevance judgment. The same document will likely be judged more relevant if presented earlier rather than later in the evaluation process. Adding to the already mounting complexity, difficulty, and frustration in relevance judgment is that someone other than the end-user (e.g., an information professional) often makes the judgment. That happens particularly in assisted searching environments such as online systems.

Relevance is indeed a complicated notion, but it is a systematic and measurable phenomenon (Schamber, Eisenberg & Nilan, 1990). Simply put, relevance is a property that reflects the relationship between a document and the user's query. While an accurate and objective judgment of relevance appears hard to get, an estimation of its value is possible to obtain. Meanwhile, keep in mind what has been discussed in this subsection when judging relevance of retrieval results.

11.1.2.1.2 Determination of All the Relevant Documents in a System

How to define and measure relevance is only one problem in computing recall and precision. The other predicament involves the determination of all the relevant documents in an IR system. Unless a system is created for experimental purposes, there seems no way of knowing exactly the total number of documents that are relevant to a given query in a system. Yet, that number, the denominator in the formula $R = a/(a+c)$, is required for calculating recall.

Several methods have been proposed over the years to get around the problem (Large, Tedd & Hartley, 1999). Pooling is one such method. Basically, different users conduct the same search on the assumption that if the search is tried enough times eventually most, if not all, relevant documents will be found at least once. Results from all the searches will then be aggregated, and duplicates are removed. Any individual search results can then be compared with this aggregated set of relevant documents in the system to calculate recall. This pooling method is implemented, among other projects (e.g., Clarke & Willett, 1997), in the TREC series for recall computation (Harman, 1995). Consequently, a question arises as to how many repetitive searches need to be done before people using the pooling method are confident that enough relevant documents have been collected.

Another approach in estimating the total number of documents in a system is to ask one or more experts with both searching experience and subject knowledge to conduct the searches, and to assume that these experts will find all the relevant documents in the system. Results obtained by other searchers, such as novices, can then be checked against these expert searches to measure recall. This approach can be called the expert method.

In addition to the pooling method and expert approach, Large, Tedd and Hartley (1999) also describe a subset method. That is, documents in a small subset of the system database are examined one by one to locate relevant ones. The underlying assumption is that the subset is representative of the entire system, suggesting that a random sampling procedure must be applied for choosing the subset. The estimation based on the subset then becomes the denominator for calculating recall.

As can be seen, getting the recall measure for evaluating retrieval performance is similar to counting the number of fish in a lake. The task is close to impossible because the system database is dynamic and constantly changing. All the methods discussed here are thus at best good estimates and at worst plain guesses (Large, Tedd & Hartley, 1999).

11.1.2.1.3 Other Criticisms of Recall and Precision

Apparently no satisfactory answers have been found to the two previous questions regarding relevance and the total number of relevant documents in a system. Nevertheless, more criticisms have been made about recall and precision as evaluation measures. For example, it has been pointed out that recall and precision are incomplete measures for evaluation because factors such as interactivity, cost, and speed of retrieval should also be taken into consideration (e.g., Large, Tedd & Hartley, 1999). Miller and Tegler (1986) further argue that:

> The traditional methods of evaluating information searches – recall and precision – have completely overlooked this generative, creative aspect of a search. By evaluating the product and not the process, recall and precision limit our understanding of information searches and fail to measure them effectively. (p. 371)

In other words, measures other than recall and precision should be applied in IR evaluation. As Salton (1992) noted, the main assumption behind the use of measures such as recall and precision is that the average user is interested in retrieving large amounts of relevant materials (producing high recall), while at the same time rejecting a large proportion of the extraneous items (producing high precision). These assumptions may not always be satisfied. Indeed, for example, users may not be interested in an exhaustive search except in cases like patent retrieval, which questions the validity of recall as an evaluation measure.

Furthermore, there is no mechanism for expressing different degrees of relevance in calculating recall. All relevant documents are usually assumed to have equal value no matter if they are marginal or fully relevant (Chowdhury, 1999). This assumption cannot be changed, particularly when the total number of relevant documents in a system needs to be estimated using the methods discussed previously in §11.1.2.1.2.

Recall and precision, as evaluation measures, appear far from perfect, and recall seems the more controversial of the two. Despite all the criticisms and debates, however, recall and precision measures have formed the basis for the evaluation of the better known studies of both operational and laboratory-type retrieval systems (Salton, 1992). Meanwhile, variations of recall and precision measures have been developed with the intention to eliminate the limitations associated with these two evaluation criteria.

11.1.2.1.4 Variations of Recall and Precision Measures

Average recall or precision is proposed to challenge the assumption of equal relevance value of retrieved documents. Relevance is no longer a binary property (i.e., relevant or not relevant) in computing average recall or precision. Rather, it is measured on an X-point scale (X = 3, 4, ... 11) to show the different degrees of relevance. For example, each retrieved document will be assigned a value of 0, 0.5, or 1.0 on a three-point scale. The assigned values will then be averaged across all the documents retrieved on a topic so that the variance of relevance in each retrieved document is taken into account. The scale point is not necessarily limited to 11 or below. But a finer division may cause extra trouble in computation. As discussed previously, however, it is harder to do average recall than average precision due to the difficulty in determining the total number of relevant documents in a system.

As an extension of the above measure, average recall or precision is often calculated for the top N (N=10, 15, 20, 30, ...) documents retrieved on a topic if the results are ranked in the order of perceived relevance. The TREC series has widely applied this measure, i.e., average recall or precision at output cutoffs (Harman, 1995). Chu and Rosenthal (1996) calculated average precision for the top 10 results retrieved when they evaluated the Internet retrieval systems AltaVista, Excite, and Lycos. Average recall or precision at output cutoffs provides a practicable alternative to regular recall and precision especially when retrieval outputs are ranked and large in number.

Normalized recall or precision, another variation of recall and precision, takes into consideration the sequence in which documents are presented to the user. Ideally, an IR system would present all relevant documents before displaying any of the nonrelevant ones. If a value of 1 is given to an ideal system and 0 is assigned to the worst possible system where all the nonrelevant documents are presented to the user before any relevant ones, that value becomes the coefficient in calculating normalized recall or precision. Korfhage (1997) and Foskett (1996) described respectively two different methods for computing normalized recall. Normalized precision can be obtained similarly. The other assumption of this measure is one's knowledge about all the relevant documents within a system, which has been the same predicament for computing recall. The potential of this measure thus again suffers from that improbable assumption. In addition, normalized recall or precision in essence requires that retrieval outputs be ranked in the order of perceived relevance.

Relative recall is the ratio of the retrieved relevant documents examined by the user and the number of relevant documents the user knows are in the system (Harter & Hert, 1997) or would have liked to examine (Korfhage, 1997). For instance, suppose the user believes that there are 20 relevant documents about a given query in the system. After conducting the search, the user retrieves 10 documents that are judged relevant. The relative recall for this search is 50 percent. Obviously, relative recall is proposed with the intention to tackle the problems associated with recall. But, how can the user know, for example, the number of relevant documents in a system? The answer is what has been suggested in §11.1.2.1.2 for determining the total number of relevant documents in the system (e.g., pooling method). The same old problem resurfaces after a detour to the so-called relative recall.

E-measure, proposed by Swets (1969), is a weighted combination of precision and recall for measuring retrieval effectiveness. It can be calculated using the following formula:

$$E = 1 - 1/[\beta P^{-1} + (1 - \beta) R^{-1}]$$

The parameter β in the formula is used to reflect the emphasis on either precision or recall. For example, $\beta = 1$ corresponds to attaching equal importance to precision and recall. $\beta = 0.5$ and 2 correspond to attaching half or twice as much importance to recall as to precision respectively. The lower the E-measure, the better the effectiveness. Two comments can be made about E-measure. First, it can put different degrees of emphasis on either recall or precision. Second, it includes both recall and precision in a single measure of effectiveness. As will be discussed later, a single evaluation measure is very much favored in the IR community.

The variations of recall and precision provide different views and alternatives of the two evaluation measures. Nevertheless, none of the variations can even substantially, let alone entirely, circumvent the problems recall and precision confront. Consequently, additional evaluation measures (e.g., fall-out) have been introduced over the years.

11.1.2.2 Fallout

Fallout, initially put forward by Swets (1963), is defined as the ratio between nonrelevant documents retrieved and all nonrelevant document in a system database. Using the notation in Table 11.1:

$$F = b/(b+d)$$

Fallout measures the inability of an IR system in excluding nonrelevant documents from retrieval results, which Robertson (1969) called noise factor. The value for fallout again ranges from 0 to 1, the same as that for recall and precision. But the smaller the fallout value, the better the IR system is from the evaluation viewpoint.

As in the case of recall computation, the total number of nonrelevant documents in a system is not known. That number, therefore, has to be estimated using the methods discussed earlier for generating recall. Overall, fallout does not appear to be an extensively used evaluation measure, though Robertson (1969) states that the recall-precision graph (a graph plotting the values of these two measures) is not as easy to interpret as the recall-fallout graph, and believes precision is not as useful a measure of performance as is fallout used in conjunction with recall.

11.1.2.3 Generality

Generality is defined as the proportion of documents in a system database that is relevant to a particular topic. According to the notation given in Table 11.1:

$$G = (a+c)/(a+b+c+d)$$

The higher the generality number (or the greater the density of relevant items in the database), the easier the search tends to be (Lancaster & Warner, 1993). But generality is, strictly speaking, a measure for the database quality from the perspective of relevance rather than for retrieval performance directly. In addition, it is always difficult to determine the number of relevant documents not retrieved from the system, i.e., the value of c in Table 11.1.

11.1.2.4 Single Measures for IR Evaluation

One of the criticisms for recall and precision is their incompleteness as evaluation measures (see §11.1.2.1.3). That is why recall and precision are normally used in combination, and possibly along with other criteria for evaluation purposes. It would be ideal if a single evaluation measure could be used by including related factors in the computation. E-measure is one close example of a single measure for evaluating information retrieval. Cooper (1973a; 1973b) also suggested a utility measure that is based on a user's subjective judgment of an IR system in terms of its usefulness. The utility of a system can be measured differently as long as it is in accordance with Cooper's utility theory. For instance, Su (1991) asked users to rate the usefulness of search results according to a seven-point Likert scale by treating the value of search results as a whole. She found that this utility measure was the best single measure of interactive information retrieval performance among the 20 measures she had selected for her study.

Utility measures can also be defined differently, e.g., worth of retrieved documents as a whole versus time spent, worth assigned in dollars, and contribution to problem resolution (Saracevic & Kantor, 1988; Saracevic et al., 1988). But no matter how utility is defined in evaluation, the measure always relies on the user's subjective judgment. The subjectivity of this measure would lead to the same concern people have when making relevance judgment for the calculation of recall and precision.

11.1.2.5 Other Evaluation Measures for Information Retrieval

Griffith (1986) once commented that only three numbers should be used in evaluating an IR system: number of relevant items retrieved, number of nonrelevant items retrieved, and total number of items in a system database. All three numbers can be obtained without any estimation or guess. The ratio between the number of relevant items retrieved and total number of items in a system database would illustrate the system's ability in locating relevant documents. Similarly, the ratio between the number of nonrelevant items retrieved and total number of items in a system database would demonstrate the system's discriminating power, i.e., the ability to reject nonrelevant items. However, few evaluation projects implemented Griffith's idea.

Evaluation measures for information retrieval have gone through a long journey that is still continuing. Among all the measures discussed here, recall and precision have received the most attention as well as the most criticisms. Nevertheless, they are the *de facto* measures for the majority of evaluation efforts because they are easy to interpret in terms of the retrieval of wanted items and the rejection of extraneous ones (Salton, 1992). Recall and precision will remain the key evaluation measures for information retrieval unless better alternatives are developed and proven.

11.2 Evaluation Criteria for IR Systems

Recall, precision, and other measures discussed previously are basically for evaluating retrieval performance. Retrieval performance apparently only represents one aspect of information retrieval even though, as indicated earlier, the end-user pays more attention to it. In order to get a complete view of how well an IR system works, measures other than those for evaluating IR performance should be considered. Different measures should be used for different types of IR systems. The following discussion examines evaluation criteria for each of the four types of IR systems: online systems, CD-ROM systems, OPACs, and Internet retrieval systems.

11.2.1 Evaluation Criteria for Online Systems

Online systems have had the longest history among the four major types of IR systems (see Chapter 8), and consequently have been the subjects of many evaluation studies. The criteria used for evaluating online systems are designed in different ways.

According to Lancaster and Warner (1993), evaluations of online systems can possibly be done at three levels: 1) evaluation of effectiveness, 2) evaluation of cost-effectiveness, and 3) cost-benefit evaluation. The first level, evaluation of effectiveness, considers cost, time, and quality of the system. Such evaluation tries to find out if the system functions effectively with regard to the user's need. The second level, evaluation of cost-effectiveness, associates the cost factor to system effectiveness so that two different IR systems can be easily contrasted at this level. For example, how much does it cost to retrieve one relevant document from an IR system? The same kind of comparison would be hard to do at the first level because those measures are not normalized. The third level, cost-benefit evaluation, goes even further than the previous two levels by assessing the cost of running an IR system against the benefits received as a result of having the system. As the level of evaluation goes up, so does the sophistication of the evaluation criteria. Level one criteria (e.g., response time or database coverage) tend to be straightforward. Level two measures need some computation. In comparison, level three criteria require judgment and reasoning, far beyond a simple appraisal. Evaluation criteria at all three levels are possibly being applied in one evaluation project. In practice, however, measures for levels one and two, particularly those of level one, are used most of the time in evaluating online systems because of their feasibility and practicability.

Although various criteria have been established for evaluating online systems, a consensus seems to have been reached about what aspects should be inspected. Lancaster and Fayen (1973) recapitulated them in the form of six criteria: 1) coverage, 2) recall, 3) precision, 4) response time, 5) user effort, and 6) form of output. It is surprising to see that searching capability is not included in this set of evaluation criteria.

Coverage is a typical measure for evaluating the system database. Specific facets of database coverage include types of documents (e.g., patents, journal articles, and technical reports), number of documents, update frequency, and retrospectiveness. The coverage of a system database determines what can be retrieved later from the system.

Recall and precision are part of the evaluation criteria for measuring retrieval performance. These two measures, as pointed out in §11.1.2, become the regular components in most evaluation efforts. But no standard has been set for satisfactory recall and precision ratios for two reasons. One is that different users would have different expectations of recall and precision in different circumstances. For example, if the user intends to do a state-of-the-art review of a subject, high recall will be anticipated. If the user is only interested in the newest development of a field, high precision would be expected. The other reason for not having a standard for acceptable recall and precision ratio is the inverse relationship presumably existing between the two measures. An increase of one measure would likely lead to a decrease in another. It is then difficult to find an optimal point for both recall and precision. Besides, the size of the system database also affects the determination of satisfactory recall and precision. Low precision ratios may be less tolerable in a larger database than in a smaller one. For instance, a user may be willing to look at 60 retrieved records to identify that 20 are useful, but much less willing to examine 600 to find 200, although in both cases the precision ratio (33 percent) is the same (Lancaster & Warner, 1993).

Response time refers to the time needed between the submission of a query and return of results. The criterion appears indispensable particularly in the online systems of early days because information technology (e.g., telecommunication and computing power) was at its infant stage at that time and information retrieval using online systems was expensive. If an IR system can process queries rapidly, the cost of using it will be minimized, which explains the importance of having this criterion in the evaluation.

User effort as an evaluation criterion implies several elements, all of which measure how much effort a user must make to conduct searches in the online retrieval environment. For example, how long does it take for the user to learn about or become familiar with one system? How friendly is the user-system interaction? What kinds of support (e.g., printed manual or online help) are provided for the user? The less effort the user needs to make, the better the online system is. One unique feature of online systems is that information professionals as intermediaries often conduct searches on behalf of end-users, and are better trained than end-users. This difference should be remembered when considering the factor of user effort in evaluation.

Form of output constitutes the last criterion devised for evaluating online systems. Output of online searches can be presented in a variety of ways (e.g., bibliographic information only or bibliographic information plus abstract). Online systems usually offer many output options but do not automatically rank search results since the use of the ranking facility (e.g., the RANK command in DIALOG) turns out to be quite expensive. Retrieval results from online systems are typically presented in reverse chronological order, i.e., items most recently added to a system are presented first. As depicted in §10.3.2.2, flexibility is the keyword for getting a top rating in this regard.

In sum, coverage, recall, precision, response time, user effort, and form of output have served as evaluation criteria for online systems even though variations are seen occasionally. In addition, these criteria may also provide some baseline for evaluating other types of IR systems.

11.2.2 Evaluation Criteria for CD-ROM Systems

CD-ROM systems are basically, as explained in §8.1, online systems in CD-ROM medium. Therefore, criteria for evaluating CD-ROM systems are derived from comparative studies of online and CD-ROM databases (e.g., Large, 1989; Nahl-Jakobovits & Tenopir, 1992) and research conducted specifically on CD-ROM system evaluation (e.g., Harry & Oppenheim, 1993a).

Evaluation criteria for comparing online and CD-ROM systems focus on the difference between the two. For instance, response time, coverage, content, and cost are the main factors being considered (Nahl-Jakobovits & Tenopir, 1992). Evaluation measures developed exclusively for CD-ROM systems appear more comprehensive. For example, Harry and Oppenheim (1993a) suggested the following criteria for evaluating CD-ROM systems: installation, document and support, database, user interface, searching, output, and reliability. Richards and Robinson (1993) looked at user guidance, index, search features, general output features, record display, and database management in their study. Rowley and Slack (1997) identified criteria specifically for the evaluation of interface design on CD-ROMs. In addition, the numerous models and checklists created to assist libraries and information centers in making their purchase decisions also contribute to the evaluation endeavor.

Although there exists no common list of evaluation criteria for CD-ROM systems, as in the online environment, similarities among the different sets of measures for evaluating CD-ROM systems can be easily discerned with respect to hardware and software considerations, database, searching facilities, user friendliness, and output features.

In contrast to the criteria listed for online systems, hardware and software considerations are a new measure because CD-ROM systems are stand-alone, different from the centralized online systems. To be more specific, this criterion includes hardware and software requirements, installation process, and other technical matters. For example, the installation of a CD-ROM system is expected to go smoothly and be guided through. An eventful installation exerts negative impact on the quality of the system as a whole. Compatibility in both hardware and software could be another concern since an institution usually has to acquire different CD-ROM systems from different producers or publishers. It is certainly undesirable for the same user to switch from one setting to another in order to search different CD-ROMs.

Database, as an evaluation criterion for CD-ROM systems, has analogous implications as in the case of online systems. Scope of database coverage (in terms of time and content), full-text or otherwise, and update frequency are some of the factors that need to be considered in this evaluation category. Update frequency is of particular concern in evaluating CD-ROM systems because they cannot be updated as frequently as online systems; a quarterly update is more desirable than an annual one if the subject area of the database is rapidly developing or on the cutting edge.

Searching facilities, not included as a criterion for evaluating online systems, are selected by many in the evaluation of CD-ROM systems. What needs to be examined in this respect consists of the facilities available to perform the search (e.g., Boolean searching, truncation, proximity searching, case sensitivity, and field searching) and additional features such as search history display and search modification. The more searching facilities a CD-ROM system provides, the more capable the system is.

User friendliness is one aspect of CD-ROM systems that attracts a lot of notice. Every single set of evaluation criteria created for CD-ROM systems includes at least one measure for user friendliness. Common user-system interaction features such as user level, navigation options, and user support should be considered in evaluating the user friendliness of CD-ROM systems. In addition, there are some parameters that are unique in this criterion for CD-ROM systems. For example, since the storage capacity of individual CD-ROM disks is limited (e.g., 700 megabytes), multiple disks might be needed to hold a complete system. Then, will the switching between disks be easy and intuitive? Rowley and Slack (1997) proposed a checklist for CD-ROM system interaction features in reference to the work of other researchers (Harry & Oppenheim, 1993a & 1993b; Richards & Robinson, 1993). The checklist divides all the interaction features into four parts: operational (e.g., break, escape), navigational (e.g., navigation between records), communication (e.g., screen titles and layout), and support (e.g., online tutorial).

Output features, referring to the options available to the user for obtaining results, form another aspect for the evaluation of CD-ROM systems. Questions commonly asked during the evaluation include: Are there appropriately predefined formats? Are users allowed to define their own formats when needed? Can users specify how results are sorted? Can results be saved, printed, or e-mailed as desired? If the printing option is chosen, can users define printing parameters such as font and paper size? As discussed in

§10.3.2.2, output features to a large extent determine the user friendliness of an IR system. The same holds true for CD-ROM systems as users naturally expect flexible and self-explanatory output features.

As shown, recall and precision are not explicitly listed as evaluation measures for CD-ROM retrieval. The reason behind this phenomenon is not given in the literature. One possible explanation could be that some CD-ROM systems (e.g., encyclopedia) are built for retrieving known items rather than for locating information on a subject. Within that context, the calculation of recall and precision becomes meaningless. Therefore, hardware and software considerations, database, searching facilities, user friendliness, and output features comprise the major criteria for evaluating CD-ROM systems.

11.2.3 Evaluation Criteria for OPACs

Online public access catalogs, designed for finding bibliographic information about a library collection, stand for a unique type of IR systems. Evaluation criteria for OPACs have been developed mainly through comparative studies; the report by Hildreth (1982) appears to be the most influential. Jones (in Hildreth, 1982, p. xii) even predicted in the foreword that no subsequent effort in this field could escape being affected by Hildreth's report. Indeed, the framework presented in the report has shaped subsequent efforts in evaluating OPACs (e.g., O'Rourke, 1987; Salmon, 1983) although the research was not intended as an evaluation of the 10 OPACs studied (Hildreth, 1985). After consulting relevant research on the topic (e.g., Hildreth, 1982), O'Rourke (1987) created for evaluation purposes a checklist of 95 questions divided into five categories: 1) operational features, 2) access points, 3) search features, 4) display features, and 5) user assistance features. These five categories could reasonably serve as evaluation criteria for OPACs.

The criterion of operational features relates to how the user actually interacts with an OPAC. For example, how does the user log on or exit the system? Does the system allow the user to select a target (e.g., a local library collection or a collection of a library consortium) for doing searches in addition to the default option? Can the user modify a search or change system default settings (e.g., display short records)? Is it easy for the user to move from one display level to another, from one record to the next or the previous? Interface (i.e., command language versus menu selection) was a major consideration at the time when those evaluation criteria were established. The same aspect, however, is less relevant to today's OPACs as few of them still apply command language. The switching from card catalogs to OPACs has a great impact on user-system interaction, which seems to be the chief justification for choosing this criterion for evaluating OPACs.

Access points decide how OPAC information can be searched, and make up another criterion for OPAC evaluation. In the early years (i.e., the 1980s) of OPAC development, author, title, call number, ISBN, and ISSN were the common access points. Keyword and subject headings have been added since. Theoretically speaking, the more access points an OPAC provides, the easier it is for the user to locate the information in the system. However, some of the access points (e.g., ISBN and subject headings) are not frequently used because users, particularly novices, know little about their implications. By contrast, access points per se did not become an evaluation criterion for online and CD-ROM systems partly because there are so many of them in these two retrieval environments. Field searching in search facilities can be chosen instead to cover the dimension of access points.

Search features of OPACs vary from system to system. When OPACs are evaluated from the perspective of search features, several elements are observed. First, what kinds of searching capabilities are supported? Are all three Boolean operators available? How about truncation and proximity searching? Second, does the system offer any search-related features such as a list of subject headings online, cross references, and suggestions for improving searches? Third, can users limit their searches by publication year, document type, or the like? The more options a system can support, the better the system.

Display features, a broader concept than output options, are chosen as a measure for the evaluation of OPACs. This criterion can be further broken down to record length (e.g., brief or full display), number of records per listing, and other display-related features. Full records may also be displayed in MARC format, a feature used mostly by information professionals. O'Rourke (1987) posed more specific questions for checking OPAC display quality. For example, will a system automatically display the record when it is the sole response to a search term? Are tags (e.g., TI for title) self-explanatory in tagged record displays? Are record displays free of abbreviations, codes, and jargon? In addition, questions can be asked about font type, style, size, or cases used in OPAC displays. All uppercase type and small font size (e.g., 10-point), for instance, are not recommended for displaying information on OPACs.

User assistance comprises another criterion for evaluating OPACs. The more assistance a system can provide to the user, the less likely the user is to feel helpless when interacting with the OPAC. Many facilities may be designed for helping OPAC users. Examples include an introductory message describing the OPAC in general, a list of accessible files or searchable fields, explanations for error messages, online tutorials, and operation-specific online help. The OPAC should also be checked to see, for example, if search history can be shown, and if procedural or guiding comments are routinely given. No assumptions should be made about users' familiarity with the system when discussing user assistance. Help messages ought to be clear, simple, and precise.

These five evaluation criteria were created in the 1980s when OPACs were first adopted in libraries. Improvements and new features have been introduced and should be considered in evaluating current versions of OPACs. For example, many OPACs are now networked, allowing remote access from home, office, and locations other than the library. Is the remote access convenient? Are adequate supports provided for helping the user gain remote access? On the other hand, as discussed in §8.3, a large number of OPACs today serve as a gateway to other information sources and IR systems. What facilities are available for users to take advantage of this feature? Attention should be given to these new features and developments of OPACs for evaluation purposes in addition to the five criteria discussed here.

11.2.4 Evaluation Criteria for Internet Retrieval Systems

Relatively few evaluation projects have addressed Internet retrieval systems, representing the newest member in the family of IR systems, although some researchers (e.g., Chu & Rosenthal, 1996; Ding & Marchionini, 1996; Leighton, 1995; Leighton & Srivastava, 1997) have attempted to examine their retrieval performance. As retrieval performance represents only one aspect in evaluating IR systems, other dimensions of Internet retrieval systems should be considered in an evaluation.

Chu and Rosenthal (1996) proposed an evaluation framework for Web search engines, the dominant type of Internet retrieval system as of this writing. The framework is derived from the 1970s evaluation criteria that Lancaster and Fayen (1973) established for online systems, with additions and revisions tailored for Internet retrieval systems. Because of the changes brought to Internet retrieval systems as a whole, some aspects specified in the five broad evaluation criteria (i.e., composition of Web indexes, search capability, retrieval performance, output, and user effort) at the time of the study are outdated today. However, the conceptual framework remains pertinent for evaluating Internet retrieval systems.

The composition of indexes in an IR system is an important component for evaluation because the content of indexes determines how information in the system can be retrieved. For example, whenever a Web search request is issued, it is the Web index rather than the Web pages themselves that has been checked for retrieving information. Coverage, update frequency, and the portions of Internet documents indexed (e.g., the title plus the first several lines, or the entire document) are the three elements examined. While the extent of all three components depends largely on the power and sophistication of the hardware and software that manage the index or database, larger coverage, frequent updates, and full-text indexing do not necessarily result in better Internet retrieval systems in other measurements. There are other factors (e.g., the interface and search capability) that play a role in having quality Internet retrieval systems.

Search capability constitutes another criterion for evaluating Internet retrieval systems since variance is the norm rather than the exception in this case. Search facilities that are basic and common may not be found in major Internet retrieval systems. For example, Google does not fully support the Boolean AND operator at present. On the other hand, retrieval features (e.g., fuzzy searching) that could only be seen in laboratories in the past are now implemented in some Internet retrieval systems. A competent Internet retrieval system must include the fundamental search facilities that users are familiar with, which include Boolean logic, phrase searching, truncation, and limiting facilities (e.g., limiting by field). Because the searching capabilities of an Internet retrieval system ultimately determine its performance, absence of these basic functions will severely handicap the system.

Retrieval performance is traditionally evaluated on three parameters: precision, recall, and response time. While the three variables can all be quantitatively measured, extra caution should be exercised when one judges the relevance of retrieved items and estimates the total number of documents relevant to a specific topic in a network-based system. Since representations of Internet documents (e.g., summaries or extracts) are mostly done with automatic means, relevance judgment based on such representations could cause more concern about reliability. Furthermore, the dynamic and flux nature of the Internet makes it virtually impossible to determine the total number of relevant documents in an Internet retrieval system. Recall, therefore, is even harder to calculate in the Internet environment than for other kinds of IR systems. As for response time as a performance parameter, it is becoming less and less important as Internet retrieval systems are increasingly improved in terms of processing power.

Output, as an evaluation criterion for Internet retrieval systems, should be examined from three perspectives: accessibility, content, and format. Thanks to the hyperlink feature, the user can access full documents of retrieved outcome if the links function properly. But there exist dysfunctional links such as broken links (e.g., links to sites that have changed URLs) or dead links (e.g., links to sites that are no longer available). An ideal Internet retrieval system should keep the number of dysfunctional links to a minimum, thus allowing maximum accessibility to final results. The output content, to a certain degree, is decided by the way an Internet retrieval system is constructed. That is, does the system purely extract or actually index what it includes when building its database? The answer should be apparent. Extracts are not of much help to the user in determining the aboutness of retrieved results.

Another facet relating to output content is the amount of duplication in the results. Currently, only some of the meta-Internet retrieval systems are capable of removing duplicates. The concern about output formats of Internet retrieval systems, however, is less of an issue because systems tend to predefine all possible output formats, and source documents represented by the output can be easily viewed if so desired. Therefore, accessibility and content are the two output features unique and important to the evaluation of Internet retrieval systems.

User effort in the current context refers to documentation and interface because these two factors critically affect users' efforts in learning and using Internet retrieval systems. Well-prepared documentation and a user-friendly interface play a notable role in users' selections of Internet retrieval systems. Unlike other types of IR systems, Internet retrieval systems are generally free and the distinction among them does not appear obvious. The attractiveness of each Internet retrieval system is therefore expressed to its users mainly via its interface and documentation. In other words, users will not choose an Internet retrieval system unless they are comfortable with its interface and able to read and comprehend its documentation when consulted. Internet retrieval systems, as a group, have tried to minimize users' efforts by implementing form fill-in and graphical modes of interaction, and by providing online help facilities. When Internet retrieval systems are evaluated from the viewpoint of user effort, one needs to examine particularly if the screen is too busy or if the help message is too technical and terse as such concerns do seem common for some of the systems. On the other hand, users of Internet retrieval systems are different from those of other IR systems. They are the most heterogeneous group in terms of IR skills and experiences. They may not have received any form of training before actually using an Internet retrieval system. Yet there is usually no intermediary, as in the case of online systems, to perform the search task for the user. The absence of intermediary and the inexperience of most Internet retrieval system users set a stricter requirement for the system to minimize user effort than in any other IR environment.

In addition to the aforementioned five evaluation criteria, passage retrieval, multilingual retrieval, and cross language searching should also be considered in the evaluation of Internet retrieval systems. The concept of passage retrieval is explained in §1.2.1 before Internet retrieval systems are specifically discussed. Since the Web has become one of the major Internet applications and Web documents take the hyperlink structure, it seems increasingly necessary to have passage retrieval on the Internet. The traditional approach of retrieving the entire document offers little help to the user of Internet retrieval systems in pinpointing the needed information in part due to the hyperstructure of Web documents. The desired piece or passage of information could possibly be buried deep in the structure and the sheer size of some Web documents poses a problem in itself. For this reason, passage retrieval is a desirable feature for Internet retrieval systems to support. The famous TREC series started a research task called the Question Answering track on passage retrieval in 1997 (Voorhees, 2000).

Multilingual retrieval or cross language searching, discussed in §9.1, deals with the language dimension of IR systems. As depicted in Chapter 9, information in languages other than English is increasingly being posted on the Internet, suggesting that the language factor is becoming increasingly important for evaluating Internet retrieval systems. Other types of IR systems do carry multilingual information, but not reaching a level comparable to that of Internet retrieval systems. According to the research firm Aberdeen Group, non-English speaking users will be a majority on the Internet by 2005 (NewsFactor Network, 2001). It seems only reasonable then to subsume the language dimension in the evaluation of Internet retrieval systems. Both multilingual retrieval and cross language searching are studied in TREC (Voorhees & Harman, 2000).

Passage retrieval, multilingual retrieval, and cross language searching in fact all belong to the evaluation criterion of searching capability. They are discussed separately in this case, however, to emphasize their significance and to reflect the changes in the evaluation framework Chu and Rosenthal (1996) proposed for Internet retrieval systems.

11.3 Major Evaluation Projects for Information Representation and Retrieval

Almost half a century has passed since the first evaluation study in information retrieval was conducted in 1953 (Lancaster, 1979). Numerous projects have been carried out to evaluate information representation and retrieval since that time. The Cranfield tests (e.g., Cleverdon, 1962), the MEDLARS (MEDical Literature Analysis and Retrieval System) project (e.g., Lancaster, 1968), the SMART experiment (e.g., Salton, 1981), the STAIRS (STorage And Information Retrieval System) study (e.g., Blair & Maron, 1985) and the TREC series (e.g., Harman, 1993; Voorhees & Harman, 2000) are some of the major projects in this category. Of all the major evaluation studies, the Cranfield test and TREC series will be examined in detail as they are the most influential in the history of IRR evaluation. Problems and issues surrounding IRR evaluation projects will also be discussed.

11.3.1 The Cranfield Tests

The Cranfield tests were carried out in two phases, named Cranfield I and Cranfield II respectively, between 1957 and 1967. They are the first extensive evaluation projects undertaken with the leadership of C.W. Cleverdon, then a librarian at the College of Aeronautics in Cranfield, England. Although the Cranfield tests were about the evaluation of manual IRR systems, the methodology devised in the project has subsequently been used for evaluating many digital IRR systems. Studies similar to the Cranfield tests are often referred to as Cranfield-like projects.

11.3.1.1 Cranfield I

Cranfield I was designed to test the comparative efficiency of four indexing systems on retrieval performance in an environment involving many other variables such as indexer, document, and search question. Recall and precision were used to measure retrieval performance in this project, the first such practice in large scale IRR evaluation experiments. Moreover, it is possible to calculate recall in Cranfield because the test collections, created specifically for the project, are closed and known. The four indexing systems chosen for Cranfield I are:

- Universal Decimal Classification (UDC)

- An alphabetical subject catalog

- A faceted classification scheme

- A uniterm system of coordinate indexing

11.3.1.1.1 Test Design

Three indexers were chosen for the test and they had various types of experience and familiarity with the systems being tested: one with subject knowledge, one with indexing experience, and one straight from a public library without either subject knowledge or indexing experience. The 100 documents, taking a convenient number, were obtained equally from the general field of aeronautics and the specialized field of high-speed aerodynamics. Each indexer was asked to index each of the 100 documents five times, spending 2, 4, 8, 12, and 16 minutes per document. The average number of indexing terms assigned to each document is 2 to 10 (Cleverdon, 1962). Search questions for the test were "manufactured" as members outside the project examined each document and then formulated the questions to which a given document would be relevant. A total of 400 search questions were created, and they were used in three rounds of searches in the form of 1,200 (400 × 3 rounds) queries.

The searching was mainly done by project staff. The first search round was conducted on the first set of 400 queries as a pretest. The second search round was designed to tackle the two problems encountered in the pretest, using a second set of 400 queries derived from the 400 questions. First, how long was a searcher justified in continuing a search when the one relevant document was known to be in the file somewhere? Second, how could the searcher decide exactly what constituted a different search strategy when using terms particularly from the four index languages? A stopping point for the search was then prescribed in the second round, and changes of search strategies for the same query were required to be both in general and in terms of each indexing system in as fair a manner as possible. Failure analysis of the results for the second round revealed cases where a search on one indexing system had succeeded but the same query on another system had failed due to search formulation. So a third round of search using another set of 400 queries was constructed to eliminate searcher and search strategy variations by adopting a standardized and fixed strategy for all four systems.

11.3.1.1.2 Test Findings

The most important finding in Cranfield I is that the uniterm system gave the best recall among the four different indexing systems included in the test (see Table 11.2) although all systems achieved a similar level of performance efficiency (Cleverdon, 1962).

Table 11.2   Recall Ratio of Four Indexing Systems

Indexing System	Recall (%)
Uniterm	82.0
Alphabetical subject	81.5
UDC	75.6
Faceted classification	73.8

Cranfield I also revealed that increased time in indexing increased recall to a certain level, after which the positive correlation between indexing time and recall might reverse as shown in Table 11.3 (Cleverdon, 1962).

While the three indexers are different in terms of indexing experience and subject knowledge, no significant difference was observed in retrieving documents indexed by them or in their indexing performance. In addition, success

Table 11.3   Indexing Time vs. Recall Ratio

Indexing Time (minute)	Recall (%)
2	72.9
4	80.2
8	76.2
12	82.7
16	84.3

rates in retrieving documents on the general area of aeronautics were noted to be 4–5 percent better than those on the specialized field of high-speed aerodynamics. Other findings of Cranfield I include:

- There is an inverse relationship between recall and precision.

- A 1 percent increase in precision could be achieved at a cost of 3 percent loss in recall.

- Systems operated at recall 70–90 percent and precision 8–20 percent.

Among all the results summarized here, three of them are beyond expectation or even contradictory to some general beliefs held in the IRR community. First, in terms of recall, the uniterm system outperformed three controlled vocabulary systems included in the project in spite of the theory that controlled vocabulary yields better retrieval performance. This finding has indirectly promoted research on automatic indexing, which relies heavily on uniterms or keywords. Second, the finding was that the performance of an indexing system on retrieval does not depend on the indexer's experience or subject knowledge, while the traditional thinking was the opposite—that the indexer's experience and knowledge would help improve performance. Third, Cranfield I found that increased time in indexing would not necessarily increase recall. To the contrary, there was even a decrease in recall when the indexing time was increased from four minutes to eight (see Table 11.3). While the recall ratio increased again as a result of longer indexing time, the gain in retrieval performance does not appear to be in proportion to the indexing time spent. For example, the recall ratio increased only by 4 percent (i.e., from 80.2 percent to 84.3 percent) whereas the indexing time was quadrupled (i.e., from 4 minutes to 16).

11.3.1.2 Cranfield II

Cranfield II was designed to assess the effects of different indexing devices on retrieval performance. Indexing devices are measures employed by the indexer to improve either recall or precision. Examples of indexing devices include synonyms, generic relations, coordination, links, and roles. The explanation about the test was given in Cleverdon's project report (Cleverdon, 1962):

> We started from the belief that all index languages are amalgams of different kinds of devices. Such devices fall into two groups of those which are intended to improve the recall ratio and those which are intended to improve the precision ratio. ... The purpose of the test was to investigate the effect which each of these devices, alone or in any possible combination, would have on recall and precision. (p. 17)

11.3.1.2.1 Test Design

About 200 research papers were gathered, each generally having 5–10 references. Then, each author was asked to state, in the form of a search question, the basic problem that was the reason for his or her investigation on the assumption that a research paper is written as the result of an investigation undertaken to provide the answer to a question or questions in the author's mind. Each author was also requested to write up to three additional questions describing any subsidiary questions that arose in the course of the research. After that, abstracts of these references (i.e., cited documents) were obtained along with some noncited papers identified by graduate students at the college on titles or via bibliographical coupling (i.e., two documents are bibliographically coupled when their reference lists have one or more documents in common). The author was asked to indicate the relevance of the references and noncited papers to each question on the scale of 1 to 5, with 1 being the most relevant, on the assumption that the references were made because they must have something to do with the subject of the paper (Cleverdon & Mills, 1963). The authors identified a total of 1,961 cited documents fully or partially relevant to the 279 questions they posed, from which 1,400 documents and 221 questions were finally selected for Cranfield II.

The test collection of 1,400 documents is mainly in the field of high-speed aerodynamics and aircraft structures. Each document was "indexed" in three ways. First, the most important concepts were selected and recorded in natural language of the document. Second, the single words in each of the chosen concepts were listed. Third, the concepts were combined in different ways to form the main themes of the documents. Each term was also given a weight (i.e., 1, 2, or 3 with 1 being the most important) at the time of indexing to indicate its relative importance. Various indexing devices were applied as well during the indexing process in order to probe their effects on retrieval performance.

Searching was done by making use of the various indexing devices implemented in three major types of indexing languages: single term, simple concept, and controlled term index languages. Specifications about these indexing languages were detailed in Figure 3 to Figure 5 of Cleverdon (1967). Indexing languages formed by keywords in the titles and abstracts were also tested in the project. Queries were decomposed into individual words, and a search was first made for a match for all the words. The matching was then done at different levels by dropping one query term at a time and for all possible coordination with remaining terms. For a query with five individual words, for instance, the first search was done with all the five terms. The second search would be done with any four out of the five terms by dropping off one from the query. Then a search was made with any three terms, any two, until only one term was left for matching. Synonyms, broader terms, narrower terms, and other facilities could be used to replace the original words. The searches were carried out in such a way that all the factors were kept constant except one. In the previous example, the number of terms in a query was the only factor allowed to vary while all other parameters were kept constant. Both hits and false drops were recorded for every search so that recall and precision ratios could be calculated.

The entire design was noted for its volume, variety, and complexity. The test was by no means trivial, especially given that it was done manually.

11.3.1.2.2 Test Findings

Recall and precision ratios of all the searches in each language were averaged and used to measure the effects of indexing devices on retrieval performance in Cranfield II. The test reported the following findings:

- Single term indexing languages were superior to any other type in terms of performance.

- When single terms were used for indexing, the inclusion of collateral classes and, in particular, quasi-synonyms worsened the performance.

- When concepts were used for indexing, the performance worsened with the inclusion of superordinate, subordinate, and collateral classes along with the original concepts.

- When controlled terms were used for indexing, the inclusion of narrower and broader terms worsened the performance.

- Indexing languages formed out of titles performed better than those formed out of abstracts.

It was quite astonishing and seemingly inexplicable that, as shown in Cranfield II, the best performing index languages were composed of uncontrolled single words derived from documents. No explanations about the surprise could be found by the research participants (Cleverdon, Mills & Keen, 1966). This finding also conforms to one of the Cranfield I findings, i.e., that the uniterm system outperformed three other controlled vocabulary systems included in the project in terms of recall. According to Cranfield II, it seems that the original terms always performed better alone without any additional variations (e.g., broader or narrower terms). Title-based indexing languages offered better performance than abstract-based ones because titles are in general more indicative and precise than abstracts. The inverse relationship between recall and precision was further confirmed in Cranfield II when indexing devices became part of the experiment environment.

11.3.1.3 Problems with the Cranfield Tests

A large number of reviews and criticisms (e.g., Harter, 1971; Swanson, D.R., 1965, 1971; Vickery, 1966, 1967) have been published since the conduct of the Cranfield tests, pointing out various problems with the tests. Harter and Hert (1997) categorized these problems into four types: validity and reliability, generalizability, usefulness, and conceptual issues. In consideration of the fact that the conceptual issues (e.g., how to define and measure concepts like relevance and satisfaction) exist in all IRR evaluation projects, the following discussion will only center around three types of problems relating specifically to the Cranfield tests, namely, validity and reliability, generalizability, and applicability.

The validity and reliability of the tests were questioned because of several arguments. For example, the documents actually submitted to authors who posed the questions for relevance assessments with respect to the corresponding questions might favor the simple term matching techniques at the expense of the more complex matching systems. Large numbers of potentially relevant but not retrieved items were never included in the evaluation. Yet, the system was not penalized for not retrieving these items. There were also unwarranted or untested assumptions in the tests. For instance, one must assume that relevance judgments made on a number of documents for a given question are independent of each other. Furthermore, the connection of the source document and question in Cranfield II is much less narrow than that in Cranfield I. All these affect the validity and reliability of the Cranfield tests, i.e., whether the tests actually measured what they intended to measure, and whether the tests are repeatable if the same procedure is followed.

The Cranfield results are not generalizable because no random sampling was applied in the tests. In addition, the test collections were small (i.e., 100 and 1,400 documents respectively) compared with the actual number of documents in an IRR system. Some of the findings, as discussed earlier, appear contradictory to common beliefs and experience of the IRR community. All these facts caused concerns about the generalizability of the tests.

The applicability of the tests in operational systems becomes questionable as artificiality is reflected in several aspects of the Cranfield tests. First, there was no real user involvement throughout the tests. Second, search questions were manufactured rather than asked by real users. Third, the testing system is not an operational one. Rather, it is designed merely for the experiments. Obviously, it is impossible to control test variables (e.g., number of terms in a query, time spent on document retrieval) involved in an operational system. Therefore, what has been found in the artificial Cranfield test environment may not be applicable to operational IRR systems.

11.3.1.4 Significance of the Cranfield Tests

In spite of all the criticisms, the Cranfield tests have exerted a great impact on many other evaluation projects in the following ways. First, the Cranfield tests identified the major factors that affect the performance of retrieval systems. Indexing languages and indexing devices are some examples of such factors. Second, the Cranfield tests developed for the first time a methodology that is still with us in TREC despite its many defects. Third, the Cranfield tests have manifestly influenced our view of IR systems and how we should study them, almost entirely for the good (Sparck Jones, 1981). Fourth, the Cranfield tests also pointed the way forward to effective and attainable automatic indexing methods because they demonstrated that uniterm and natural language systems tend to perform the same as, if not better than, controlled vocabulary systems.

The significance of the Cranfield tests cannot be overstated even though their problems appear serious. As far as the evaluation of IRR systems is concerned, all major projects, including the TREC series, are influenced by the Cranfield tests in one way or another. Not a single large-scale evaluation project becomes an exception in the field of information representation and retrieval. That is the very reason why the term "Cranfield-like projects" was coined.

11.3.2 The TREC Series

The TREC (Text REtrieval Conference) series constitutes a succession of conferences that have been held in the United States annually since 1992 (i.e., TREC-1) with the intention to meet the following goals (Anonymity, 2000):

- To encourage research in text retrieval based on large text data collections

- To increase communication among industry, academia, and government by creating an open forum for the exchange of research ideas

- To speed the transfer of technology from research labs into commercial products by demonstrating substantial improvements in retrieval methodologies on real-world problems

- To increase the availability of the appropriate evaluation techniques for use by industry and academia, including development of new evaluation techniques more applicable to current systems

The conferences have been jointly sponsored by the National Institute of Standards and Technology (NIST), the Defense Advanced Research Projects Agency (DARPA), and other related agencies or institutions (e.g., the Advanced Research and Development Activity – ARDA office of the Department of Defense) in the United States.

By the end of 2001, 10 TREC conferences had been held. Although specifics about the TREC series have been changed over the years, e.g., participants and tracks (i.e., subproblems in information retrieval), the goals for the largest evaluation endeavor in the history of information representation and retrieval remain the same.

11.3.2.1 The Design of the TREC Series

The TREC series, unlike the Cranfield tests, is an ongoing evaluation undertaking that involves various participating teams that develop their own retrieval systems. Every time, teams that decide to take part in a particular TREC obtain the test collection and related information provided by the conference sponsors. The actual retrieving is completed at the home base of the participating teams. Top-ranked retrieval results are submitted to the sponsors for evaluation. The participating teams of each TREC also meet at a preset time to exchange their viewpoints and experience, and make plans for the next TREC.

11.3.2.1.1 Participant Teams

Participating teams of TREC (e.g., Bellcore, Carnegie Mellon University) come from industry, academia, and government as well as from countries other than the United States. Participation in TREC was by invitation only in the beginning, but is now open to all who are able to take part in the project. Table 11.4 gives the number of participating teams in the first nine TRECs.

Table 11.4   Number of Participating Teams in TREC

TREC	Year	Number of Teams
TREC-1	1992	25
TREC-2	1993	31
TREC-3	1994	33
TREC-4	1995	36
TREC-5	1996	38
TREC-6	1997	51
TREC-7	1998	56
TREC-8	1999	66
TREC-9	2000	69

The participating teams are able to choose from three levels of participation: full participation, full participation using one-quarter of the full document set, and participation in evaluation only to allow commercial systems to protect proprietary algorithms (Harman, 1995).

11.3.2.1.2 Test Documents

The test documents were collected mainly from newspapers (e.g., *Wall Street Journal*), newswires (e.g., Associated Press Newswire), and other kinds of sources (e.g., Federal Register). They were uniformly formatted into Standard Generalized Markup Language (SGML) and distributed as CD-ROMs with about 1 gigabyte (GB) of data each. TREC-1 started with two disks of test data, the number of disks used in the experiments eventually increased to five. Disk 4 and 5 contain data for the ad hoc task to be described below. The document lengths range from 300 to 400 terms to several hundred pages. The test set consists of more than one million documents.

11.3.2.1.3 Topics and Queries

Topics for retrieval are written by people who are actually users of a retrieval system and devised to mimic real users' needs. The topics are constructed by doing trial retrievals against a sample of the document set, and then those topics that have roughly 25 to 100 hits in that sample are selected. Each topic is formatted in the same standard method (i.e., in SGML with a sequential number, a short title, one sentence description, and the like) to allow easier automatic construction of queries. The same 50 topics are created for the routing task in every TREC, and 50 new additional topics are generated for each TREC for the ad hoc task. The ad hoc and routing retrieval tasks of TREC will be explained shortly. Training topics are also prepared for participants to get to know the test data set. The quality of topics for TREC-1 and TREC-2 was so high that it was possible to reach a very good level of performance without unduly demanding indexing and searching strategies. Therefore, the topics have been prepared from TREC-3 onward with an eye to great realism while recognizing diagnostic interests in laboratory evaluation (Sparck Jones, 2000).

Retrieval queries are constructed based on the questions either automatically or manually. The manual method could possibly be used with some machine assistance. Some ad hoc queries were formulated using relevance feedback.

11.3.2.1.4 Retrieval Tasks

Two types of retrieval tasks, ad hoc and routing, are examined in TREC. Ad hoc tasks correspond to retrospective retrieval, i.e., finding all the information on a certain topic, while routing retrieval matches with Selective Dissemination of Information (SDI) by locating newly produced information about a query.

Starting from TREC-4, a set of additional retrieval tasks, called "tracks," has been introduced, each focusing on a particular retrieval subproblem. Sparck Jones (2000) explained about tracks by making the following apt analogy:

> Informally, TREC as a whole can be seen as a wheel, with a central hub (the ad hoc task) and radiating spokes (tracks) linked both to the hub and round the rim to one another. New spokes can be inserted, existing ones strengthened, or worn-out ones removed. We can thus look for a continuously improved TREC IR wheel, and indeed not just with more and better spokes, but with hub and rim redesign and reinforcement as well. (pp. 43–44)

Table 11.5 lists the tracks covered from TREC-4 to TREC-10, which is also known as TREC 2001. In recognition that sufficient infrastructure exists to support researchers interested in retrospective retrieval task, the ad hoc task was discontinued in TREC-9 so that more TREC resources could be allocated to building evaluation infrastructure for tracks (Voorhees, 2000).

Given the fact that the routing task has been merged with the Filtering track since TREC-7, all the retrieval tasks probed in recent TRECs are in the form of tracks.

A total of 14 tracks had been created by 2001, reflecting the research focuses of the IR community in recent years. While some tracks have been discontinued, new ones have also been established to investigate emerging problems in information retrieval. Based on the overviews and reflections

Table 11.5 An Overview of TREC Tracks

TRACKS	TREC-4	TREC-5	TREC-6	TREC-7	TREC-8	TREC-9	TREC-10
Interactive	X	X	X	X	X	X	X
Database Merging	X	X					
Multilingual	Spanish	Spanish Chinese	Chinese				
Confusion	X	X					
SDR			X	X	X	X	
Filtering	X	X	X	X	X	X	X
NLP		X	X				
VLC		X	X	X			
CLIR			X	X	X	X	X
High Precision			X	X			
Query				X	X	X	
QA					X	X	X
Web					X	X	X
Video							X

prepared for all the TRECs held so far (e.g., Harman, 1995; Sparck Jones, 1995 & 2000; Voorhees 2000; Voorhees & Harman, 2000), a brief description is provided for each track listed alphabetically below.

- *The Confusion track* represented efforts in dealing with corrupted data that would come from, for example, OCR or speech input. Data of that nature is also called noisy or confused data. It was run in TREC-4 and TREC-5. This track is related to the fuzzy searching discussed in §5.1.2.1 of this book.

- *The Cross-Language (CLIR) track* is a task in which documents cover several languages (e.g., English, German, French, or Italian) and topics are in each language. The focus of this track is to retrieve documents in one target language using topics written in a different language. Participants also performed monolingual runs in the target language to act as a baseline. In TREC-10, the focus of this track was on retrieving Arabic documents using English or French topics.

- *The Database Merging track* was only run in TREC-4 and TREC-5, not in any other TRECs. It investigated methods for handling heterogeneous collections such as producing a single document ranking for queries when the underlying data sets were diverse.

- *The Filtering track* is regarded as the "real" form of the routing task, which has been merged with this track since TREC-7. The Filtering track deals with the task in which the topics are stable and some relevant documents are known. But there is a stream of new documents being added into the system. For each document, the system must make a binary decision as to whether the document should be retrieved as opposed to forming a ranked list. It is one of the two tracks (the other being the Interactive track) that have been run in every TREC so far.

- *The Interactive track* is a task for studying user interaction with text retrieval systems, and for developing methodologies for interactive evaluation. It is one of the two tracks (the other being the Filtering track) that have been investigated in every TREC so far. The task in TREC-10 involved observing subjects using the live Web to accomplish a specific task (Voorhees & Harman, 2002).

- *The High-Precision track* tested the effectiveness, efficiency, and user interface of participating systems in TREC-6 and TREC-7. Using the same 50 topics and documents set as the ad hoc task, a user was asked to find 10 documents that answer the topic within five minutes. Users could not collaborate on a single topic, nor could the system or user have prior knowledge about the topic. Otherwise, the user was free to consult any available sources as long as the retrieval time did not exceed the limit of five minutes.

- *The Multilingual track* considered issues of retrieval in languages other than English. A preliminary Spanish test was carried out in TREC-4, with a formal track in TREC-5. Chinese retrieval was examined in TREC-5 and TREC-6.

- *The Natural Language Processing (NLP) track* explored in TREC-5 and TREC-6 if the NLP techniques (syntactic and semantic) available were mature enough to have an impact on IR, and if they could offer an advantage over purely quantitative (e.g., statistical) retrieval methods.

- *The Query track* was introduced in TREC-7 to foster research on the effects of query variability and analysis on retrieval performance. Participants each constructed several different versions of existing TREC topics, mostly concentrating on different natural language versions of the topics. All groups then ran the various versions. The track ceased to be a track after TREC-9 and would evolve into a "station." That is, the TREC Web site (http://trec.nist.gov) will serve as a repository for both query statements and retrieval results produced from those queries.

- *The Question Answering (QA) track* started in TREC-8 to take a step closer to information retrieval (i.e., passage retrieval) rather than document retrieval. For test questions, systems produce a text extract that answers the question. Different runs will have different limits on the maximum length of the extract, ranging from a short phrase (2–3 words) to an entire document (1,000 words). TREC-10 conducted a pilot study using questions that require information from multiple documents to be combined to form a correct answer (Voorhees & Harman, 2002).

- *The Spoken Document Retrieval (SDR) track* is a successor of the Confusion track, investigating a retrieval system's ability to retrieve spoken documents (i.e., recordings of speech). This track is being offered with the support of the speech group at NIST. Participants compared the effectiveness of their retrieval system on human-produced transcripts of broadcast news, on transcripts produced by a baseline speech recognition system, and, optionally, on transcripts produced by their own recognizer. The SDR track is discontinued in TREC-10.

- *The Very Large Corpus (VLC) track* had a trial run in TREC-5 and was discontinued in TREC-7. It performed ad hoc searches on approximately 20 gigabytes (GB) of text, exploring the effectiveness and efficiency of retrieval. Participants were evaluated on precision of the top 20 documents retrieved, query response time, data structure building time, and some cost measures.

- *The Video track*, new in TREC-10, focused on content-based access to digital video to continue TREC's interest in multimedia retrieval (Voorhees & Harman, 2002).

- *The Web track* features ad hoc tasks whose document set is a snapshot of the World Wide Web. The main task involves approximately 10GB of Web data. Participants are encouraged to investigate a variety of Web retrieval strategies such as whether links can be used to enhance retrieval. The track started in TREC-8 and would continue in TREC 2002.

The previous description of all the tracks illustrates the magnitude and extent of retrieval tasks investigated in TREC. Some of the tracks actually go beyond the goals TREC initially set. For example, TREC is essentially an evaluation project in text retrieval. Yet, a track on video retrieval was run in TREC-10. Such tracks, as Sparck Jones (2000) put it, are extensions of TREC.

11.3.2.1.5 Evaluation and Relevance Judgments

Evaluation in TREC has used traditional recall and precision measures so relevance judgment is a must. People who created the topics are also assessors for making evaluation. The pooling method described in §11.1.2.1.2 was used to form the data pool for assessment in all TRECs. Each participating team submits to the sponsors the top 100 documents retrieved in each run for a given topic, as a ranking algorithm is implemented in all the test systems to output retrieval results in the order of perceived relevance.

An assessor on average judges approximately 2,000 documents per topic. The completeness and consistency of TREC judgments were checked in separate studies, and the outcomes appear positive (Voorhees & Harman, 2000). A standard evaluation package is used to record each of the submitted runs. The evaluation measure used most frequently in TREC is the average precision we discussed in §11.1.2.1.4. Other kinds of recall- and precision-based evaluation measures are also computed in TREC. Sparck Jones (2000) summarized track performance measures applied from TREC-4 to TREC-6 in her review.

11.3.2.2 Findings of TREC

The findings in TREC are too many and diversified to be enumerated in this short subsection. Therefore, only the general ones are recapitulated as follows:

Many very different approaches give similar performance, indicating that "All roads lead to Rome" and different methods can be sought to achieve the same objective.

Automatic processing (i.e., query construction or retrieval) is as good as manual processing, but may not be quite so convincing for poor queries.

Statistically based indexing and searching techniques are cheap and competitive, particularly for large collections or databases. They can do much better than simple term baselines although they need to subsume some collection training.

Simple phrases along with single terms contribute something, implying additional promise for automatic methods in the field.

Relevance feedback is valuable, and moderate query expansion seems helpful. However, there is not much progress in TREC toward the goal of designing effective individual query, as opposed to query class, strategies for the ad hoc task. In other words, a system still cannot automatically analyze a request for the implications of its term makeup and choose one particular query formation strategy that is likely to give best results.

11.3.2.3 Problems with TREC

The main criticism to TREC is that it basically follows the footsteps of the Cranfield tests by using an artificial test environment, and choosing recall and precision as retrieval performance measures.

The artificiality of the TREC series is threefold. First, the test documents, consisting of mainly newspapers, are gathered for the project rather than a collection naturally built over the years. While newspapers can be a valuable source for many other purposes, they are not heavily consulted for most research endeavors. Second, TREC does not have genuine and hands-on users. The topics or search requests, as in Cranfield, are manufactured specifically for the project. The retrieval is done by system developers, and retrieval performance is judged by assessors who also created the topics. Third, the tests are done in the traditional laboratory environment with a certain degree of control and manipulation. It is hard to relate such an environment to the real, operational system.

In addition, there are problems associated with the evaluation methodology adopted in TREC. On one hand, the limitations of using recall and precision as evaluation criteria for retrieval performance are all present in TREC because recall and precision are the major selected measures for assessment in the project. On the other hand, only the top-ranked results retrieved from each system are pooled for evaluation. The TREC assessments would consequently appear better than the cases if all the results were included in the evaluation. According to the research reported by Zobel (1998), the recall in TREC was overestimated. Moreover, the need for more statistical evaluation seems obvious as the recall-precision curves provided by each participating team are often close, and there is a need to check whether there is truly any statistically significant differences between two systems' results or two sets of results from the same system. It also seems necessary to get beyond the averages to better understand systems performance. In addition, it is very difficult to perform failure analysis on the results because of the huge number of test documents involved and the threshold set for retrieval outputs (Harman, 1995).

Overall, TREC uses the black box approach for evaluation, with systems compared as wholes for performance through their team run results (Sparck Jones, 2000). Little knowledge has been gained about how a particular strategy or device makes the system performance change even though TREC has been held since 1992. The glass box approach is apparently needed for the evaluation task.

11.3.2.4 Significance of TREC

With many of its unique features (e.g., test document size and the increasing number of participating teams), TREC holds a significant place in the history of information representation and retrieval evaluation. Its significance has been reflected in the following aspects.

First, it provides an open and stimulating forum for evaluating information representation and retrieval. By being an open forum, it has encouraged participation by many institutions and organizations from home and abroad. By being a stimulating forum, it has motivated participants to further improve their systems. Indeed, for instance, significant improvement in retrieval performance was observed in TREC-2 over that in TREC-1 (Sparck Jones, 1995).

Second, many different approaches have been tried in TREC, which include passage retrieval, data fusion, statistical and probabilistic indexing, and term weighting strategies. The Boolean retrieval mechanism, although important, is no longer dominant in the project. In addition, the test collection size reaches the magnitude of gigabytes instead of megabytes as in earlier evaluation efforts, thus getting closer to the real-life situation in terms of volume. TREC has been evolving to equate closer to a real-world operational environment that allows transition of the test results to the inclusion in commercial products with known benefits (Kowalski & Maybury, 2000).

Third, TREC is more generalizable than many other projects in part because it is a continuing research effort. It attempts to answer many questions, which can be put into such broad categories as indexing and retrieval models, indexing vocabulary, document descriptions, indexing sources, queries and query sources, search strategy, scoring criteria, and learning ability of IR systems (Sparck Jones, 2000).

In all, TREC is of great importance to the field. New research possibilities have also been suggested for the future, which include:

- Hold TREC less frequently so that time can be spent on digesting the results obtained so far.

- Concentrate effort on fewer tasks or tracks to pursue them in more depth.

- Get real users involved in the project to improve the applicability of the research findings.

- Place the application of IR test findings up front, and move TREC more firmly toward studies of retrieval in operational contexts.

- Adopt the glass box evaluation approach by engaging individual teams at the particular strategy, device, or even parameter level rather than using the black box approach by comparing systems as wholes for performance through their team run results.

- Embark on multiple-task studies by applying the TREC experience in it. Retrieval will be examined as only one component of a system, which also offers, for example, automatic summarization of retrieved texts.

11.4 A Final Word on IRR Evaluation

The Cranfield tests and TREC series symbolize the problems and issues in IRR evaluation. Generally speaking, most evaluation projects are carried out in laboratories rather than real-life situations with artificial collections and manufactured requests. The size of test collection is usually small although the TREC series is an exception. Recall, precision, and fallout are predominantly used as evaluation measures. Yet they are unreliable since, among other concerns, they are based on subjective judgments of relevance. In addition, most evaluation projects focus on these individual criteria (e.g., recall and precision) without a framework for evaluating the entire system. After all the efforts, we have learned what happens in such systems, but it is not quite clear as to why it happens and how it happens because of the black box evaluation approach.

Proposals and suggestions have been made to advance research in evaluating information representation and retrieval by going beyond the existing models and implementing methodology pluralism. For example, Harter and Hert (1997) described an emerging framework for IRR evaluation, emphasizing the use of multiple dimensions and methods, and evaluation from the perspective of several IRR system stakeholders. They also believe strongly that user-system interaction must be considered during the evaluation process in the digital age. On the other hand, future evaluation projects should be done in a real-life environment and use measures other than recall, precision, and fallout to overcome the two most notorious limitations of previous assessments in the field, namely, subjectivity in judging relevance and inability to determine the total number of relevant documents in a system.

References

Anonymity. (2000). Overview [of TREC]. http://trec.nist.gov/overview.html. (June 17, 2001)

Bell, Hazel K. (1991). Bias in indexing and loaded language. *The Indexer, 17(3),* 173–177.

Blair, D.C., and Maron, M.E. (1985). An evaluation of retrieval effectiveness for a full-text document retrieval system. *Communications of the ACM, 28(3)*, 289–299.

Chowdhury, Gobinda G. (1999). *Introduction to modern information retrieval.* London: Library Association Publishing.

Chu, Heting, and Rosenthal, Marilyn. (1996). Search engines for the World Wide Web: A comparative study and evaluation methodology. *Proceedings of the 59th Annual Meeting of the American Society for Information Science, 33,* 127–135. Or, http://www.asis.org/annual-96/Electronic Proceedings/chu.html.

Clarke, S.J., and Willett, P. (1997). Estimating the recall performance of Web search engines. *Aslib Proceedings, 49(7),* 184–189.

Cleverdon, C.W. (1962). *Report on the testing and analysis of an investigation into the comparative efficiency of indexing systems.* Cranfield: College of Aeronautics.

Cleverdon, C.W. (1967). The Cranfield tests on indexing language devices. *Aslib Proceedings, 19,* 173–192.

Cleverdon, C.W. (1984). Optimizing convenient online access to bibliographic databases. *Information Services and Use, 4(1-2),* 37–47.

Cleverdon, C.W., and Mills, J. (1963). The testing of indexing language devices. *Aslib Proceedings, 15(4),* 106–130.

Cleverdon, C.W., Mills, J., and Keen, E.M. (1966). *Factors determining the performance of indexing systems, Vol. 1 – Design.* Cranfield, England: Aslib Cranfield Research Project.

Cooper, William S. (1973a). On selecting a measure of retrieval effectiveness. Part I. *Journal of the American Society for Information Science, 24,* 87–100.

Cooper, William S. (1973b). On selecting a measure of retrieval effectiveness. Part II. *Journal of the American Society for Information Science, 24,* 413–424.

Ding, Wei, and Marchionini, Gary. (1996). A comparative study of Web search service performance. *Proceedings of the 59th Annual Meeting of the American Society for Information Science, 33,* 136–142.

Foskett, A.C. (1996). *Subject approach to information.* 5th ed. London: Library Association Publishing.

Froehlich, Thomas J. (1994). Relevance revisited—Towards an agenda for the 21st century: Introduction to special topic issue on relevance research. *Journal of the American Society for Information Science, 45(3),* 123–134.

Fugmann, Robert. (1993). *Subject analysis and indexing: Theoretical foundation and practical advice.* Frankfurt/Main: Indeks Verlag.

Griffith, Belver C. (1986). Evaluation of information systems: Class notes. Philadelphia: Drexel University, College of Information Studies.

Harman, Donna. (1993). A special conference report: The first Text Retrieval Conference (TREC-1) Rockville, MD, U.S.A., 4–6 Nov. 1992. *Information Processing & Management, 29(4),* 411–414.

Harman, Donna. (1995). Overview of the second Text Retrieval Conference (TREC-2). *Information Processing & Management, 31(3),* 271–290.

Harry, Veronica, and Oppenheim, Charles. (1993a). Evaluation of electronic databases, Part I: Criteria for testing CD-ROM products. *Online & CDROM Review, 17(4),* 211–222.

Harry, Veronica, and Oppenheim, Charles. (1993b). Evaluation of electronic databases, Part II: Testing CD-ROM products. *Online & CDROM Review, 17(6),* 339–347.

Harter, S.F. (1971). The Cranfield II relevance assessments: A critical evaluation. *Library Quarterly, 41,* 229–243.

Harter, Stephen P., and Hert, Carol A. (1997). Evaluation of information retrieval systems: Approaches, issues, and methods. *Annual Review of Information Science and Technology, 32,* 3–94.

Hildreth, Charles R. (1982). *Online public access catalogues: The user interface.* Dublin, OH: OCLC.

Hildreth, Charles R. (1985). Online public access catalogs. *Annual Review of Information Science and Technology, 20,* 233–285.

Hooper, R.S. (1965). *Indexer consistency tests – Origin, measurements, results and utilization.* Bethesda, MD: IBM.

Ingwersen, Peter. (1996). Cognitive perspectives of information retrieval interaction: Elements of a cognitive IR theory. *Journal of Documentation, 52(1),* 3–50.

Keen, E.M. (1971). Evaluation parameters. In Gerard Salton. (Ed.), *The SMART retrieval system: Experiments in automatic document processing* (pp. 74–111). Englewood Cliffs, NJ: Prentice Hall.

Kent, Allen, et al. (1955). Machine literature searching. VIII. Operational criteria for designing information retrieval systems. *American Documentation, 6(2),* 93–101.

Korfhage, Robert R. (1997). *Information storage and retrieval.* New York: John Wiley & Sons.

Kowalski, Gerald, and Maybury, Mark T. (2000). *Information storage and retrieval systems: Theory and implementation.* 2nd ed. Boston: Kluwer Academic Publishers.

Lancaster, F.W. (1968). *Evaluation of the MEDLARS demand search service.* Bethesda, MD: National Library of Medicine.

Lancaster, F.W. (1979). *Information retrieval systems: Characteristics, testing and evaluation.* 2nd ed. New York: Wiley.

Lancaster, F.W. (1998). *Indexing and abstracting in theory and practice.* 2nd ed. Champaign-Urbana, IL: University of Illinois, Graduate School of Library and Information Science.

Lancaster, F.W., and Fayen, E.G. (1973). *Information retrieval online.* Los Angeles: Melville Publishing Co.

Lancaster, F.W., and Warner, Amy J. (1993). *Information retrieval today.* Arlington, VA: Information Resources Press.

Large, Andrew. (1989). Evaluating online and CD-ROM reference sources. *Journal of Librarianship, 21(2),* 87–108.

Large, Andrew, Tedd, Lucy A., and Hartley, R.J. (1999). *Information seeking in the online age: Principles and practice.* London: Bowker-Saur.

Leighton, H. Vernon. (1995). Performance of four World Wide Web (WWW) index services: Infoseek, Lycos, WebCrawler, and WWWWorm. http://www.winona.msus.edu/library/webind.htm. (June 11, 2001)

Leighton, H. Vernon, and Srivastava, Jaideep. (1997). Precision among World Wide Web search services (search engines): Alta Vista, Excite, Hotbot, Infoseek, Lycos. http://www.winona.msus.edu/library/webind2/webind2.htm. (June 11, 2001)

Miller, C., and Tegler, P. (1986). Online searching and the research process. *College and Research Libraries, 47(4),* 370–373.

Mizzaro, Stefno. (1997). Relevance: The whole history. *Journal of the American Society for Information Science, 48(9),* 801–832.

Nahl-Jakobovits, Diana, and Tenopir, Carol. (1992). Databases online and on CD-ROMs: How do they differ? Let us count the ways. *Database, 15(1),* 42–50.

NewsFactor Network. (May 31, 2001). English still rules on Web, but times are changing. http://www.newsfactor.com. (June 1, 2001)

O'Rourke, Victoria. (1987). Selection of an online public access catalog: A checklist approach. *Information Technology and Libraries, 6(4),* 278–287.

Richards, T., and Robinson, C. (September 1993). Evaluating CD-ROM software: A model. *CD-ROM Professional,* 92–101.

Robertson, Stephen E. (1969). The parametric description of retrieval tests. Part I: The basic parameters . *Journal of Documentation, 25(12),* 1–27.

Rowley, Jennifer, and Slack, Frances. (1997). The evaluation of interface design on CD-ROMs. *Online and CD-ROM Review, 21(1),* 3–11.

Salmon, Stephen R. (1983). Characteristics of online public catalogs. *Library Resources & Technical Services, 27(1),* 36–67.

Salton, Gerard. (1981). The SMART environment for retrieval system evaluation: Advantages and problem areas. In Karen Sparck Jones. (Ed.), *Information retrieval experiment* (pp. 316–329). London: Butterworth.

Salton, Gerard. (1992). The state of retrieval system evaluation. *Information Processing & Management, 28(4),* 441–449.

Saracevic, Tefko. (1975). Relevance: A review of the literature and a framework for thinking on the notion in information science. *Journal of the American Society for Information Science, 26(6),* 321–343.

Saracevic, Tefko, and Kantor, Paul. (1988). A study of information seeking and retrieving. Part II: Users, questions, and effectiveness. *Journal of the American Society for Information Science, 39(3),* 177–196.

Saracevic, Tefko, et al. (1988). A study of information seeking and retrieving. Part I: Background and methodology. *Journal of the American Society for Information Science, 39(3),* 161–176.

Schamber, Linda. (1994). Relevance and information behavior. *Annual Review of Information Science and Technology, 29,* 3–48.

Schamber, Linda, Eisenberg, Michael B., and Nilan, Michael S. (1990). A reexamination of relevance: Toward a dynamic, situational definition. *Information Processing & Management, 26(6),* 755–776.

Sparck Jones, Karen. (1981). The Cranfield tests. In Karen Sparck Jones. (Ed.), *Information retrieval experiments* (pp. 256–284). London: Butterworths.

Sparck Jones, Karen. (1995). Reflections on TREC. *Information Processing & Management, 31(3),* 191–314.

Sparck Jones, Karen. (2000). Further reflections on TREC. *Information Processing & Management, 36(1),* 37–85.

Su, Louise T. (1991). *An investigation to find appropriate measures for evaluating interactive information retrieval.* Unpublished Ph.D. Dissertation. New Brunswick, NJ: Rutgers, the State University of New Jersey.

Swanson, Don R. (1965). The evidence underlying the Cranfield results. *Library Quarterly, 35(1),* 1–20.

Swanson, Don R. (1971). Some unexplained aspects of the Cranfield tests of indexing performance factors. *Library Quarterly, 41(3),* 223–228.

Swanson, Rowena Weiss. (1978). Performing evaluation studies in information science. In D.W. King (Ed.). *Key papers in design and evaluation of retrieval systems* (pp. 58–74). New York: Knowledge Industry.

Swets, John A. (1963). Information retrieval systems. *Science, 141,* 245–250.

Swets, John A. (1969). Effectiveness of information retrieval methods. *American Documentation, 20(1),* 72–89.

Vickery, B.C. (1966). Review of Cleverdon, Mills, and Keen. *Journal of Documentation, 22,* 247–249.

Vickery, B.C. (1967). Review of Cleverdon and Keen. *Journal of Documentation, 23,* 338–340.

Voorhees, Ellen M. (2000). Report on TREC-9. *SIGIR Forum, 34(2),* 1–8.

Voorhees, Ellen M., and Harman, Donna. (2000). Overview of the sixth Text REtrieval Conference (TREC-6). *Information Processing & Management, 36(1),* 3–35.

Voorhees, Ellen M., and Harman, Donna. (2002). Overview of TREC 2001. *Proceedings of the Tenth Text REtrieval Conference (TREC 2001),* (pp. 1–15). NIST Special Publication 500-250. http://trec.nist.gov/pubs/trec10/papers/overview_10.pdf. (September 2, 2002)

Wellisch, Hans H. (1995). *Indexing from A to Z.* 2nd ed. New York: H.W. Wilson.

Zobel, J. (1998). How reliable are the results of large-scale information retrieval experiments? *Proceedings of the 21 Annual International Conference on Research and Development in Information Retrieval—SIGIR-98* (pp. 307–314). New York: Association for Computing Machinery.

CHAPTER 12

Artificial Intelligence in Information Representation and Retrieval

Artificial intelligence (AI) is a field aiming to make machines do things that would require intelligence if done by people. The IRR community has shown great interest in AI research, hoping to bring AI applications to information representation and retrieval. Although AI researchers have experienced excitement as well as disappointment in pursuing their goals, their enthusiasm has not waned. To the contrary, an increasing number of attempts have been made to develop AI applications for representing and retrieving information particularly since the Web became the major platform for IRR. This chapter provides an overview of AI research in the context of information representation and retrieval. Two active AI research areas for IRR, natural language processing and intelligent agents, are discussed, in addition to the limitations and potential of AI research for information representation and retrieval.

12.1 Overview of AI Research

Artificial intelligence has been established as a research field at least since 1956, when the Dartmouth Conference was held (Sparck Jones, 1991). The goal of AI is to develop systems that behave intelligently, using computers to carry out tasks that require reasoning on world knowledge. Knowledge in AI should be interpreted as a combination of information, facts, rules of thumb, or even the intuition and common sense necessary for intellectual activities such as solving problems and making decisions. More importantly, AI is supposed to have a component that is able to reason, like human beings, in situations where only partial knowledge or indirect connectivity is available. For example, an AI system for information representation should be able to generate broader, narrower, and related terms according to the content of a document. In other words, the system needs to be able to identify and establish relationships among the terms contained in the document. The system must have artificial intelligence, mimicking human intelligence, to complete the task.

Knowledge in AI is obtained via the knowledge engineering process in which the knowledge engineer acquires knowledge from the domain expert, a person extremely knowledgeable about a specific area or domain, by such methods as interview, observation, and thinking-aloud protocols. The acquired knowledge is then represented using, for instance, production rules, semantic networks, or frames to form a knowledge base. The knowledge base, along with other provisions (e.g., inference engine and self-learning facility), makes up an AI application.

AI researchers aspire to develop applications for many areas (e.g., robotics and pattern recognition), and information representation and retrieval is one of them. Efforts have been made in IRR to apply AI to, among other things, information representation, query formulation, search performance improvement, output ranking and visualization. Natural language processing and intelligent agents appear to be the two AI research areas that may contribute the most to the field of information representation and retrieval.

12.2 Natural Language Processing

Natural language processing (NLP) is an area of research and application that explores how the natural language text, entered into a computer system, can be manipulated and transformed into a form more suitable for further manipulation (Chowdhury, 1999). It draws heavily from natural language understanding, a subdivision of AI research, which includes question and answering, speech recognition, machine translation, machine learning, and expert systems.

12.2.1 The Role of Natural Language Processing in IRR

Language, spoken or written, is an essential component in both information representation and information retrieval, as information has to be expressed in a language when being processed, transferred, or communicated. Natural language in IRR, as opposed to any other artificial language, is the language people would naturally use to represent information or form a query. Natural language can be processed in AI at phonological, morphological, lexical, syntactic, semantic, and pragmatic levels (Doszkocs, 1986), and each holds implications for information representation and retrieval.

The phonological level analysis involves treatment of speech sounds. This type of processing could be important in sound retrieval (see §9.2.2), which includes, for example, voice input or spoken information. The "sound like" feature in information retrieval (e.g., find documents containing terms that sound like "music") can only be implemented at the phonological level of natural language processing.

The morphological level of processing deals with constituencies used to make up individual words, e.g., word stems or bases, prefixes, infixes, suffixes, and compound words. For example, the word *uniterm* consists of the prefix *uni* and word base *term*. Truncation is a retrieval technique that derives from this level of processing. Information representation such as automatic indexing can also be done, to a certain degree, with documents processed at the morphological level.

Lexical level processing typically refers to the signification and application of words, for example, determining whether *book* is meant as in a publication or as in making a reservation. Implications for IRR with this level of language analysis include: 1) stop-word removal, 2) automatic search term substitution and augmentation (e.g., thesaurus lookups), 3) spelling error detection and correction, and 4) the handling of acronyms and abbreviations through lookups in word lists.

The syntactic level analysis parses sentences to make the grammatical relationships between words in sentences clear. For example, is the structural unit in a sentence, a phrase, or a clause? This process also involves the need for a grammar that describes the possible word order and different rules of agreement. Noun phrases, for instance, identified in the syntactic level analysis can be candidates for indexing terms. Phrase searching and proximity searching are all applications of language processed at the syntactic level.

Semantic level processing tries to assign meaning to the various syntactic constituents in a sentence. Various semantic aids (e.g., thesaurus) might be needed to conduct language analysis at this level. Sample applications in this regard for IRR consist of automatic display of cross references, synonyms, and related terms. However, semantic level processing cannot be successfully completed without language analysis at the pragmatic level.

The pragmatic level, the highest level of language processing, attempts to decide the meaning of the language by considering the surrounding context, the author, the user, and knowledge of the real world. This level of processing presents the greatest challenge to AI researchers in natural language processing. Indeed, human beings depend on context and other knowledge to understand language and eliminate meaning ambiguity. Yet the complexity and difficulty involved in the process are still not fully comprehended, and systems have not yet been developed that can imitate how human beings process language at this level. The application of this process to IRR would be extraordinary and of fundamental significance if a breakthrough in NLP at this level can be achieved. Many applications that have been dreamed of in IRR, e.g., automatic summarization and natural language query, could then come true. Vocabulary switching, briefly described in §4.4 as a mechanism for automatically changing from one IRR language to another across different subject domains, would also benefit from this line of AI research.

If language processing can be done successfully at the semantic and pragmatic level, the semantic Web envisioned by Berners-Lee, Hendler, and

Lassila (2001) would become a reality in processing the semantics of Web pages (e.g., here a site about artificial intelligence, there a link to an AI research lab) rather than merely parsing Web pages for layout and format specifics (e.g., here a header, there a link to another page). The authors even optimistically predict that the semantic Web will not "merely" be the tool for conducting individual tasks such as knowledge representation as described in their writing: if properly designed, they believe it can assist the evolution of human knowledge as a whole. Again, this will not happen until natural language can be effectively processed at the semantic and pragmatic level.

The six different levels involved in natural language processing define what NLP can do for information representation and retrieval. While the first four levels of processing can be done reasonably well today, further research into performing language analysis at the semantic level, and especially the pragmatic level, is called for. Research efforts in computational linguistics, linguistics in general, philosophy of language, and socio-linguistics would facilitate AI research in natural language processing (Cercone & McCalla, 1984).

12.2.2 The Natural Language Model

The natural language model in IR relies largely on NLP research, which is a feature shared by the so-called linguistics model in IR. The linguistic model is converging with the natural language model as research in NLP progresses. For this reason, the linguistic model will not be discussed separately nor any further in this book.

The core of the natural language model is the use of natural language for information retrieval. Natural language in this context means the use of language for retrieval without artificial elements or close human involvement. For example, the user no longer needs to do concept analysis, select search terms, and consider search strategies when formulating queries in IR systems that support the natural language model. Instead, the user can just enter the query in phrases, sentences, or any other form of natural language. Ask Jeeves, for instance, allows users to enter a query the same way as they ask a question (e.g., why is the sky blue?). The NLP track set up in TREC-5 and TREC-6 was devoted to the topic of natural language processing (Voorhees & Harman, 2000).

The natural language IR model is actually implemented in two different ways. One is to offer a natural language front-end so that the onerous tasks of, for example, converting a natural language query into what the IR system can understand take place behind the scene. Ask Jeeves falls into this category because it prepares answers to preconstructed questions that the user may ask. If the user happens to ask a question that matches one of those anticipated by Ask Jeeves, the answer could be literally perfect both in terms of quality and quantity. If the question is not anticipated, retrieval output can range from zero hits to results entirely out of scope. The second implementation of the natural language model truly accepts and processes natural language inputs. These inputs would be analyzed, as described previously, at various natural language processing levels for retrieval purpose. DIALOG's TARGET, LexisNexis' FREESTYLE, and Westlaw's WIN, for example, are online system search facilities close to the natural language model (Tenopir & Cahn, 1994). IR systems that are genuinely natural, however, remain a research area.

The constraints of the natural language model lie mainly in the bottlenecks of NLP research, i.e., its inability to analyze language successfully at the semantic and pragmatic level. Users would appreciate the benefits of using natural language in the retrieval process, and this model should have a considerable impact on the user friendliness of IR once it is fully established. In addition, it seems that the natural language model, if applied in conjunction with other methods (e.g., statistical methods) or models (e.g., probability models), would result in better IR systems. As mentioned in §7.6.3, multi-model systems are emerging in the field of information retrieval.

12.3 Intelligent Agents

Intelligent agents, employing assorted AI techniques and in the form of software programs, are able to perform certain tasks without human intervention. Expert systems, on the other hand, are defined as software programs that inform, make recommendations, or solve problems in a manner and at a level of performance comparable to that displayed by a human expert in the field. In essence, expert systems are intelligent agents on a larger scale or the predecessor of intelligent agents. Besides, the word *bots* (i.e., an abbreviation of *robots*) is increasingly used as a synonym for intelligent agents. According to Hendler (1999), an ideal intelligent agent should have four features:

1. Communicative—the ability to understand the user's goals, preferences, and constraints

2. Capable—the ability to take options rather than simply provide advice

3. Autonomous—the ability to act without the user being in control the whole time

4. Adaptive—the ability to learn from experience about its tasks and its users' preferences

The applications of intelligent agents are many and varied, both inside and outside of the IRR field. No matter for what purpose an intelligent agent is created, it should possess the four characteristics Hendler specified. Intelligent agents can be used in many different settings, ranging from our everyday life to complex R&D projects. A great number of agents, mostly in the public domain, can be found at BotSpot (http://www.botspot.com).

Intelligent agents for information representation and retrieval target specific subdivisions of the field. In general, IRR tasks that are well understood, can be explicitly specified, and have a clearly defined boundary would be feasible at present for intelligent agents to accomplish. Selective Dissemination of Information (SDI) is one such example. Intelligent agents monitor one or more IR systems and notify the user when new information appears in the system on a given topic. Categorization of retrieval results, common in Internet retrieval systems because of their huge amount of output, represents another such example. The best-known examples of intelligent agents in IRR are the data collection programs for Internet retrieval systems, referred to variously as crawlers, robots, or spiders. These agents periodically visit target sites, copy certain information, and send it to the system database.

Integrating information retrieved from different sources should, likewise, not be an insurmountable task for intelligent agents. Intelligent agents for more challenging IRR tasks such as query formulation and information representation are being researched. For example, the question-and-answer mechanism implemented in some IR systems is intended to find out by asking questions what a user really wants when making a request for information. Attempts to develop intelligent agents that can compile automatic summaries and abstracts are also on the rise, especially for news and business information. The success of these efforts ultimately depends on research in artificial intelligence.

12.4 AI and Information Representation and Retrieval

How far can AI go in information representation and retrieval? The answer to the question is yet to be found, chiefly because it is not a trivial task to build and program a machine that can successfully imitate the intellectual activities of human beings. This should be the most difficult nut to crack in AI research (Pescovitz, 1999).

The role of AI in information representation and retrieval today is therefore limited and should not be overstated for two reasons. First, complex tasks in IRR depend on extensive world knowledge and on deploying it in a flexible and constructive way. Second, many IRR operations are only shallowly done even by people (Sparck Jones, 1991). Swanson (1988) once commented: "Although the goal of much advanced IR research is to make computers do humanlike things, the possibility that people can be human-like should not be overlooked."

Indeed, the role of people in developing AI applications for information representation and retrieval should not be overlooked. A computer does not have the subtlety, depth, range, and richness of human intelligence because it is still a million times simpler than the human brain (Hefner, 2000). Nevertheless, AI in its current state can make a contribution to situations where the knowledge base or inference can be limited either intrinsically or the user can complement the limitations. AI is also applicable to circumstances where AI algorithms are used in conjunction with other techniques (Sparck Jones, 1991).

Applications for information representation and retrieval based on AI alone or in combination with other techniques are mushrooming. For example, DolphinSearch (http://www.dolphinsearch.com) enables the computer to recognize what a document is about with human-like context-based understanding. ClearForest (http://www.clearforest.com) employs semantic and rule-based technology for reading and analyzing enormous amounts of information from internal sources such as e-mail and company documents, and external sources such as newswires, research archives, and Web sites. It also can understand and visualize context by mapping out interrelationships existing in data, and present the results in a single screen view. Autonomy (http://www.autonomy.com), an AI application that uses pattern recognition, enables the computer to extract meaning from text and then to use that meaning to better categorize and deliver useful information (Silberman, 2000).

Various AI elements are incorporated into these and other applications for information representation and retrieval. Where is the field of information representation and retrieval heading as we enter the digital age? Research and development in artificial intelligence have at least suggested some possibilities.

References

Berners-Lee, Tim, Hendler, James, and Lassila, Ora. (May 2001). The semantic Web. *Scientific American*, 35–43. http://www.scientificamerican.com/2001/0501issue/0501berners-lee.html. (April 24, 2001)

Cercone, Nick, and McCalla, Gordon. (1984). Artificial intelligence: Underlying assumptions and basic objectives. *Journal of the American Society for Information Science, 35(5),* 280–290.

Chowdhury, Gobinda G. (1999). *Introduction to modern information retrieval.* London: Library Association Publishing.

Doszkocs, T.E. (1986). Natural language processing in information retrieval. *Journal of the American Society for Information Science, 37(4),* 191–196.

Hefner, Katie. (December 28, 2000). Artificial intelligence hasn't peaked (yet). *New York Times,* http://www.nytimes.com/2000/12/28/technology/28ARTI.html. (December 28, 2000)

Hendler, James. (March 11, 1999). Is there an intelligent agent in your future? *Nature,* http://helix.nature.com/webmatters/agents.html. (March 11, 1999)

Pescovitz, David. (March 18, 1999). Look what's talking: Software robots. *New York Times,* http://www.nytimes.com/library/tech/99/03/circuits/articles/18bots.html. (March 18, 1999)

Silberman, Steve. (February 8, 2000). The quest for meaning. *Wired,* http://www.wired.com/wired/archive/8.02/autonomy.html. (March 18, 2000)

Sparck Jones, Karen. (1991). The role of artificial intelligence in information retrieval. *Journal of the American Society for Information Science, 42(8),* 558–565.

Swanson, Don R. (1988). Historical note: Information retrieval and the future of an illusion. *Journal of the American Society for Information Science, 39(2),* 92–98.

Tenopir, C., and Cahn, P. (1994). TARGET and FREESTYLE: Dialog and Mead join the relevance ranks. *Online, 18(3),* 31–47.

Voorhees, Ellen M., and Harman, Donna. (2000). Overview of the sixth Text REtrieval Conference (TREC-6). *Information Processing & Management, 36(1),* 3–35.

About the Author

Dr. Heting Chu became an associate professor in the Palmer School of Library & Information Science at Long Island University, New York, in 1994 after being an assistant professor at St. John's University for one year. She obtained her BA from Peking University in Beijing, China. Her master's degree was completed at McGill University, Montreal, Canada. She earned her Ph.D. from Drexel University in Philadelphia. Her educational background plus her teaching and research experience in information representation and retrieval enabled her to write this book. She has published many articles and two monographs (both in Chinese) on information representation and retrieval. She has received numerous requests for reprints and citations of those publications from people all over the world. In addition, she does research on e-books, e-journals, scholarly communication, scientometric analysis of hyperlinks, and Web sites.

Index

Entries are filed word-by-word. Locators followed by *t* indicate tables; locators followed by *f* indicate figures.

More ASIST Titles from Information Today, Inc.

Introductory Concepts in Information Science

Melanie J. Norton

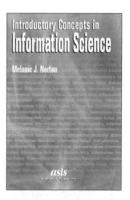

Here is a unique introduction to the practical and theoretical concepts of information science that also examines the impact of the Information Age on society. Drawing on recent research into the field, as well as from scholarly and trade publications, the monograph provides a brief history of information science and coverage of key topics, including communications and cognition, information retrieval, bibliometrics, modeling, economics, information policies, and the impact of information technology on modern management.

2000/127 pp/hardbound/ISBN 1-57387-087-0

ASIST Members $31.60 • Non-Members $39.50

Statistical Methods for the Information Professional

Liwen Vaughan

For most of us, "painless" is not the word that comes to mind when we think of statistics, but author and educator Liwen Vaughan wants to change that. Here, Vaughan clearly explains the statistical methods used in information science research, focusing on basic logic rather than mathematical intricacies. Her emphasis is on the meaning of statistics, when and how to apply them, and how to interpret the results of statistical analysis. Through the use of real-world examples, she shows how statistics can be used to improve services, make better decisions, and conduct more effective research.

2001/240 pp/hardbound/ISBN 1-57387-110-9

ASIST Members $31.60 • Non-Members $39.50

Intelligent Technologies in Library and Information Service Applications

F.W. Lancaster and Amy Warner

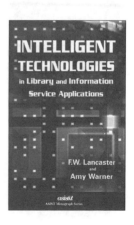

Librarians and library school faculty have been experimenting with artificial intelligence (AI) and expert systems for 30 years, but there has been no comprehensive survey of the results available until now. In this carefully researched monograph, authors Lancaster and Warner report on the applications of AI technologies in library and information services, assessing their effectiveness, reviewing the relevant literature, and offering a clear-eyed forecast of future use and impact. Includes almost 500 bibliographic references.

2001/214 pp/hardbound/ISBN 1-57387-103-6

ASIST Members $31.60 • Non-Members $39.50

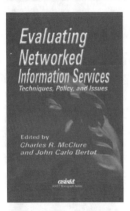

Evaluating Networked Information Services Techniques, Policy, and Issues

Edited by Charles R. McClure and John Carlo Bertot

As information services and resources are made available in the global networked environment, there is a critical need to evaluate their usefulness, impact, cost, and effectiveness. This monograph brings together an introduction and overview of evaluation techniques and methods, information policy issues and initiatives, and other critical issues related to the evaluation of networked information services.

2001/300 pp/hardbound/ISBN 1-57387-118-4

ASIST Members $35.60 • Non-Members $44.50

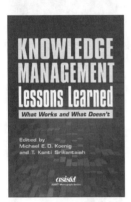

Knowledge Management Lessons Learned

Edited by Michael E. D. Koenig and T. Kanti Srikantaiah

A follow-up to Srikantaiah and Koenig's ground-breaking *Knowledge Management for the Information Professional* (2000), this new book surveys recent applications and innovations in KM. More than 30 experts describe KM in practice, revealing what has been learned, what works, and what doesn't. Includes projects undertaken by organizations at the forefront of KM, and coverage of KM strategy and implementation, cost analysis, education and training, content management, communities of practice, competitive intelligence, and much more.

2003/550 pp/hardbound/ISBN 1-57387-181-8

ASIST Members $35.60 • Non-Members $44.50

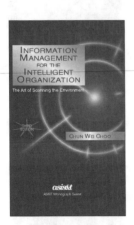

Information Management for the Intelligent Organization, 3rd Edition

By Chun Wei Choo

The intelligent organization is one that is skilled at marshalling its information resources, transforming information into knowledge, and using it to sustain and enhance its performance in a restless environment. This updated and expanded monograph shows how an organization may manage its information processes more effectively in order to achieve these goals. It includes new sections on information culture, information overload, and organizational learning; a new chapter on Knowledge Management (KM) and the role of information professionals; and numerous extended case studies of environmental scanning by organizations in Asia, Europe, and North America.

2001/352 pp/hardbound/ISBN 1-57387-125-7

ASIST Members $31.60 • Non-Members $39.50

To order or for a complete catalog, contact:

Information Today, Inc.

143 Old Marlton Pike, Medford, NJ 08055 • 609/654-6266
email: custserv@infotoday.com • Web site: www.infotoday.com